INSIDE
THE BEVERLY HILLS
SUPPER CLUB FIRE

RON ELLIOTT

Turner Publishing Company
200 4th Avenue North • Suite 950
Nashville, Tennessee 37219
(615) 255-2665

www.turnerpublishing.com

Inside The Beverly Hills Supper Club Fire

Library of Congress Number: 2010928782

ISBN: 978-1-59652-751-5

Printed in the United States of America

10 11 12 13 14 15 16 17— 15 14 13 12 11 10 9 8 7 6

Table of Contents

Dedications

This book is respectfully dedicated to those who lost their lives in the Beverly Hills Supper Club fire May 28, 1977.

Marian **Adkins**
Amelia P. Arthur
William E. Arthur
Walter W. **Backus**
Ruth C. **Backus**
Warren G. Baker
Jean I. Baker
Daniel Barker
Mabel M. Barker
Martin H. Barker
John B. Beavers
Ann L. Beer
Donald N. Bezold
Patricia M. Bezold
Barbara Bohrer
Jane L. Bohrer
Judith A. Bohrer
Mary L. Bohrer
Raymond W. Bohrer
Thomas W. Bohrer
Doris C. Brown
James K. Brown
Patricia W. Brown
Charlotte Bums
Robert D. Bums
Maxine Mae Butler
Roy O. Butler
Howard B. Carson, Sr.
Josephine Carson
Helen V. Castelli
Norbert J. Castelli
Stewart P. Coakley
Geraldine Cole
Ellen Cooksey
Fred Cooksey
Carol W. Cottongim
Robert P. Cottongim

Orville Coulter
James C. Cox
James B. Crane
Harold D. Daly
Rosemary Dischar
Gloria Sue **Duncel**
Mary N. Dwyer
Rosemary M. Dwyer
Shelia A. Dwyer
Elmer L. Ellison
Nora L. Ellison
Grace W. Fall
William Fawbush, Sr.
Marilyn L. Finch
Virginia Fitch
Helen W. Floyd
James W. Fowler
Anna I. Freshner
Fredrica H. **Fryman**
M. Scott **Fryman**
Tracy O. **Fryman**
Willard **Fryman**
Lenora Gentry
Allen Gorrnan
Anna Gorham
Russell O. Gray
Carol Ann Greer
Frank M. Greer
Clarence F. Gripshover
Donnie Clyde **Grogan**
Felton B. Harrison
Douglas G. **Herro**
Harry R. Hodges, II
Barbara J. Hous
Dottie D. Isaacs
Mary L. Ittel
Ruth J. John

Lillian R. Jutzi
Raymond C. Jutzi
Robert E. Kettman
Susan A. Kettman
Tammy C. Kincer
Lucy King
Paul G. Kiser
Minnie Knight
Donald E. Koontz
Dorothy M. Koontz
Carl **Krigbaum**, Jr.
Diane Lape
Etta E. Leis
Gary Littrell
Sharon Littrell
Leona S. Long
James P. Lyon
Monica A. Lyon
Margart E. **Malowan**
Sharlene **Matthews**
Clark **Mayfield**
Sara **McClain**
Collis W. Mitchell
Minda M. Moford
Agnes **Muddiman**
Everett H. **Neill**
Paula L. **Neill**
Jean Darlene Noe
Mildred **Overton**
Ruth M. Patterson
Harold R. **Penwell**, Jr.
Lawrence G. Phelps
Hilma C. Pfieffer
Margaret E. Phillips
Alberta C. **Pieper**
Mary L. Pitsenbarger
Nolan Pitsenbarger

Richard K. **Pokky**

Dorothy V. Wilson **Polley**

George C. **Polley**

Ethel Prugh

Gary Prugh

L. J. Prugh

Virginia **Raitt**

Virginia K. Ramler

Anna L. **Reineke**

Nell O. Reynolds

Elma B. Rhinehart

Charles J. Rist, Jr.

Maymia Rist

Robert R. **Roden,** Jr.

Terri L. Rose

Alma Schnapp

Joseph J. Schrantz

Mary A. Schrantz

Rosalie A. Schuman

Robert G. Seaman

Percy Shepherd

Charles D. Sherwood

Evelyn M. Shough

Donna Sue Skaggs

Paul H. Smith

Ann L. Stations

Fred K. Stratton, Sr.

Opal L. Stewart

John R. Strom

Laura J. Sykes

Robert E. Sykes

Stephen H. Taylor

Barbara A. Thornhill

Baby Thornhill

Carolyn **L.Thornhill**

Darlene Thornhill

Robert Thornhill

Rosemary Tilley

Glenna K. Turner

John Twaddell

Baby Tyra

Diana Lou Tyra

Doris Tyra

Phyllis Tyra

Mary S. Vogel

Ottillia Vollman

Fred E. Wade

Martha E. Wade

George R. Walker, Jr.

Beatrice Wenning

Gertrude Williams

Betty Wilson

Mary Ann Work

Robert F. Zadek

George Zorick, Jr.

George Zorick, III

There are some things that need to be forgotten, but there are some things that must be remembered. The safety of our citizens demands that the tragedy of the Beverly Hills Supper Club fire not be forgotten. The events of that night will forever be implanted in my memory. My determination while Governor of Kentucky to identify the cause of the tragedy and take specific action to prevent a similar diaster, are also well implanted in my memory.

My Prayer from that first night has been that God grant the hurting and grieving relatives strength to endure their loss. While surely the love of God has healed most of those hurts, His wisdom has given us the constant vigiliance to preclude such a tragedy from ever happening again. This publication, allowing us all to remember a great catastrophe in our Nation's history, is a great opportunity for us to rededicate the memory of the Beverly Hills Supper Club fire to responsible action to preserve the safety of all our citizens.

Julian M. Carroll
Governor of Kentucky
1975-1980

Preface

December 7, 1941. November 22, 1963. Anyone who was alive on either of those dates and was old enough to remember can tell you exactly where he or she was and what was going on in their life that day.

For many people in Kentucky, Indiana, Ohio and surrounding states, May 28, 1977 falls into the same category. Those who were on the highway that evening wondered where all the fire trucks, ambulances and police cars were going in such a hurry. Those in the Northern Kentucky area heard the sirens screaming through the soft spring air. Those at home throughout the tri-state area of Kentucky, Ohio and Indiana quickly received the news that the Beverly Hills Supper Club was on fire. Those who were within five miles saw the column of black smoke smudging the evening sky.

Beyond the fact that it existed atop a hill somewhere near Cincinnati, most of us knew little of the Beverly Hills. Some knew that it was a fabulous night spot which attracted top name entertainers to the area and served excellent food, all at modest prices. Others knew that it was the place to hold your organization's annual banquet or that special wedding ceremony and reception.

Old-timers may have remembered some of the history of the Beverly Hills from when it was the classiest of the myriad illegal gambling casinos which existed in the vicinity of **Newport** through the **30's**, 40's and **50's**. Most of us had some recollection, however vague, of the scandal that occurred in 1961 when George Ratterman ran for county sheriff, promising to clean out the vice in the area.

In the early **70's**, as we sailed along on 1-75, we wondered why Newport hadn't dried up and blown away after Mr. Ratterman managed to survive the Mafia's attempt to discredit him and accomplished what his campaign promised.

When Mr. Richard Schilling purchased the property and announced his plans to rebuild, few outside the contracting business took much notice. Someone did, though. Soon, the Beverly Hills was in the headlines again, this time in a swirl of controversy surrounding arson as the possible (probable?) cause of the fire that destroyed the building during its remodeling.

The grand reopening was accompanied by enough fanfare to make most citizens take notice. In operation as a night club, the reputation grew until almost everyone knew that the Beverly Hills was there.

What very few people knew was the ways and means by which the structure had been constructed, improved, inspected and approved.

Those who did know kept it quiet. The ignorance of the population was maintained, somehow, despite the newspapers' best efforts to dispel it.

Then, on a lovely Memorial Day Saturday night, the Beverly Hills Supper Club burned to the ground. When the blaze was extinguished, the building was gone, and 165 people's lives had been extinguished, too. As with all tragedies, the public demanded to know how such a thing could have happened. Unfortunately, the process of finding out became so long and drawn-out that most of us lost interest before the question was answered.

If, in fact, one chooses to consider that the Commonwealth of Kentucky did answer the question. An investigative team appointed by Governor Julian Carroll was assigned the chore. After examining a mountain of evidence, the team submitted a lengthy report to the Governor, who felt that criminal proceedings might be in order. But, a Campbell County Grand Jury said no. Governor Carroll then appointed an independent investigator who dug through the evidence once again. On the investigator's recommendation, no criminal action was ever pursued.

Although a great amount of civil litigation followed the Beverly Hills disaster, most of the major cases were settled out of court. Hence, with no criminal trials and no major civil suits heard in court, the full facts of the causes behind the fire were never brought under the scrutiny that such actions would have provided.

This book, then, is an effort to present as many of those facts as could be unearthed, from the perspective of one who had a personal involvement with not only the Beverly Hills Supper Club and its owners, but who also got up close and personal with the fire.

My writing style dictates that I create the preface after the text is finished so that I have a more complete idea of what I might need to say to the reader. Therefore, from my perspective, these are the closing words of this text. Appropriately enough, I'm writing this paragraph on May 28, 1996, the nineteenth anniversary of the Beverly Hills fire. I've been so involved with it that I feel as if I actually knew some of the victims. During the production of this book, most nights after an evening of relating the terrors many endured, I've had difficulty in getting to sleep. I can remove the words from my vision by the mere flick of a switch on my computer, but eliminating the horrors from my brain is an entirely different matter. I've tossed and turned, not so much over the accounts of those who escaped the fire, or even those who died, but rather the agony of those children and parents who sustained the losses. The stories they relate are not easily dismissed. Tonight, with these people on my mind, I expect to be no different. These tales, presented in the last section of this book, define the true measure of tragedy. I fervently hope we all learn something from them.

I would like to thank Joyce King, John Snell and Ron Bryant for their help, patience and encouragement, former Governor Julian Carroll for the data he provided, Wayne Darnrnert for his leg work and keeping me straight on which way the hallway ran, and last but not least, Doug Sikes of Turner Publishing Company. Doug, you earned your keep on this one, son.

Ron Elliott

Part One

THE GOOD OLD DAYS

Built early that year, this June 14, 1937 file photo of the Beverly Hills Country Club's front drive was accompanied by the caption, "Swank Beverly Hills, plain on the outside, but said to have cost $1,000,000.00, is one of five great gambling establishments in Newport. (The Courier-Journal)

Chapter 1

My lungs still rebelling against all the smoke I'd inhaled, I rounded the comer of the building to the garden area at the rear of the Beverly Hills Supper Club. My brain could hardly comprehend the scene which met my eyes. Police cars, fire trucks and ambulances, red and blue lights blazing, gave an ethereal aura to the soft spring air. Had it not been for the bodies covering large areas of the pavement and grass, the setting might have been from some not-very-well done movie.

Despite my narrow escape from the building, I had not realized — until I saw the lights and bodies—that the fire was as disastrous as this. Moving numbly toward the garden area, I stumbled over a man sitting on the grass. Mumbling an apology, I noticed a woman lying on the grass beside him. I looked at the man, but he took no notice of me, apparently staring at some distant object. The woman, dressed in a powder blue sheer dinner gown, appeared to be asleep. As no one else was around, I decided to see if I could help.

"Is this your wife, sir?" I asked.

The man, his gray hair telling his age at about 60, made no reply. Just as I started to think he had not heard me, he nodded slowly. "Yes," he said, his voice barely audible.

The lady looked so peaceful, sweet and lovely. Her angelic face and silver hair made me think of my mother. Even though I was certain that she was dead, I said, "Would you like me to try to revive her with **mouth-to mouth resuscitation?'**

Again, the gentleman did not answer right away. I waited. At length, he replied, "Yes, if you think it'll help. Please do anything you can to help her." His voice was hollow and distant.

I didn't think it would help. As I bent down to open the lady's mouth, tears streamed uncontrollably down my cheeks. Noticing that she was already cold to my touch, I almost wished I hadn't volunteered for this grisly chore. Just as I was about to place my mouth over her's, someone placed a hand on my shoulder and said, "Do you need help?'

I looked up to see my own family doctor, Joseph Braun, standing over me. Straightening, I asked, "Dr. Braun, what are you doing here?'

"We had a doctors' party here tonight," he replied, brushing by me to kneel beside the lady on the grass.

Stupid question, I thought. I knew that the doctors' party was at the Beverly Hills tonight - I'd noticed it on the booking schedule earlier in the evening. Of all the events that had conspired to create this tragedy, the doctors' party was the single favorable circumstance. Having many doctors present prevented injuries from becoming more serious, and doubtlessly saved lives. Mutely, I watched Dr. Braun conduct a quick examination of the lovely woman. Standing to face me, he announced, **"She's** dead, Wayne," confirming my fears. Dr. Braun hurried away to apply his medical **skills** where they would do some good.

The man seated on the grass at my feet, having heard the doctor's verdict, started to weep. Witnessing his anguish, my tears began anew. I sat beside him and placed my arm around his shoulders. He leaned into me, as if to draw strength from my body. Little does he know how weak I am, I thought. Never in my life had I felt so helpless.

"Your wife is with God now," I sobbed. "Please be brave; God loves you." I hoped he found more comfort in my words than I thought I had power to give. He continued to weep softly, saying nothing.

In a few minutes, the thought of covering her occurred to me. "Let me have your jacket to cover her," I suggested. Still, he said nothing, but started to struggle out of his coat. When it was free, I gently placed it over the dead lady's face and stumbled away. I never learned the names of either of those two people.

A fellow Beverly Hills employee was standing over a woman lying a few steps away. Her face was covered with soot, and her clothing appeared quite wet, perhaps from perspiration, perhaps water from the burst pipes. Already inured to the situation, I asked, "Is she dead?'

"I think so," he mumbled.

"I think they're collecting bodies at the rear of the garden," I said. I don't know what made me think that. "Let's carry her there."

He stared at me blankly for a moment, then bent to pick up her feet. I took the shoulders. As we lifted her from the turf, a soft moan emanated from her body. "She's alive," I cried, and we hurried to the rear of the garden.

In a mass of injured, a doctor was **working** feverishly. "Help this lady," I pleaded, "She's alive." We placed her at the doctor's feet.

After a quick examination, he said, "No, she's gone."

"But we heard her moan," I protested.

"That's perfectly normal, son," he said, turning to help someone else.

Finding a cloth napkin on the grass, I placed it over her face. Something inside me made me place my hand on her forehead and offer a brief prayer. I asked God to please, in His mercy, receive her into His kingdom, a ritual I was to repeat at least fifty times this night.

I glanced around the garden. At least 100 bodies covered the ground, making it look more like a battlefield than the lovely spot where sparkling fountains, pagodas, and flowers had saluted many a radiant, just married bride's promenade. How well I could recall their beaming faces' disclosure of the dreams alive in their hearts. Now the garden hosted the dead, their blank eyes staring unseeing; their dreams tragically and abruptly ended.

Inside the glass enclosed Garden Rooms, tables blazed, flames reflecting off their mirrored surfaces. Whiskey bottles from the portable bars exploded; each "pop" spewing fresh fuel for the conflagration. Sparks leaving a ghastly red trail spiraled into the night air as a section of the roof collapsed.

Movement off to my left attracted my attention. Turning in that direction. I saw a hundred or so patrons — survivors — being shepherded by policemen down a rocky hillside into an area where I-471 was under construction. I could see the mud oozing over the dress shoes of the men and ruining the hems of the ladies' ankle-length evening gowns. A rope line, provided by the firefighters, guided them down the hill. I thought then that the spectacle of these well dressed people stumbling down the steep, muddy slope clinging to the slender life-line would remain forever in my mind's eye.

A commotion occurred behind me. Wearily turning, I saw a policeman with his knee on the back of a prostrate young man. Handcuffs reflected the light of the fire above my position. "What'd he do?' I yelled.

Handcuffs in place on the youth's wrists, the policeman looked at me. "I caught him rifling the pockets of the dead," he said, emotionlessly. I watched as he jerked the lad to his feet and lead him away. I decided to find somewhere to sit and keep watch over the victim's personal effects.

I stumbled over to a low stone wall near the rear of the garden and sat. As soon as I was seated, I noticed that my mouth was parched and exhaustion overtook my entire body. My mind quite dazed, I analytically pondered how this horrible event could have happened At my work station upstairs, I knew that some of us had trouble getting out of the building, but I had simply not realized the extent of the catastrophe. Perhaps the survival of myself and those in my care had blocked the bigger picture. My reverie was abruptly interrupted by an explosion from the main building. I spun just in time to witness the Beverly Hills' death rattle as the main section of the roof collapsed. As I watched the faltering flames consume what was left of the building, I slowly began to realize that this night had witnessed not only the destruction of the magnificent Beverly Hills Supper Club, but the tragic end of many, many lives.

Then as I sat there, drained physically and emotionally, performing the protective chore I'd assigned myself, my mind wandered back over the events that brought me to this morbid vigil.

Me and my beloved 1957 Chevrolet Bel Aire convertible: 1959. (W. Dammert)

Chapter 2

The city of Cincinnati sits on the northern bank of the Ohio River which serves as the border between Ohio and Kentucky. To those of us who live in the region, it has always seemed that when any event draws a national focus, the media describes the area as "Greater Cincinnati" if the attention is positive, but "Northern **Kentucky**" when it's less than flattering. Perhaps that perspective is an indicator of the reputation of the Cincinnati suburbs separated from the "Queen City" by the Ohio River.

And the reputation is not undeserved. **Newport,** Covington, Southgate, and some of the other towns south of the river have a long and checkered history replete with gambling, prostitution, drug trafficking, and **murder-for-hire**; all illegal, all reputedly with Mafia influence, and all under the nose of the local law. Bookies and slot machines were so prevalent in the '30's, '40's and '50's that you could place a bet on any ball game or horse race, or, if you wanted, even on which bird would fly first from the wire. In the March 26, 1960 issue, *The Saturday Evening Post* reported that in earlier times, "...violence became commonplace in Northern Kentucky, and law enforcement about on a par with that in Cicero, Illinois, in the heyday of Chicago mobsters' activities there... "

Such is the environment to which I, fresh out of the U. S. Navy and a few days past my twenty-first birthday, returned in the spring of 1957 to begin a search for employment. After several days of "don't call us, we'll call **you**," I took a day off to vent my frustrations on a golf ball. As most of my high school friends were working or had gone elsewhere, I drove alone in my new, black '57 Chevrolet convertible to the Summit Hills Country Club in Edgewood, where I was a member. Just the drive lifted my spirits somewhat — it was a beautiful June day, and I was a free man in a sharp car. After three and a half years of Navy discipline, the wind blowing my hair (and it being long enough for the wind to blow) was just what the doctor ordered.

The starter was an old friend. "Wayne Dammert!" he cried on see-ing me. "Where the hell have you been?"

"Sailing the seven seas for Uncle Sam," I replied.

"You alone?"

"Yep, just me."

"Well, wait a while and I'll match you up with somebody to make up a foursome," he said and we stood there chewing over old times for a few minutes. Eventually, a threesome showed up, and he placed me in that group. I introduced myself, and, in introducing himself, one of the men mentioned that he was a "boss" at the Beverly Hills Supper Club. I didn't know what being a boss meant, but I was nonetheless impressed.

My first thought was to ask him about a job, but then, I had second thoughts. While the Beverly Hills was, by consensus, the most plush of the gambling spots in the area, the just-as-common belief of Mafia con-nections with the establishment gave one pause.

Finally, over a beer at the nineteenth hole, I worked up my nerve. "I'm just out of the service," I ventured, "do you suppose there might be a job for me at the Beverly Hills?"

My heart was in my throat as he stared, obviously sizing me up. At length, he said, "Yeah, I see no problem," and he gave me the name of a man to see. "Come up to the Club tonight, and he'll put you to work."

My spirits were really soaring as I drove home — I'd found a job! And at the fabulous Beverly Hills. I'd never been there, but it was well known that the "Beverly" had a total Las Vegas-type environment, com-plete with a huge restaurant, after-dinner shows and even a resident chorus line. Such big-name entertainers as Joe E. Lewis, Martha Raye, Guy Lombardo, the Andrews Sisters, **Liberace,** and the Mills Brothers were regular attractions. As Cincinnati had both major league baseball and NBA basketball teams, many of the visiting players were regular Beverly patrons, as were any movie stars who happened to be in the vicinity. I was so thrilled at the prospect of working in such an envi-ronment that I hadn't even bothered to ask what I'd be doing. It really didn't matter.

Where are you preaching **tonight?**" **my** mother asked, noticing my suit and tie.

"I have a job interview," I announced.

"Oh, yeah? Where?"

"The Beverly Hills," I said, pride in my voice. "I'm not sure what I'll be doing, so I thought I'd dress up."

"The Beverly Hills!" she nearly shrieked. "The Mafia **runs** that place,

Sailor Wayne Dammert at the Acropolis in Athens, Greece; Summer 1955. *(W. Dammert)*

you'll get in trouble up there! They've got illegal gambling and Lord only knows what else."

"NOW, Mom," I said, "it's the nicest place around, you know that. They have a pretty big restaurant — maybe I'll be working there. Anyway, I'm just going to look things over, if there's any problem, I won't take the job." With that assurance, I was in my car and headed south on US 27, headed for the Club's location in Southgate. I found a spot in the **parking** lot and ignored my thumping heart as I headed for the front door.

Inside, I was met by a **maitre** d' — I'd soon learn they were called "Captains" — who asked if he could help me. I gave him the name of the man I'd been told to ask for. "Wait here," he said and disappeared around a comer.

I stood there drinking in the fantastic atmosphere for a few minutes until I heard someone say, "Are you the guy **lookin'** for a job?' I turned to see a large, ugly man glaring at me. The swarthy skin and the general demeanor made me think of every gangster movie I'd ever seen.

"Yes," I answered, hesitantly. Suddenly, the atmosphere didn't seem quite so charming.

He looked me up and down. "Come with me," he mumbled and started down the hall. We walked first through the bar, then a huge dining room that looked to hold about 800 people. A large stage with footlights and a sound system adorned the front of the vast room. I followed along through what seemed a dozen turns and locked doors — checkpoints — my confidence ebbing with each step. Finally, I was standing before the man I'd come to see.

"Do you have any experience?' he asked.

My first impulse was to say, "At **what?**" **After** thinking a moment, I stammered, "I'm just out of the service."

He stared at me for a moment, then consulted some papers on his desk. "You know how to play blackjack*?,

Note: For those unfamiliar with the game, blackjack is a casino card game in which each player bets against the (house) dealer Initially, each player receives two cards. At The Beverly Hills, all cards except the dealer's hole card were dealt face up. The object of the game is to come as near to

a total count of twenty-one as possible without going over, counting an ace as eleven, face cards as ten, and all others at face value. The player has the option to stop with the cards he has (stand) or request another card (hit). If a player goes over twenty-one he is "bust" and loses his bet. If he is closer to twenty-one than the dealer, he wins. In casinos, the dealer is required to hit with sixteen (or less) and to stand on seventeen (or more).

"Sure." I didn't know it then, but the man I was facing was in charge of hiring for the casino. I'm sure I didn't think about my mother's warning.

"All right, then. We need blackjack dealers, we'll start you out there." He pushed a buzzer under his desk — visions of Edward G. Robinson and Humphrey **Bogart** flashed through my mind — and another man appeared to take me to work.

Unhindered by the fact that gambling was illegal in Kentucky, this early inside photo of the Beverly Hills casino reveals its presence and popularity. In this June 14, 1937 article it was said of the Beverly Hills that "It runs wide open, puts on a good floor show, and provides gambling facilities after the show." (The **Courier-Journal***)*

"I'm Earl Williams," he said as we went out the door. We walked out of the office, through the dealers' break room and into the casino. The scene which met my young eyes was beyond anything I'd ever even dreamed. In the "pit," three steps below the level where I was standing, a chuck-a-luck table with its hour-glass shaped cage containing three dies, eight blackjack tables, three roulette wheels, and four dice (craps) tables sat on the plush carpet. As it was early, no customers were in the casino yet.

Earl took me over to one of the blackjack tables . With me playing customer and him acting as dealer, he gave me a quick lesson in how the operation was run. I understood blackjack pretty well (having played more than a few hands in the Navy) and so didn't have many questions. Earl showed me a metal box, slightly larger than a standard dollar bill and about six inches deep with a hinged lid. "Keep your money in here," he advised. Little did I envision how many bills I'd stuff into that box in just one night.

Finally, he consulted his watch. "All set?" he asked with a smile.

"I guess so," I replied, hoping my voice did not betray my uncertainty.

"OK, then, I'll see you in a couple of hours." He walked away, leaving me wondering what to do.

I didn't wonder long. In a few minutes, the doors flew open and a throng of patrons rushed into the room as if headed for **Macy's bargain**-basement-day sale. The stream of gamblers flowed down into the pit and distributed itself among the various games. Before I had time to think about it, all the high stools at my table were taken, and I was dealing cards and raking money into the metal box.

After a few hands, my anxiety departed, and I started to have fun. The players were friendly and helped me over the rough spots. The only part I didn't like was the way my pit boss, Marty Meyer, kept constant watch over me. Earl had told me that Marty's brother, Mitch, was one of the big bosses. I tried not to let him bother me, hoping that his vigilance was due to the fact that I was new on the job and would subside in time.

Most of the players were men who took the play seriously. A few women sat at my table, and it seemed that they were more interested in flirting with the other players and me than they were the cards. One beautiful lady in particular was wearing a revealing red dress and perfume that smelled heavenly. Each time our eyes met, she flashed a smile that melted the ice in my water glass. Marty evidently didn't like that.

As I finished a hand, he stepped between me and the table. "I'm moving you to another table," he announced, curtly.

"OK," I said, placing the money in the box.

He took me to another table and relieved that dealer. On the second hand I dealt at the new station, the lady in the red dress arrived. She took a seat, flashed that smile on me and said, "Hello again." Two hands later, Marty moved me again. The lady followed me to the new table.

Once again, Marty stepped in. "I'm moving **you,**" he snapped.

"Oh no, you're not!" the lady declared. "I have a perfect right to play at any dealer's table and I'm damn tired of your childish tricks."

Marty glared. "I'm the pit boss," he said.

"And I'm the customer," she shouted, drawing other patron's attention. "Shall I speak to the manager?"

Without a word. Marty spun and walked away. The lady and I continued to smile at each other until I was relieved at break time. I expected trouble with Marty.

In the dealer's room, Earl Williams was sitting, smoking with several other dealers. He stood and smiled as I entered. Earl was tall and **big-boned,** and his smile made his good nature evident. "Welcome to the Beverly Hills, Wayne," he said. "How'd it go?"

"Oh, all right, I guess."

"Good." He turned to the other men. "Wayne Dammert, meet George Billinger." George stood to shake hands. His gray hair bespoke many years in the business, and he looked the part, too. He could have passed for a riverboat gambler.

"I'm on the roulette wheels," he said, smiling.

Earl introduced me to Leon Wagner, Sam Sherman, and Ivan Jaeger. Sam was a perfect double for television star Phil Silvers, and the guys called him "Flash." We made small talk for a while, just getting acquainted. At length, Earl asked if I was hungry.

"Yeah," I replied. "Can we eat here?"

"Yes," Earl said. "You can get a good meal at a decent price from the restaurant." After a pause, he added, "That is if you ain't as tight as Flash and Ivan." Everybody laughed.

"What's the joke," I inquired.

"Just teasing," Earl informed. "Flash and Ivan are regular gourmets. Flash's wife usually sends him to work with roast pheasant or some such, while Ivan is a connoisseur of the finest bologna sandwiches to be had at any price." Through the giggles, Earl added, "the rest of us generally eat in the restaurant."

After we'd chatted for a while, being comfortable with these men, I decided I'd ask some questions that'd been bothering me. "Say," I began, "what we're doing here is illegal as all hell, isn't it?"

The jocularity abruptly stopped. All nodded solemnly.

"Well, then are we liable to get **raided?**" I'd heard of the police bursting in on such operations.

Everyone's laughter broke the tension I'd created. "Not likely," George answered.

I waited, but he did not elaborate. In a minute, Ivan said, "they pay off the local law, so they ain't gonna bother us." He was not joking.

"How come there's no slot machines in here?" Almost every joint in the whole area had slot machines.

Earl spoke up. "Despite the pay-off's," he said, "there's precautions in place. The man out front can push a button that sounds an alarm back here if he gets suspicious. You'll have to learn the drill, but when the alarm rings we can tear the casino down and have the place looking like the Wednesday afternoon poetry society meeting inside of two minutes."

"Does that ever happen?" I could envision the panic a raid would cause.

"Oh, we've had a false alarm or two," Leon said.

"What about the slot machines?" I persisted.

"There's too much tax on 'em," Ivan ventured.

That made no sense to me. "How can there be tax? They're illegal."

"They're illegal in Kentucky, but there's a federal tax of $250 per machine," Ivan said. "I understand the feds are pretty strict on 'em."

George snorted, his shaggy silver head shaking. "It can't be very strict. Hell, they're everywhere."

After a moment's thought, Earl commented, "As heavy as those things are, they'd be damned hard to hide quickly." I suppose that explained why the Beverly had no slot machines.

When the break ended, I was back at the blackjack table. After about an hour, a man sat down and handed me a slip of paper. I didn't know what it was; the customer usually handed me cash to exchange for chips. As I hesitated, Marty Meyer approached. "That's a Vegas credit slip," he said. "Treat it just like cash."

"What's the deal on that?" I asked as I counted out the chips.

"We've got an arrangement with one of the Las Vegas casinos," he explained. "Some of the high rollers transfer their credit with them to us. If someone brings one of those slips in, it's already been approved up front." Just as I'd been led to believe, this was no fly-by-night operation!

The remainder of the night passed with no major excitement. At one point, a woman with a very unusual shade of dark red hair came to my table with a well-heeled gentleman. Her hair was such a deep red that it seemed to have a purplish cast when the light was just right. On about her third hand, when I asked if she wanted a card, she looked plaintively at me. "Should I hit or stand?"

She had an eight and a ten showing, so she had eighteen and clearly should stand, but I didn't see it as the dealer's responsibility to advise the players. "It's up to you."

She frowned and screwed up her face in puzzlement. "Oh, hit me," she said.

I dealt her another card, a deuce. By all odds, she should have gone bust and lost her bet. I thought she didn't understand much about the game and had been incredibly lucky.

When my shift ended, Earl walked with me across the casino. Seated around a table were a dozen women, any one whom would qualify as the most beautiful I'd ever seen. "Who are they?" I asked, my mouth dropping open.

"The chorus girls," Earl said.

"What are they doing?"

"The bosses make 'em stay until 2."

"Why?" I continued to stare.

"I don't know," Earl said, taking my arm to pull me along. "I guess they just like having those gorgeous creatures around."

"Gorgeous is the right word," I said, reluctantly turning my head to look where I was going. I didn't ask, but from Earl's attitude, I assumed that the Beverly's policy toward those girls must be "if you want to keep your job, you can look but you better not touch ." Damn!

◌⅍◌

The nights turned into weeks and the weeks into months as I settled into the job. I became so comfortable with the routine that I didn't worry much about what I was doing being illegal, but I suppose the thought that I might end up in jail was always in the back of my mind.

But those thoughts were usually pretty far back because the life was exciting. Celebrities flocked to the Beverly Hills. During this period, Milton Berle, Gordon and Shelia **McRae**, Steve Lawrence, and Edie **Gormet** appeared in the nightly shows. Steve and Edie were not married then, but it was apparent that they were pretty close. They tied the knot soon after their stints at the Beverly Hills. I got to meet most of the stars when they came to play at my blackjack table.

Additionally, the Beverly played host to the likes of baseball great Stan Musial (when the St. Louis Cardinals were in town), Dean Martin, Frank Sinatra, Jerry Lewis, Shirley **McLain,** and Sal Mineo. All these people sat at my table and while I tried not to be too star-struck, my autograph collection was growing. One night, Paul Homing, who is from Louisville and was a big star for football's Green Bay Packers at the time, helped us close the place down. It was the thrill of my young life to walk out to the parking lot with his friendly arm draped over my shoulder.

One evening, I was dealing blackjack when Gloria Graham walked

Pictured opposite page: The Beverly Hills Chorus Line. Southgate, KY. Top row, from left: Mary Ann, Nancy Lee Williams, and Nora Ford Culbertson. Middle row, from left: Betty Silva Dammert and Ann Daly Mayo. Bottom row, from left: Marilyn Derrick Conte, Jay Maxwell, Alice Kinman Wolfson, and Georgia Carrier Hatridge. (W. Dammert)

into the casino. I'd been totally entranced with her, as boys will do, since I witnessed her performance as "Angel" in *The Greatest Show on Earth* when I was an adolescent. She strolled into the room, looked around and walked over to my table. My heart was in my throat as that beautiful lady smiled at me and purred "Hello, handsome." The Beverly Hills was the place to be!

The lady with the reddish-purple hair showed up at least once a week, always with a different man. Two things soon became evident: she was a prostitute, and she was unbelievably lucky at blackjack. I really didn't understand why the owners let her in, as her profession was obvious, but because she always came with an escort, I suppose they looked the other way. The management absolutely allowed no woman to pick up men at the Club.

Although I saw this woman a lot, I never learned her name. But I did learn her trick. Just as she had done the first night I worked there, at some point during the play, she'd always ask me if she should hit or stand. Usually, she'd ask when she had sixteen or seventeen. I'd never answer her, and she'd invariably take another card. After several instances, it dawned on me that her object was to make her escort think that she'd never been in the casino before. Tricks of the trade, I suppose. The fact that amazed me, however, is that most of the time when she took a hit when most players would have stayed, she'd get a low card, and win the bet.

After I'd been dealing for several months and was comfortable with the job, she walked up to my table, fresh escort in tow. I was in a foul mood about something that evening. On her fourth hand, she had a seven and a king showing, and I knew what was coming. Looking soulfully at me, she asked, "What should I do now?"

With the largest contempt I could muster, I said, "You know damned well what to do, you do it every week." She took a hit, went bust and stomped away. Although she was never to darken my table again, we hadn't seen the last of that lady.

"What the hell is that?" I wondered as Earl Williams and I exited the dealers room to begin our shift. The casino was draped with red velvet ropes, attached to the roulette, blackjack and chuck-a-luck tables, forming corridors throughout the room.

"Management installed those to keep the spectators from getting behind the tables, I think," Earl opined.

I descended into the pit and navigated through the rope aisles to my station. Soon, the casino was full of players, and the ropes were forgotten. A couple of hours later, I noticed the door of the dealers room fly open. Earl burst forth, excitement written on his face. He charged down the steps, headed in my direction, entirely oblivious to his surroundings. He ran right through one of the rope barriers. Tables tumbled, chips, cards and money flew in all directions, and pandemonium reined as the ropes yanked at their moorings. Needless to say, play was disrupted until we could reassemble the equipment.

"Earl, what the hell were you **thinking?**" I **asked** as we resumed work.

"I was so excited, I forgot about the damned ropes," he answered, embarrassed.

"What's the excitement?'

He looked puzzled for a moment as if he'd forgotten. "Oh, yeah. I was going to tell you 'Bust' is in the house."

I didn't know what he meant. "What?"

Earl nodded toward a big man across the room. "I don't know what his name is, but we call him 'Bust,'" he said. "Don't call him that to his face, but get ready for the show."

"Why do you call him that?"

Earl simply smiled and hurried away. In a little while, "Bust" wandered up to my table.

"How are you, sir?' I greeted him.

"**Doin'** good, so far," he said, handing me a one-hundred dollar bill. "Deal me in."

I placed his money in the box and handed him a stack of 20 five-dollar chips.

"No, no," he said, refusing the chips. "I only play with one-dollar chips."

Player's eccentricities are just part of a dealer's life. I counted out 100 one-dollar chips and dealt the cards. At that time, all of the table's eight player positions were occupied. "Bust" played in a normal fashion for 30 minutes or so, betting from five to twenty dollars on each hand, his **one-**dollar chips in one neat stack high enough to contain the desired sum. He'd split the hand or double down whenever the rules allowed. Nothing was all that unusual, so I began to wonder what Earl had been **talking** about. Then, the man seated next to "Bust" collected his chips and walked away. "Mind if I play that hand?' "Bust" asked.

House rules allowed for anyone to play as many hands as they wanted. "Not at all," I said.

Over the next 90 minutes, this action was repeated until "Bust" was playing all eight hands the table accommodated. On the second round of him playing the whole table, he had about $200, total, on the table. My show card was a five. Adding the jack I had face down, my hand totaled fifteen. "Bust" and I both knew that the house rules required that I'd have to hit the hand. The odds dictated that I'd bust.

I pointed at the hand on my far left where sixteen was showing. "Stay!" he shouted.

The next hand, moving clockwise, had an nine and a four, totaling thirteen. "Stay!"

His emphatic "Stay!" answered each hand regardless of the cards, until it was my turn to play. Nervously, I glanced up to see that a large crowd had gathered to observe the action. Nearest me was Earl Williams, grinning like a 'possum. Most of the pit bosses were also watching.

I pulled my card from the shoe. The seven made my hand total 22; I was bust — over 21 — and he won all eight hands. Raising a massive arm high over his head,

Leon Wagoner (left) and George Billinger (right) and me in front of a casino in Nassau, where they worked six months each year. The other six they worked at The Beverly Hills. Leon worked the dice tables and George worked the roulette tables. Spring, 1959. (W. Dammert)

he yelled, "That's the way, boy. Bust!" With that, he slammed his fist down on the surface, laughing. The bedlam created by the noise and flying chips rivaled Earl's earlier announcement of "Bust's" presence. "Bust" stayed quite a while longer, the large crowd in attendance with him.

Some wild times were had in the dealer's break room. The whole bunch of us got along well, and we had a lot of fun playing practical jokes on each other. Aggravating George Billinger was one of our main sources of entertainment. We had a television in there and each of us saw it as a duty to prevent the others from enjoying their favorite programs. George loved the Lennon Sisters, so we did everything possible to disrupt him when they appeared on the Lawrence Welk Show.

One Saturday evening we filed into the break room prepared to prevent George from seeing the Lennon Sisters, only to discover that he'd put the television on the station he wanted and then removed all the knobs from the set. We looked high and low to see where he had hidden the knobs, but they were not to be found.

Later that night, we were riding home together. As we crossed the bridge into Cincinnati, George fished the television knobs from his pocket and with a flourish, flung them from the car window into the Ohio River. His smug grin said, "Got ya back, didn't I?'

My job varied from time to time. Sometimes, when I reported for work, the pit boss would put me on the roulette, and sometimes on the dice tables. I enjoyed most of it, but I didn't like the dice tables. The game has so many combinations that can be played that even an experienced dealer can sometimes have difficulty keeping everything straight. The pit bosses stood right over the dice tables, expecting the dealer to catch and correct any mistake. I wasn't that knowledgeable about the game, so I was usually very nervous. Additionally, if the dice got "hot," meaning that any player was winning consistently, the pit boss would blame the dealer. The only thing I liked about the dice tables was the tips the customers gave the dealer. I'd get twice as much in tips at dice than at blackjack, although that didn't matter much at the time, as all tips were pooled and divided equally among the dealers. Fortunately, I wasn't often asked to work the dice tables.

"Wayne, can I see you a minute?" the voice called as I entered the door. An ill omen — such a happening on Monday usually meant a change in assignment for the week. I turned, fearful that I'd be given the dice table. Rather than one of the pit bosses, it was Artie Jaeger who had spoken to me. "The Casino's closed," he said. "You're working the bingo this week."

"Why's it closed?"

"The grand jury's in session," he answered, irritably. "Get Earl to help you set up the bingo."

I found Earl backstage in the show room. The orchestra was just finishing the show, which starred Jimmy Durante. "Why's the casino closed," I asked Earl.

"The grand jury's in session," he replied.

"Artie told me that," I said. "So what?"

"They can't pay off the grand jury," he said, matter-of-factly. "So, they close the casino down, the bosses go to Florida, and you and I get to work the bingo."

Being twenty-one, I didn't question the logic.

He pushed the caller's machine over to me. "Take that out on the stage. You know how to call bingo?"

"You think I haven't put in my time at the Knights of **Columbus?**" I asked, laughing.

Before he could reply, Jimmy Durante came around the curtain, dressed in a tuxedo. "Hello, Earl," he said, passing toward the dressing area. I was struck by the fact that his distinctive voice was coming from a real person ten feet away.

"Good evening, Mr. Durante," Earl said. "Good show tonight."

"Thanks." Turning to me, he asked, "What's your name?"

"Wayne," I stammered, flustered at being face-to-face with one of television's biggest stars. "Wayne Dammert."

"Good to see you," he said with a smile and moved on down the hall.

Recovering a little, I said, "What's the deal on this bingo, Earl?"

"Just plain bingo," he said. "We can do it, grand jury or not, 'cause it's legal."

"The money goes to charity?'

"I guess so," he said moving toward the front with a stack of bingo cards. Pausing at the curtain, he threw over his shoulder, "In theory, anyway."

I called the bingo that night without event. As I was leaving that evening, I overheard a heated conversation between an irate lady and one of the captains. "I come all the hell the way from California, and you expect me to be content with a sleepy singer and bingo?' she was shouting into his beet-red face. I don't think she was the only customer who expected more.

The next evening was far from uneventful. As I was backstage getting the equipment ready, Jimmy Durante came through, just as he had the previous night. He nodded, smiled pleasantly, and said, "Hello, Wayne." I was thrilled that he'd remembered my name.

During the bingo game, Errol Flynn sauntered into the show room, **looking** and acting for all the world as if he owned the place. On his arm was a beautiful girl who didn't look a day over seventeen. I guess the handsome, dashing movie star's reputation for chasing women, especially young ones, was well deserved. From what I saw, he didn't have much trouble catching them, either. He caused no disruption, but I understood that he, too, was quite disappointed to discover that the gambling was not in operation.

I called the bingo for the remainder of that week and many other times later. By far, the best part of **working** in the show room was the opportunity to watch the girls in the chorus line. There was one petite redhead in particular who seemed to be **looking** at me every time I was eyeing her. We'd smile, and that was about as far as our relationship went. This wasn't far enough to suit me. I put my young brain to work on how I could manage to meet her without getting in trouble.

Chapter 3

A few days of consideration brought the scheme of writing a note to the cute redhead. I scribbled a silly something and ended up the missive by **asking** her to meet me out front after work. Another day or so was all I required to determine how to get the note to her. When I arrived for work one evening, I gave the note to **Blackie,** the casino doorman, and asked him to pass it to her when she came in. As I handed the folded paper to **Blackie,** I glanced around like a thief, hoping no one was watching. I thought I was taking a real gamble with my job, but, damn, she was cute.

That night, I was to work the bingo game which would begin immediately following the show. The famous pianist, Liberace, was performing at the Beverly Hills. Liberace always appeared on stage wearing a brilliant white tuxedo. As he played, featuring his signature high hand motions, the gleam from that white jacket would have made a good commercial for Tide. I was standing at the rear of the show room waiting for him to finish so I could get the bingo set up. As he neared the grand climax of his performance, my friend with the reddish-purple hair jumped up from a table down front and bounded up onto the stage. She was wearing a bright red dress that clung to every curve of her body (and did she have curves!). Every eye in the house was riveted on her. "My God," I said to the captain standing next to me. "That's the whore who always comes in the casino."

The audience stirred. Perhaps some of the patrons thought she was part of the show, but the expression on **Liberace's** face said that he sure as hell didn't think so. The captain and I watched helplessly as she jiggled across the stage to the hoots and catcalls of the men in the audience. Arriving at center stage, she sat down on the piano bench right beside Liberace.

He appeared to be embarrassed, but he handled it like the professional that he was. He chatted with the woman for a minute while the gallery wondered what was going on, then she paraded back across the stage and to her seat. Liberace resumed the piece he'd been playing when she **inter-**

rupted and finished it just as nothing had happened. How I'd love to know what they found to talk about!

Just before I started back stage, I looked toward the front door just in time to see **Blackie** hand the redhead my note. She accepted it questioningly. **Blackie** nodded toward me. My heart was pounding as she quickly read my words. She looked toward me, and after an eternity, smiled and nodded "yes." She motioned out the front door. I was all smiles getting the bingo machine ready.

When the bingo game was over, I went back to the casino to begin my shift at blackjack. I walked into the dealers break room just in time to hear "Flash" say, "Damn you, Ivan. What the hell were you **thinkin'** about?" Earl and George Billinger were doubled up with laughter.

"Ivan ate Rash's dinner," Earl giggled in answer to my unspoken question..

"Seems a natural enough mistake," I said, **thinking** of two identical paper bags in the refrigerator.

"Natural mistake, hell!" Flash roared. "**Any** damned fool that can't tell the difference between breast of capon and a baloney sandwich ought not be allowed loose on the streets by himself." I joined in the laughter. Even Ivan was amused, although he tried to hide it from Flash.

When my shift ended, I went into the break room and sat around, chewing the fat with the guys. I checked my watch every couple of seconds until almost 2:00 AM. Having no interest in letting the guys know that I had a date with one of the chorus girls, I attempted to exit quietly. My timing was just a little off; the cute redhead fell in step with me as I crossed the casino. I glanced around, hoping no one saw us. I was sure I was violating company policy.

"Hi," she said with a big smile.

"Hello," I answered. Suddenly, even though I observed all the bosses watching, I didn't much care about policy.

"I'm **Jackie Foley**," she said as we walked out the front door.

"Wayne **Dammert**," I mumbled, embarrassed that I hadn't even thought to find out her name.

"Yeah, I know," she said, taking my arm.

We found my car. "Nice car," she commented.

"I bought it with my mustering-out pay from the Navy," I said, starting the engine. "Where would you like to go?'

She considered that for a moment, then suggested, "I'm hungry. Let's go to Schilling's," an all-night restaurant in Fort Mitchell.

We talked, ordered, talked, ate, and talked some more. **Jackie** was absolutely gorgeous, and I did my inexperienced best to charm her. I don't know if she tried, but she certainly did charm me. She said that she was twenty-one, but I didn't believe her — she didn't look it. Among many other details, she informed me that she'd been one of New **York's** Radio

City Music Hall's famed Rockettes. I was impressed. After a couple of hours, we left and I drove her back to the **Newport** boarding house where she was staying. We sat in the car for another hour or so and talked some more. When I finally arrived home, I happened to catch my reflection in the hall mirror. I had show-girl make up all over my face. I was glad my mother was not awake yet — I'd have difficulty explaining how I got all that make up on me by just **talking**.

When I reported for work the next night, one of the big bosses was waiting for me just inside the foyer. He didn't speak, just wiggled a finger for me to come to him. My blood froze — I knew he'd seen me leave with **Jackie** the previous evening. I still hadn't completely shaken the gangster image of some of the owners, and I thought that being fired was the best that would happen to me. Some of the tales I'd heard about cement overshoes at the bottom of the Ohio river flashed through my mind as I approached him.

"Yes, sir," I stammered.

"I saw you leave with one of the chorus girls last night." I couldn't read his mood from those words.

"Yes, sir," I repeated, awaiting my fate.

"Well," he said slowly, "it's all right if you date 'em, but don't be seen leaving the building together." I heaved a sigh of relief as he explained that as the girls were strictly "hands off' for the customers, they felt that if customers observed them leaving with employees, it would reflect badly on the Club. I went to work with a light heart.

Neva, the woman who ran **Jackie's** boarding house, was a retired show girl. That being the case, her place seemed to attract a lot of these girls, not only from the Beverly, but the other clubs in the area as well. It was a dandy place for a guy like me to hang out. They fed me at the boarding house table, and I met a lot of beautiful women. The show girls came and went with regularity. I dated **Jackie** for a while, and we had a good time, but she soon departed for greener pastures. At least she helped me get past being frightened of even speaking to the girls.

Soon after **Jackie** was gone, I made a date with another of the show girls, Kim Montgomery, who was from Hollywood, California. Wouldn't you know that the night I was to meet her, something went awry at work, and I was very late in **picking** her up. I dreaded the reception I would get, but I thought that I at least owed her an explanation. Much to my surprise, she was delighted to see me. She explained that her boyfriend having stood her up was the reason she'd left California. She said that just before I showed up, she'd decided that she wasn't going to have much better luck in Kentucky. I was the one that had the luck!

While dealing blackjack one night, one of the players informed me that he was a skater in the Ice Capades, which was performing in the **Cin-**

cinnati Gardens for the rest of the week. When I exhibited some interest, he gave me two passes for the next evening's show at the Gardens. I was delighted when he asked me to meet him at the stage door.

Larry Vincent, the lounge piano player, lived near me, and it was common knowledge that his eyesight was not good enough for him to drive at night, so he often rode to work with me. On one particular humid August evening I left the top down on my convertible. Arriving at Larry's place, I parked the car and ran across the street to a drug store. When I returned, Larry, the stolid piano player, was sitting in the front seat, sporting a black, hairy gorilla mask with a red ribbon at the top. A wisp of smoke curled up from a foot-long cigar protruding from the gorilla's mouth. When I stopped laughing, I drove to Covington, to the hoots and honks of other drivers, where, as usual, I picked up George Fisher, a friend who was a dice dealer at the club. To the amazement of George and myself, Larry handed George a platinum blond wig that would have made Mae West proud. Larry insisted that George wear the wig. So, off to work we went, good ol' Wayne with a gorilla smoking a cigar and an ugly, imitation Mae West to keep him company.

The next evening, I had the day off, so Kim and I put the Ice Capades passes to use. As arranged, we met the man who'd given me the passes at the stage door. Kim and I remained backstage the entire evening and saw how they managed the show and met most of the performers. The night ended on a sour note for me, however. When we arrived back at the boarding house, Neva handed Kim a message saying that her father had called. As it turned out, nothing was wrong, but Kim's father had arranged for her to return to California. Before I knew it, Kim was gone.

Things sailed along at the Beverly Hills. Whatever else it may have been, working there was not boring. At one point, the Andrews Sisters were appearing in our show. I loved their music, and delighted in listening to and watching their unique singing style. One evening while I was setting up for the bingo, one of the Andrews girls (I never did learn to tell them apart) walked across the stage wearing a full-length mink coat. This was not unusual; she played bingo nightly, and usually wore that coat

"Hello, there," she said with a smile, seeing me with the bingo machine.

"How ya doing," I said. "Great show tonight."

"Glad you enjoyed it." She started to walk on.

As this was another hot, humid Kentucky summer night, curiosity got the better of me. "Hey," I shouted at her, "why are you wearing that big coat."

She turned, but did not answer. Slowly, a cat-that-got-the-cream grin spread over her face. Maneuvering so that her back was to the audience, she opened the coat, revealing a tiny, sheer pink negligee that was all she was wearing beneath the coat. She gave me an eyeful and told me to be sure to call her numbers. As I stood there gasping, she calmly closed her coat then moved out into the crowd. Nope, it wasn't boring.

Nor was it boring the night the alarm buzzer went off in the casino. I was dealing blackjack when the irritating sound pierced the air. "What the hell is that," I shouted to the pit boss.

"Police raid," he shouted in return. The gambling surfaces sat on regulation pool tables. Removing the false tops transformed the casino into a billiards parlor. The customers were aware that such things might happen; I suppose they depended on us to get things in order quickly. "Get that blackjack table out of here!" he ordered.

"Where do I put it?"

"In one of the stalls in the ladies room."

Without hesitation, I snatched the blackjack surface from the table and headed down the hall. The screams of violated modesty from the women attending to business in there vaporized whatever complacency I'd developed about our operation being illegal. As it turned out, the doorman had panicked — there was no raid. Although it disrupted the entire evening and caused a few minor heart attacks, we were all glad it was a false alarm.

I was backstage getting set up for bingo when Georgia, a dancer, approached me. "Wayne," she said, "can I see you a minute?"

"Sure," I replied. "What's on your mind?"

She smiled coyly. "Well, one of the other girls asked me to speak to you."

I didn't know this girl very well, but I started to suspect she was pulling my leg. "About what," I asked suspiciously.

"Betty wants to go out with you." Her statement was so straightforward, I didn't think she was teasing. "Are you interested?"

"I don't know her," I said. "I have to see her first."

"Well, come on and I'll point her out to you."

We walked out front. All the chorus girls were sitting at the bar, waiting for the bingo to begin. Georgia pointed to the most beautiful woman in the group. "That's Betty," she said.

I'll say I was interested! I couldn't believe that she'd have any interest in me.

By the summer of 1958, I became concerned about what I was doing. The fact that the entire operation was illegal bothered me more and more. I didn't really worry about police raids — I was assured that the pay-off's took care of that — but, still, the idea of going to prison was not appealing. One of the things I liked about my job, though, was that my afternoons were free. I could play golf or cruise the Ohio in my boat all I pleased. The leisure and uncertainty elements of my job came together one afternoon when I, by chance, played a round of golf with the Campbell County sheriff. In the course of conversation, I mentioned that I worked at the Beverly Hills. The sheriff laughingly said, "Well, you tell 'em to take good care of you, or I'll come out there and shut the place down."

A few days after Betty had been pointed out to me, Jim Wolf, another of the dealers, and I were in my boat on the river. "Slow down, Wayne," Jim yelled.

"What?" I asked, pulling the throttle back. Jim pointed to a boat, near the bank, full of women. Closer inspection revealed them to be almost the entire Beverly Hills chorus line, including Betty, the girl I was to meet. I pulled alongside.

Her name was Betty Rose Silva; she was from Hillside, New Jersey. As was true for several of the other girls, she had been one of the Radio City Music Hall Rockettes before she came to the Beverly. Betty had also appeared on television's Jackie Gleason Show as one of the June Taylor dancers. As a dancer, she had toured most of the world with various groups. As we became acquainted, Jackie **Gleason's** trademark "And away we go!" kept running through my mind.

And we did go. January 1959 found me standing at the altar in New Jersey. Betty lost her job over it — she was fired as soon as the management discovered we were engaged — and neither of us were very happy about that. Despite that attitude, management did give us some very nice wedding gifts, which seemed paradoxical to me. Love bloomed at the Beverly Hills — the same scenario was repeated by several other couples.

After Betty and I had been married a year or so, my concerns about my job came to the boiling point. For one thing, we already had our first child, so my line of work was unsettling. For another, a change in management policy concerning distribution of tips collected in the casino upset me. Previously, all tips were pooled and distributed evenly among the dealers. For some reason, the management decided that tips collected at the dice tables would go to the dice dealers, blackjack tips to blackjack dealers, etc. As the biggest tips were on the dice tables, this change did not make the rest of us happy.

More importantly, the illegal activities in Campbell County were getting completely out of hand. Murder, prostitution and gambling were so pervasive throughout the vicinity that the local citizenry had decided to take action. The residents of **Newport** had formed the Committee of Five Hundred with the intent of cleaning up the area, and they were applying a lot of pressure. The publicity the Committee generated concerning illegal gambling, pay-off's and Mafia influence made everyone uneasy.

In the middle of this activity, Milton Berle was appearing at the Beverly. The place was packed for his show, and remained so for the bingo. During the game, I made some reference to the noise the customers were making. At the end of the game, one of the big bosses called me aside. "Wayne," he said, "you were out of line with that comment about the noise."

Already upset, I shot back, "Well, the bingo players couldn't hear me calling the numbers."

"As long as you've been here, I'd think you'd know that the customer is always right."

Having no good reply for that, I said, "Well, it's good that you care about the customers, because you clearly don't care about **us**."

He glared at me for a long minute. "Just what the hell do you mean by that?" His voice was not **kind**.

"I mean we're getting screwed on the tips." The look on his face told me I'd made a mistake.

"I think it'd be a good idea if you took a few weeks off." He turned and walked away.

Disgusted, I stomped out of the building, determined to never return. In a few days, I found other employment and thought I was out of the whole mess. But after a while, I got an urge to return to the Beverly. I called, and was advised to come in the next night. When I arrived, the **parking** lot was empty and the building dark. No doorman met me, but, to my surprise, the door opened when I pulled. I found all the bosses sitting dejectedly at a table in the front lounge.

"What's going on?" I asked.

Only one of the group bothered to look up. "We're closed," he mumbled. "The heat is **on**."

We were witnessing the end of an era.

Chapter 4

Throughout our rich history, Kentuckians have never wanted for political entertainment. The laws of the Commonwealth ensure that the citizens are faced with an election of some type every year, and the history books will attest to the aptness of the famous "and politics the damnedest, in Kentucky." Many, if not most, of Kentucky's election campaigns are spiced with tales of illegal voter influence, intimidation, murder, and ballot box tampering; political intrigue is a general rule.

The campaigns in Campbell County in 1961 proved no exception to that rule. County sheriff was one of the offices up for grabs. Along with two more traditional candidates, George Ratterman, former **Notre** Dame and Cleveland Brown star quarterback, brought an **NFL** "toughguy" image to the campaign. Backed by the Committee of 500 and the newly formed **Newport** Civic Association, Ratterman, family man, father of eight, and the "all American boy," entered the race as an independent, with a platform to clean up the vice in the area.

To say that those who owned and operated the myriad gambling establishments were upset would be gross understatement. Everyday throughout the spring of '61, the newspapers were filled with charges and counter charges flying among the candidates. In opposition to the reform committees, the **Newport** Businessmen and Taxpayers League contended that reform would severely cramp local business revenue.

As a citizen, I was in favor of the reform movement — the lawlessness was completely out of hand. I had major concerns about raising a family in the area. As a former casino employee, I knew the truth of what the businessmen were saying, too. Estimates of the gambling in Northern Kentucky had it at $20,000,000 per year. The amount of money that flowed through the Beverly Hills casino in just one night may have ranged up to several hundred thousand dollars. A question in my mind, however, was what benefit was all that cash flow to the community? I had no idea of where all the money went. A very small portion of it was paid to the employees. That money did, of course, support legal local business. Some larger part went to pay-off the law enforcement officials, but I could not see how that helped the area. As for the bulk of the funds, who knows? The only certainty is that none of the illegal money was going into any city, county or state tax coffers.

Just as the weather warmed in the spring of '61, so did the political battle. As the candidates and citizens groups got into the swing of the affray, the obvious contempt in which they held each other moved things far beyond typical campaign rhetoric. Ratterman, initially viewed as a political lightweight, soon proved that his tough image was more than that, with his vicious attacks on the illegal activity. In turn, he endured much abuse. At one point, when Ratterman asked his audience if they wanted the laws of the state enforced, the answer was an emphatic "Hell no!"

The height of the storm came at 2:30 AM on May 9, 1961. In response to an anonymous tip call complaining of prostitution, three Newport police officers entered the private apartment of Tito Carinci at the Glenn Hotel. In the room with Ratterman was a woman named Juanita Jean Hodges. Both she and Ratterman were partially undressed. Miss Hodges, 26 years old of Houston, Texas, was appearing in the area as a striptease dancer under the unforgettable stage name of April Flowers. Both parties were arrested: Ratterman charged with breach of peace, resisting arrest and disorderly conduct; April Flowers with engaging in prostitution.

George Ratterman and his backers immediately declared the entire situation as a frame-up to discredit him. The candidate's story was that he'd agreed to meet with Carinci, a business associate, and a mutual friend and another business associate, Thomas Paisley, that evening. Ratterman said that they had dinner and a drink in Carinci's apartment and then he began to feel groggy, so he stretched out on a bed just before Paisley left. He knew nothing else, he said, until he was awakened by a great commotion caused by several men in the room, tearing at his shirt and trousers. He did notice a woman, partially undressed, as the men, who said they were police officers, tore off his trousers and shorts as he was pushed to the floor. He claimed that the police were obviously involved in the frame as they ripped his trousers from him and refused to return them. Ratterman's statement ended with a positive spin; "This will help the cause. The decent citizens cannot help but be impressed with the low-level type opposing us and will deplore these underworld tactics."

The facts, as reported by the newspapers, seemed to support the frame-up theme. The Cincinnati Enquirer's May 10 headline declared that Ratterman was the victim of "knock-out" drops as chloral hydrate had been found in samples of his blood in tests performed by Kettering Laboratories. On the same day, Newport mayor, Ralph Mussman, appointed two policemen to investigate the Ratterman case, saying, "One matter of grave concern involves the claim that a drug was administered to Mr. Ratterman for the purpose of framing him. If these claims are truthful, I am just as much interested in seeing that he is vindicated as I would be seeing that he is prosecuted if he is found guilty."

As for Ratterman's companions, Carinci was also charged with resisting arrest because he tried to prevent the policemen from entering the room, while Paisley said that everything was perfectly normal when he departed.

Summer blew up the Ohio as the battle waxed and waned. George Ratterman demonstrated his courage by never retreating a step in his quest for the sheriff's office. Amid the police and grand jury investigations, the *Enquirer* pointed out that what had happened to George Ratterman "is a melodramatic answer to Campbell County residents who ask, 'Why can't we get more candidates of high caliber?'"

The Saturday Evening Post had another answer to that question. With reference to a previous election, the *Post* reporter said that a Newport official had told him, "...anybody who'd run for office on a platform of throwing out gambling would get about as many votes as a prointergationist candidate for a Mississippi school board... " The early sixties were interesting times.

Additionally, the newspapers reported that the same tactic had been used before. In 1951, said the paper, "Conditions had sunk to a new low even for Newport, and in revulsion voters swept in office the four Newport Civic Association (NCA) candidates... Early in the NCA's administration, the gambling and vice interests looked about for an intermediary. They fingered a young clergyman of the faith of most of the leaders of the NCA.

"Under circumstances similar to the Ratterman case, but unpublished, the clergyman, clad only in shorts, was photographed in the apartment of a gambling operator's mistress. There are those who say he was framed after being drugged or made drunk." I read the papers and went to work each morning, glad that I was no longer involved. In the furor, no one noticed, except those of us who had a personal interest, that the Beverly Hills Supper Club officially closed its doors on July 18.

George Ratterman was tried in police court trial on the three charges against him and speedily acquitted, despite the damning testimony of April Flowers.

October brought the bombshell I'd expected all along. April Flowers refuted her previous statements, claiming that she'd been double-crossed. She now said that Mr. Ratterman had been unconscious and fully clothed at all times until the arresting officers arrived. The papers quoted her as saying that she'd told this true story to the FBI and that "the racket boys" were now trying to get her to deny it. The prostitution charge against her had been reduced to breach of peace. George Ratterman said that he admired her courage. I wondered if the fact that the charge was still pending against her had any bearing on her actions.

Later in the month, the grand jury ended its six-month investigation, returning indictments against the three policemen who had arrested Ratterman, one of whom was **Upshere** White, the current **Newport** chief of police, Ratterman's friend, **Tito** Carinci, and two other men. All six were charged with conspiring to violate and actually violating Mr. Ratterman's civil rights. The grand jury's report minced no words concerning conditions in Campbell County: "...We have... reached the inescapable conclusion that there has been no effort whatsoever on the part of the local police...to enforce criminal laws...related to gambling and vice. And we have also reached the conclusion that there has been no effort on the part of the Commonwealth's Attorney, County Attorney, or City Attorney of **Newport** to do anything whatsoever to carry out their sworn duties to enforce the law, violations of which are apparent to any resident of Campbell County."

November 1961 saw Mr. Ratterman elected Campbell County sheriff, receiving almost as many votes as the other two candidates combined. Given all the circumstances of his victory and the fact that the returns reflected the sentiments of most of the residents, his mandate was clear — the vice was to come to an end.

Before long, the goal was accomplished — all of the gambling casinos were closed, the illegal liquor sales and prostitution were just memories. Most of the people involved in the gambling activities moved on to Las Vegas where they could ply their trade legally. I thought about going, too, but my roots were too firmly planted in Kentucky. When I've had occasion to visit Las Vegas, it's like old home week — many of the casino personnel, even today, are the folks I worked with in the old days. In 1979, the *Cincinnati Enquirer Sunday Magazine* ran a story titled "How **Newport** died and went to heaven" on some of these people. The conclusion amuses me: "To dozens of men who once lurked in the shadowy world of **North-err** Kentucky gambling, Las Vegas is a paradise where their games operate unbounded. But you get the idea from talking to them that somehow life was more fun beating the law back on the banks of the 0-HI-0."

Part Two

A New Beginning

Chapter 5

When the wheels of time wound around to the late 60's I was well entrenched in my job in industry. Despite the fact that Betty and I had four children, she'd still managed to find time to open a dance studio which was doing well. The Beverly Hills was a seldom mindful memory. Along with the vice in the area, the Club was gone.

When Betty and I went out to dinner, one of our favorite spots was The Lookout House, located atop a hill in Fort Wright. The establishment was owned and managed by Mr. Richard Schilling, a man I knew as he had been a frequent visitor at my blackjack table in the old days. As the previous operator of Schilling's restaurant, Mr. Schilling knew a lot about the restaurant business, and his reputation was for sparing no expense to create and maintain a first-class environment. He surpassed that reputation at the Lookout House, even going so far as to add a touch of nostalgia by offering his customers casino-type gambling — with play money, of course.

One evening in the early spring of 1970, my wife and I were dining at the Lookout House when Richard Schilling approached our table. "How you **doin'**, Wayne?' he asked, smiling and extending his hand. Mr. Schilling was always chatting with the customers, and I felt that he usually made an extra effort whenever he saw me there.

"I'm **doin'** great," I responded, shaking his hand.

"Everything going all right with your **dinner?"** His concern for the customer always came first.

"Just fine, as usual."

We talked about old times for a few minutes. Then he announced, "I've made a little purchase that'll interest you."

"Yeah?' I said. **"What's** that?'

A sly grin covered his face. "Well, I've taken this place about as far as it's gonna go."

"You sure have," I agreed, looking around. It seemed that the Lookout

House was under continual improvement. "This is the nicest restaurant around."

"Thanks," he said with a smile. "But, I'm ready for a new challenge." He paused a moment, then, grinning wider, announced, "I bought the Beverly Hills."

Now I understood his grin. "That building's been empty for seven or eight years, now," I commented.

"Well, not actually. Someone tried to make a go of it last year, you know."

"Oh, yeah, I heard about that," I said. "Failed, didn't they?'

"Yeah," he replied. "They only lasted a couple of months. I bought it right at the end of the year."

"What **kind** of shape is it in?'

"It's pretty rough," he said. "Doesn't matter, though. I'm going to remodel and try to make it into a real showplace."

"A hell of an idea. That's a prime location up there. The building's a little small though, isn't **it?"** In all my years of working there, I'd learned a little of the history of the place. The Beverly Hills building was some 35 years old at that point, and was relatively small, by night club standards.

"Yes," he said. "It's a little small for what I have in mind, but you're right, it's a prime location for a restaurant. I'm going to remodel what's there and add on to it. I've got in mind to make the Beverly Hills the finest nightclub this side of Las Vegas." The gleam in his eyes showed his excitement with the project.

"Sounds great," I said. "I wish you every success."

"Thanks," he responded with a smile. "I'm up there every day, supervising the work. Stop by sometime and let me show you what I'm doing."

"I'd love to see it," I said.

A few weeks later, after work one day, I decided to take Mr. Schilling up on his invitation. On a beautiful April evening, I drove south on US 27 and made the turn onto the steep driveway winding up to the Beverly Hills location atop the hill. The parking area was full of construction equipment and heaps of gravel. Stacks of pipe festooned the site. The light was fading and apparently the construction workers had finished for the day. **Parking** the car, I weaved my way to the front entrance.

Inside, the place was a shambles. I walked through the foyer into the barroom. The floor was covered with so much debris of various kinds that a puff of dust flew up from my every step. The walls were stripped down to the studs, and all that remained of the oval bar that was once so elegantly paneled and padded was the metal framework. To my left, the huge room that was the kitchen when I worked here was also empty — all the fixtures were missing. On my right, double doors were standing open, allowing me to look into the dealer's break room. It, too, was stripped and full of trash. I walked into the small room and looked past it into the casino. Of course, all the gaming equipment was gone. Vacant, the area looked much larger than I remembered.

I turned back into the bar area. As I walked forward into the old showroom, a harsh voice yelled, "Hey! What the hell are you doing?"

I turned to see a hefty man wearing a plaid shirt and a hard hat approaching me.

"Just **lookin'** around. Mr. Schilling invited me to stop by sometime." I smiled.

"He's not here right now. You got any business in here?" He did not return my smile.

"Nah. I just thought I'd look it over." As he continued to glare, I added, "I used to work here, in the old days."

With that, he smiled and extended his hand. " I'm the construction foreman. Has this place changed much since the last time you were in here?"

"Well," I drew out the word looking around, "it wasn't this dirty."

He laughed. "We're **workin'** on it, ain't we? Mr. Schilling's got a lot of big ideas about what he wants to do with the place."

"I'll just bet he does," I commented. "You probably know as well as I do that he's never satisfied. He told me that he planned to build this into some place."

"Yeah, he does. We're going to remodel the whole thing and do it up first class." As he looked around the room, the influence of Richard Schilling was clear — I could see the visions of elegance in his eyes.

"What's the plan," I asked.

He turned to our left. "Over there," he began, pointing, "where the kitchen used to be, is what Mr. Schilling's calling the main dining area now. The barroom will still be the bar, and this will still be the show room, although he got plans for a new show room on the back approved just the other day ." He turned to face to the right. "The old casino area is now called the Viennese Room — more dining space."

"Where's the kitchen gonna be?"

"They've built an all new one on the back comer. It's huge."

"What's going upstairs?" I asked, indicating the stairs just inside the front entrance.

"More dining rooms," he answered. "He's calling that the Crystal Rooms."

"Rooms?" I said. "Is he going to divide it up?"

"Sort of. There's a big room on each side of the hall up there. We're gonna have folding dividers that can be used to partition each side into three smaller areas." His hands drew rooms in the air above his head as he spoke.

"That'll be nice," I observed. "So it'll accommodate several small parties or a couple of big ones."

"You got the idea." We fell silent for a moment, just **looking** and dreaming of the grandeur to come. Then, he added, "You got it right about it being nice, too. All the stuff Mr. Schilling's ordered will really dress this place up. There's nothing but the best money can buy going in here." His voice was laced with pride.

As we started **walking** toward the rear of the building, someone yelled. I turned to see Lee Ramsdell, an old friend, **walking** into the room. "Lee, what are you doing here?' I **asked** with a smile.

"Hi, Wayne. I'm going to be one of the managers when it re-opens." I could hear the pride in his voice, too.

"Yeah? When do you hope to open?'

"Sometime in the fall, I guess. As you can see, there's a lot of work to be done."

"Speakin' of which, I better get at it," the foreman said. He turned and walked toward the front of the building.

Lee and I wandered on into the room. In the middle of the concrete floor were some ashes from where someone had had a fire for warmth, probably. The sight brought a vague memory to mind. "This building burned one time, didn't it, Lee?'

"Yep. 'Way back, in the thirties, I think," he replied. "The story was that Pete Schmidt, who owned the place, wouldn't sell out to the criminal syndicate who wanted control, so they torched the joint."

"I remember hearing about that," I said. "There were some people caught in it, I seem to recall."

"I think the caretaker and his family were upstairs at the time. There's no fire exit up there," he added, thoughtfully. "It seems to me they jumped out a window and were injured by the fall. Seems like a daughter or a niece or something was **killed**." Neither of us knew that there was still no fire exit upstairs, a fact which would endanger my life seven years in the future.

"What **kind** of things has Mr. Schilling ordered?' I **asked** to break the mood. I remembered the foreman's comment, and I already knew that only the best would do for Mr. Richard Schilling.

"Oh, all **kinds** of stuff," Lee answered. " He and a decorator have been all over the country **looking** to see how other night clubs are fixed up. He's taking the best of their ideas and throwing in a few of his own. The carpet will be mostly red. We're gonna cover the walls with fancy wallpaper and wood frames. Then mirrors and original oil paintings — high class stuff, all of it — will hang on that. Some of it's stored back there now. The biggest thing, though, is the chandeliers." We started **walking** back out of the building.

"Are they pretty? Crystal?' I **asked** as we neared the front door. The construction foreman joined us just inside the entrance.

"Oh, yeah," Lee answered me. The ones he's got coming in are from Europe. High class crystal. One of his ideas is to put in a spiral stairwell up there near the front." He waved in the direction of the old dealer's break room. "He's gonna have a huge chandelier hang from the roof of the building down into the middle of the spiral. It'll be the first thing you see when you come in the place, and the focus of the whole club." Again, we fell silent, each lost in our own visions of how the place would look.

We heard footsteps behind us. Turning, we saw a man wearing a construction hard hat and carrying a clip board headed toward us. "Oh, hell," the foreman sighed, "it's that damned bricklayer."

"What?"

"The city building inspector," he mumbled. "They can't get anybody to take the job, so they've got a damned bricklayer **poking** around here. All he does is try to mess up our work."

The man approached us. "How y'all **doin?**" he greeted us with a smile.

"OK," the construction man answered.

"Mr. Schilling around?'

"No. I think he's gone to Cincinnati this evening."

"Well, tell him to call me. I've got a few concerns I want to go over with him." He turned to walk away. "This is gonna be a real nice place," he said in parting.

"What's the deal on him?' I **asked.**

"Oh, just **doin'** his job, I guess," the foreman said with a sigh. "The thing is, though, he don't know his ass from a hole in the ground about building. The law requires that he approve all the plans Mr. Schilling had drawn up, and he don't know any more about what he's **doin'** than a pig knows about Sunday." He shook his head in disgust. With another sigh, he walked away from Lee and me.

The light was failing inside the building. We started to walk out toward the front entrance. I glanced to my left, trying to envision how the spiral staircase and chandelier would look. "Doesn't Mr. Schilling usually have his own ideas?'

We moved out the entrance onto the drive. "Yeah, he does, but state law requires that all plans have to be drawn by a licensed architect and, like the man said, approved by the building inspector. Mr. Schilling tells the architect what he wants, and he draws it up. As a matter of fact, I think that's where he is this evening."

I turned to look back at the Beverly Hills. The exterior of the building had not changed much from the old days. "Well," I said, "I guess I better be **gettin'** home." I extended my hand.

"I'm glad you stopped by," he said, taking my hand. I started toward the car. After I'd taken a couple of steps, Lee called, "Say, Wayne?"

"Yeah?" I said, turning.

"What are you **doin'** now? For a living, I mean."

"I'm a design draftsman. Why?"

"Oh, I just wondered if you'd be interested in **working** here. We're starting to hire staff."

I laughed. "Need blackjack dealers, do you?"

He laughed, too. "I don't think so, but we will need waiters for the banquets and stuff like that. You interested?"

The idea had not even occurred to me. "I don't know," I said with no conviction. Mixed emotions filled my mind. I had a good job, but the pride of those involved with this project was infectious.

"Well, think about it. Nostalgia is gonna be a big part of the new Club. It'd be neat to have some of the old gang around here."

"I'll think it over."

"OK. If you decide you're interested, come on back sometime and we'll talk to Mr. Schilling about it."

I didn't get back soon enough. Betty and I discussed the idea of me **working** at the Beverly Hills again and decided that giving up my job as a draftsman would not be such a good idea. The more I thought about it, though, the stronger the urge to return to the Beverly became. I knew, of course, that the old days were gone, but the attraction of the glamorous atmosphere was strong. I'd just about made up my mind that I'd go see about **working** there part time, when, on June 22, 1970, the Monday morning newspaper announced that Mr. Schilling's "$3 million dream" had gone "up in smoke."

According to the reporter's account, fire had broken out in the building about 3:00 AM on Sunday morning and was in full blaze by the time the Southgate fire department arrived. The exterior of the building had been saved, but the interior was totally destroyed, wiping out all the beautiful fixtures Mr. Schilling had installed as well as his plans for soon reopening. The paper said that the renovation was nearly complete. Now, the building and all his work was gone.

Given the history of the Beverly Hills, arson was naturally suspected. Southgate fire chief, Ray Muench, called for an investigation by the Kentucky State Police, but down-played that aspect in his comments to the newspaper. "It's normal to have an investigation in a fire like this," he said. Then he added, "Besides, we have no idea what caused the fire."

After I read the paper's account of the damage, I first felt that this would be the end of the Beverly Hills. But, knowing Mr. Schilling as I did, I was sure that he'd eventually find some way to recover from the loss and reopen the club. I remembered the gleam in his eyes as he'd told me that he intended to make it the "showplace of the nation," and knew that this was only a setback in the process.

A few days later, I read the newspaper account of the fire again paying more attention to the dollar estimates of the damage and the insurance figures, trying to gain an understanding of Schilling's financial situation. I didn't know how he'd do it, but I did know that he'd get the club open again, somehow.

Not even on the second time through, however, did the fire chief's comment register on my mind about what was in the future for the club and me. Tucked away among the comments was Chief Muench's observation, "The fire had a pretty good start on us, especially up on that hill. You've always got a good wind going up there, and it didn't help matters any."

The Beverly Hills'new Frontenac Room: Main a la carte dining room. (National Fire Protection Agency)

Chapter 6

As it turned out, I was correct in my thinking about Mr. Dick Schilling. According to the newspapers over the following weeks, he waffled on continuing with the Beverly Hills remodeling project initially, canceling all his construction contracts soon after the fire. Within a week, however, he'd changed his mind and reinstated his plans to rebuild the club. Early in 1971, when I read that the renovation was nearing completion, I decided to go check it out.

Coming up the winding drive, I immediately saw that the place was as appealing as I had read. A series of lights, atop rock pillars strung together with chains, lit the approach to the building. At the front entrance, a large canopy extended from the building to cover the pavement so that patrons could turn their cars over to the **parking** attendants without regard to the weather. As there did not appear to be too much activity, I parked beneath the canopy and ascended the stairs running perpendicular to the landing outside the entrance. On the landing, I made a right angle turn and moved up another flight of steps to the front door. The door opened when I turned the knob.

Inside the building, I faced another set of stairs. At the top of these, I found myself in a beautifully appointed foyer area tacked on to the front of the main bar. The carpet, mirrors, paneling and lighting were all in place, in stark contrast to the barrenness of when I was last here. On my left, I saw what looked like some **kind** of a store as it had a glass front and shelves. Aside from the shelving, the room was empty. Turning to my right, I walked past rest rooms and a couple of telephone booths into the office area.

Just as I entered, Lee **Ramsdell** emerged from a doorway. "Wayne! Good to see you here." He smiled and extended his hand.

"I thought **I'd** stop by to see how you're coming along," I said, shaking hands.

"It's **doin'** great," he enthused. "We'll be ready to open in a month or **so.**"

'Mid-February?"

"Yeah, somewhere around there. Want to see the place?'

"You bet," I replied. "It's a little different from when I was here last."

"Yes, it is," he said, a hint of sadness in his voice as he remembered. "This place was a hell of a mess after the fire." He ushered me back into the main bar area. "This," he announced proudly, "is the Empire Cocktail Lounge."

"Looks like the bar to me," I commented.

"Of course it is," he said with a smile, "but Mr. Schilling's given every room a more elegant name. You'll notice that after you get through the foyer, you have to go through here to get anywhere in the club."

"Good planning," I thought aloud. "I see the bar itself has been re-built." I took in the elegance of the room. "How many people will this room hold?'

'"Bout 100, I guess," he replied. Gesturing at the oval bar, now back in its grandeur, he added, "Maybe 50 at the bar, and the same number at the tables on the floor. At the far end of the room, you'll see the stage and the dance floor. We'll have live entertainment in here every night."

I nodded understanding. "What's that over there?' I asked, indicating the area I'd thought looked like a store.

"That," he answered, stepping in that direction, "is the ladies' bou-tique. You'll notice that not only will it have the finest in ladies fashions and jewelry, but there's dressing rooms for them to try on the clothing." Spreading his arms, he made a pirouette, a huge smile covering his face.

"Nice."

We walked to the left of the bar, past the boutique, into the room which was the kitchen in the old days. It had been totally redone and now ap-peared to be circular inside. A massive stone fireplace in the center ac-cented the roundness of the room. "This," Lee announced, "is the Frontenac Room."

"A la carte dining?' This room was exquisite. I could imagine a fire in the hearth, the glow reflecting from the crystal prisms on the opera-type candle sconces highlighting the murals lining the walls.

'You got it," he said. 'We can seat about 150 people in here for dining. As you observed, we plan to use it for those that just come in to eat."

I noticed a couple of small alcoves along the outside of the room. "Private parties?' I inquired.

"Yep. Each of those will hold a party of six or eight."

"This is as far as we go this way, isn't it?'

"That's the outside wall," he said, pointing to the left. "Let's go back out front." We retraced our steps, moving back through the main bar to the right into a hallway running from the front of the building. The left wall was lined with mirrors. "This is the Hallway of Mirrors," Lee informed.

Before I could reply, the scene on the right of the hall caught my attention. The spiral staircase leading to the second floor had been improved. Beneath the stairs, goldfish swam in a rock-lined pool being fed by a waterfall at the rear. The waterfall trickled down the wall I knew to be the old dealer's room. Looking up, I saw a huge, beautiful chandelier suspended to hang in the center of the curve of the stairs. The gurgle of the water cascading into the pool and the reflections in the mirrors opposite enhanced the beauty of the setting. 'Wow!" I exclaimed.

"Gorgeous, isn't **it**?" **Lee** asked, rhetorically. "You know, there'll be lots of weddings here at the Club. We think this'll be a favorite spot for pictures."

"Should be," I agreed. "It's certainly picturesque."

"That's the idea. I think the performers will probably sign autographs here, too." Moving down the hall, he indicated the small L-shaped room on the right beside the stairs. "You've been in there, I think?'

"A time or two," I said. It was the area we used for the dealer's break room. The memory of all the jokes we'd played in there and the time the dinners got mixed up brought a smile to my face. "What's going to be in there'?'

"Nothing. We plan to just use it for storage." We walked the length of the hall to where it intersected a perpendicular hallway running the entire length of the building from front to back. A couple of steps into this hall, we passed through double doors and descended two steps into what I knew to be the old casino. "This is the Viennese Rooms," he said.

The huge room was decorated mostly in gold. The same kind of sconces I'd seen before adorned the walls, and six crystal chandeliers hung from the ceiling. At the far end of the room, a dance floor separated the seating area from a built-in bar. "Banquets?' I ventured.

'You seem to understand the plan," he said. 'We think this room will hold about 250 people."

"You said 'rooms?'" I remembered.

"That's right. They're not in yet, but we're going to have folding partitions which will break this area up into three rooms if need be."

"Or, you can leave it open for big parties. Good idea."

Lee smiled. "Mr. Schilling's tried to think of everything and told the architect how he wants it done."

"So I see. I'd say he hasn't skimped on the fixtures, either." The carpet, chandeliers, paneling and all the fixtures were strictly first class.

'You got that right. I'm not sure how he managed it — 1 mean the financing and all — but this is a hell of a long way from the pile of ashes this place was back in July."

We went back across the hall into the old **showroom**. The huge stage at the rear center made me think that it was still the show area. "This is the

Empire Room," Lee informed. The decor was a pleasant pink and red accented by five large chandeliers. A big opening at the front of the room would allow patrons to enter at the front door, pass through the bar and move directly into this room. "Wow!" I exclaimed, "this is nice."

"This area was totally wiped out in the fire," Lee said. "We had to rebuild this from scratch." Again, I could see his pride.

"You're going to have shows in here?'

"No," he said. "We've built a new showroom on the back."

"Lee! Where the hell are you?' someone shouted.

"In here," Lee yelled. We turned to see Dick Schilling enter from the bar.

He smiled when he saw me. "Hello, Wayne. What do you think of the joint?' We shook hands.

"It's fabulous," I said, honestly. "First class."

"Thanks," he replied. "I'm trying to make it live up to the billing — 'Showplace of the Nation.'"

"It's right there," I commented. "A long way to come from the fire, wasn't it?"

"Sure was. I was real discouraged right after the fire, but what the hell, something like that wasn't going to stop me."

"I'm glad you went on. This is going to be great."

"Thanks, again," he said. "What are you doing here?'

"Oh, just **looking** around."

"Wayne may be coming to work with us." Lee said.

That comment hit me as a shock. The last time we'd talked about it was back in the spring, before the fire. As Mr. Schilling waited for my response, the thought occurred that I'd probably had that in the back of my mind when I decided to drive up today. Although it had been a while, Betty and I had discussed my working at the Beverly, and pretty much decided that **working** part time might be fun. "Do you have anything for me?' I finally asked.

Mr. Schilling looked at Lee. "I thought Wayne could work as a banquet waiter," Lee said.

"You interested?' Mr. Schilling asked.

"Yes," I said. "I'm not ready to give up my job, but I thought I might do it part time." After a pause, I added, "At first, anyway."

"Good!" Mr. Schilling exclaimed, to my delight. "We're going to have a lot of nostalgic objects around here, you know, from the old days. It'll be good for business."

"I hope you're not counting me as a nostalgic object," I joked. "Hell, I'm not that old."

"No, no," he laughed. "I was just thinking that some of the old time customers will probably still be around, and a familiar face will just add to their enjoyment of the place. We'll be glad to have you." He shook my hand again.

"Lee," he said, turning, "there's a letter from the State on your desk. It seems the fire marshal has some concerns about the building. Would you take care of it?"

"Yes, sir." Lee hurried toward the office.

"Are you pretty much through with the building?' I asked.

"Oh, **no**," Mr. Schilling replied. "Just getting started."

"Oh?' I said, surprised. "Looks about ready to me."

"Yeah, it is, but I've got lots of plans for improvement and enlargement. For example, the showroom isn't big enough to suit me."

"I haven't seen it," I commented.

"You don't have to twist my arm," he said with a huge grin. "Let's go." He escorted me down the main hallway past the end of the Viennese Rooms into a huge new showroom. "This," he said with pride, "is the Cabaret Room."

The room was big and fabulously decorated. Glancing around at what I considered to be the vast area, I said, "And this isn't big enough?'

"Oh, no," he replied

"It looks like this will hold five or six hundred," I said, glancing around the room.

"That's right, but I want to build a *big* showroom." He spread his arms wide, indicating the space he envisioned. "Also, we're putting in a garden area in the rear, and I'm **thinking** about building another dining room back there with a glass wall **overlooking** the garden." I could just see the dreams swirling in his mind as he spoke.

"What **kind** of entertainment do you plan?' I **asked.**

The question seemed to break his reverie. "Just like the old days," he replied. "I can't give you any names just yet, but I'm after the biggest stars there are. We're going to have the likes of Bob Hope and Frank Sinatra in here, if I can get 'em."

"I'm sure you will."

He turned and started **walking** toward the bar. "If I don't, it won't be because I didn't try. My sons and I plan to make this the finest restaurant and club to be found anywhere."

"I'd like to help." I found that I'd warmed to the idea of **working** here. We had moved into the front of the building.

"Glad to have you. Well, I've got work to do." We shook hands again.

"Mind if I wander around a little more?'

"**Help** yourself," he said, **walking** into the offices. "See you soon."

I conducted myself throughout the building. Every detail was first class, even the **kitchen** and dish washing area. I climbed the service stairs from the **kitchen** to the second floor. Up there, a hall ran the width of the **build-**

ing, dividing the second floor into two large dining areas, one toward the front of the building, the other opposite. I shivered as it was cold up there. Although they were not in place, I could see the tracks for the folding partitions that would break up each room into smaller sections as necessary. Inside the front room, I looked out the window overlooking the roof of the front part of the club and the highway down the hill.

I guess I stood there a long time, reliving scenes from the past and envisioning those yet to come. I was sure that the new Beverly Hills would

The spiral stairway at The Beverly Hills. (National Fire Protection Agency)

be every bit as exciting as the old place had been. I knew that Mr. Schilling would complete every plan and build it into the finest to be found. In the old days, **working** there was just like going to a party every night, and the new club would be just the same. **Walking** down the hall, I thought about Mr. Schilling's and his sons' reputations, and I knew that it'd be hard work — he was demanding — but the enjoyment of the customer was the object, so it would not be onerous.

Halfway down the hall, I noticed an opening in the wall. The cold wind howling through the aperture explained the low temperature. Thinking that the door had blown open, I looked out, expecting to close the door. However, there was no door — it was just a hole in the wall, apparently where a door had once been. There was no where to go out there, it just led onto the roof of the front part of the lower part of the building. As there was nothing I could do about it, I just walked on down the hall toward the spiral stairway. As I wound down the stairs, the beauty of the setting struck me once again. I stopped in the hall at the bottom and gazed back up, drinking in the atmosphere of the new Beverly Hills Supper Club. I did not know that fire codes require all stairways to be enclosed, with a fire-proof door at the top and bottom. Neither I, nor Mr. Schilling, nor the architect, nor even the Southgate building inspector were aware that the staircase — the central physical feature of the club — was in violation of city, state and federal fire safety standards.

Front view of the club pre-1971. (W. Dammert)

Chapter 7

The new, improved Beverly Hills Supper Club opened, as scheduled, on February 10, 1971, less than 24 hours after the city of Southgate issued a certificate of occupancy for the rebuilt structure. A few nights later, I worked my first banquet. I was excited and nervous that first evening, but I managed to get through it without incident. Everything was just as I had expected. Mr. Schilling and his sons, Rick, Ron and Scott ran the place with an iron hand. They were very demanding of the employees, but expected nothing that they were not willing to do, and didn't do, themselves. Most nights, the Schilling sons could be seen carrying trays of food to the dining rooms and placing plates into the dishwashers. The furnishings, food and entertainment were all top notch and the customer was king. The environment was hectic most of the time, but quite exciting. About the only thing that surprised me was the prices. One could have an excellent dinner and see a first-class show for a very modest price. Given all of that, it's no wonder that the new club was an instant success.

The swirl of excitement surrounding the new club was interrupted on the morning of February 26. Along with everyone else associated with the club, I was astounded to see the Enquirer's headline: BEVERLY HILLS SUPPER CLUB A SAFETY RISK, SAYS STATE. In the article, we learned that the state fire marshal had not granted final approval of the building because of deficiencies in "stairway enclosures," "insufficient exits," and "interior furnishings."

At work. the newspaper's findings caused no great stir among either the employees or the patrons. One evening, when we'd been discussing the situation on break, I had occasion to ask my boss.

"Is Mr. Schilling aware of what the paper had to say?'

"Of course, he is," he replied. "You know he supervised every shovel-ful of dirt that's been moved around here."

"Well, what's being done?' I asked. "Is the Club safe?"

"Why, hell yes. Mr. Schilling's doing his damnedest to comply with every detail that any of the inspectors have pointed out." I went back to work, whatever small concerns I had, allayed.

One evening while **working** at a banquet upstairs in the Crystal room, I accidentally spilled a drink on a lady. She was upset, of course, and I did my best to make it up to her by paying special attention and giving her and her party a free drink. As they were leaving, I went over to apologize once again.

"I'm really sorry about your dress."

Her reply was one I was to hear repeated many times in the years I worked at the Beverly Hills. "It's OK," she said, "but it's just that I bought this dress especially for the occasion."

Such was the typical patron's attitude about spending an evening at the new Beverly. For a night out, it was the place to be.

Although Mr. Schilling had tried to provide for every aspect of the business, there were still some problems at the beginning. I was **working** a small banquet in the Viennese room one evening when the captain in charge approached me and another waiter.

"Is everything under control in here?" he asked.

"Yes," I said, not knowing what to expect.

"Good. Go move your car."

I really didn't understand why I had to move my car, but once I got a look at the parking lot, I realized that the Club did not have enough parking space to accommodate all the patron's cars. So, we were enlisted to drive our cars down to the **Newport** shopping center, a distance of about four miles. When six or seven of us were at the shopping center, another employee would come in his own car to take us back to the club. I can tell you, some wild rides were had with carloads of us getting back and forth.

On many occasions, we had thirteen bars set up in the Club. Most of the time, whoever had the responsibility to ensure that the bars were always stocked had all they could do to carry bottles from the storeroom to the various bars. Mr. Schilling did not intend for his customers to get thirsty.

Within a month of the opening, Mr. Schilling was called to appear before the Campbell grand jury that had been convened as a result of the newspaper article concerning the safety of the Club. Not much was reported about their meetings — they're secret, of course — but it was known that the fire chief, the building inspector, and the state fire marshal also testified. About a week later, the grand jury's report was released to the public. It said that "We... are satisfied that Beverly Hills has complied

with all fire and safety regulations... We have been informed that the operators of Beverly Hills will train their employees in fire prevention and
fire fighting... as soon as the employment situation stabilizes."

Soon after that report was released, I happened to overhear a conversation between Mr. Schilling and a patron. He still loved to talk to the
customers and made every effort to make them comfortable in the Beverly.
As I walked by they were apparently discussing the Club's safety, as I
heard Mr. Schilling say, "I believe with all my heart that this building is as
safe from fire as any structure in the United States."

Every night was, indeed, a party. Actually, several parties. The schedule was arranged so that while some patrons were having dinner before
they moved into the Cabaret Room for the show, others were having pre-
dinner cocktails in the bar, while still others were attending private func-
tions in some of the smaller rooms. Exact timing was required to fit in all
this activity, and we worked hard at it. There were large, electrically-heated
carts that could hold up to a hundred dinners, keeping the food hot without
drying. These carts were loaded in advance and positioned so that the dinners would be at the right place at the right time. Salads, fruit cups and
appetizers were also prepared in advance and stored on mobile, refrigerated carts. As needed,
these carts were posi-
tioned so that all the busboys had to do was add
the dressing and croutons
before serving. The serv-
ing area was sometimes a
mad house when several
parties were scheduled at
the same time. Busboys,
waiters and waitresses,
and captains all pouring
salad dressing and getting
dinners from the carts
while others were work-
ing from steam tables
where the chef and cooks
were putting meat, sauce
and vegetables onto hot
plates. Occasionally, there
was a glitch in the system,
but we usually managed
it, and in many instances,

Fellow waiter Abraham and me in late 1971. (W. Dammert)

we did so well that a patron would schedule his party's banquet for the following year before he left the club. We considered that fact as a tribute to the Club's personnel.

Some of those nights were very long. Not only with the dining activity, but when that was over — sometimes very late — we'd begin setting up for the next night's business. This was one of the most unpleasant chores we had to perform. After a hard night of serving patrons, the last thing we wanted to do was set tables, place napkins and clean silverware. But, it was part of the job, so we did it. Many times, patrons leaving the late show at maybe 2:00 AM would see a group of employees, including the Schillings, setting up for another round.

In July 1972, I reported to work early one evening to observe a group of employees standing out front watching some activity. I'd been appointed

as a captain — still part time — so I felt a little more responsible. As I approached the group, I asked, "What's going on?'

"They're beginning a new facade for the building," someone answered.

Moving into position, I could see that equipment was in use digging a trench along the front of the building. "Pouring footers?"

"Yep."

"What's it going to look like?'

"I'm not sure," he said. "Mr. Schilling and his architect have been to Las Vegas, looking at buildings. I guess he saw something he liked and is putting it up here."

He was right. Within a month, the facade was in place along the front and the east side of the Beverly Hills. It gave the place the "Las Vegas look", all right. With the false front, statues and fountains, the exterior of the club was every bit as attractive as the interior.

Front view of the club about 1976. (W. Dammert)

Entertainment at the Beverly Hills had no rival east of Las Vegas, either. During the early seventies, such big names as Ray Charles, the Mills
Brothers, Milton Berle, Jim Nabors and Bobby Goldsboro appeared regularly in the show room. When Bobby Goldsboro performed, we, along
with the patrons, usually got a special treat as Johnny Bench, the Cincinnati Reds star catcher, would show up and sometimes participate in the
act.

My favorite performer, however, was Joey Heatherton. Joey was a
singer; blond, petite, and drop-dead gorgeous. On a Sunday night, she finished her stint at the Club, playing to a packed house, as usual. After the
last show, I happened to walk near the service bar in the show room where
she was passing out bottles of liquor to the members of the orchestra in
thanks for their performances in her show. As I walked by, she asked, "And
what do you prefer, scotch or bourbon?'

Stunned, both by her looks and the question, I stammered, "Uh, I'm
not in the orchestra."

She stared at me a moment as if she didn't understand. "Well, an hon-
est man," she said with a smile that would melt ice, and handed me a
bottle, anyway. I walked away with a wide smile.

Joey got up on a chair and was giving a little speech to all the folks
who had helped her in the show, telling them how much she appreciated
their work. I walked a few steps to the bar and was talking to a friend when

Joey Hetherton performing in the Cabaret Showroom: 1977. (W. Dammert)

I noticed Joey staring at me. When she finished her talk, she walked over to where I was standing.

"Hi," I said.

"Hello, again."

"I really love your show."

"Thanks," she said. "It's always a little sad to finish the run, I love the Beverly Hills so."

"I'm glad you feel that way. We love it, too." After a few moments, I got bold. "Would you like a drink?'

"Sure. I'll have a double old fashioned."

I turned to the bartender who, obviously paying close attention to the conversation, was already mixing the drink for her. In a moment, he handed the glass to me and I handed it to Joey. "There you go."

"Thanks," she said, taking a sip.

"You know," I said with a grin, "when Connie Stevens plays here, she always gives me a big **kiss** on her last night." It wasn't true, but what the hell.

She flashed that beautiful smile on me. "Thanks for the drink," she said and walked away toward the dressing room.

"Nice try, Wayne," the bartender said as I headed for the **kitchen.**

A bustle of activity was going on in the **kitchen,** which was unusual as it was about 2:00 AM. In response to my question, I was informed that at the last minute, Joey had decided to throw a birthday party for one of the girls who worked for her. I enlisted Larry Wetenkamp, another captain, to help me set up one of the upstairs rooms while the chef prepared some food. We'd just finished when the people started arriving.

It wasn't a large party, maybe about thirty members of Joey's road show staff and band, and Larry and me. We served some canapes, drinks, punch, steaks and baked potatoes, but mostly drinks. When the steaks were served, I sat a large platter loaded with foil-wrapped potatoes on a table in the center of the small room. I'd only just stepped away when someone asked for a potato.

"I'll get it for you," Joey shouted. She walked to the tray, grabbed a potato, and threw it across the room to the guy who had requested it. When the hot missile landed in his hands, he juggled it a moment, then with a grin, threw it back at Joey. She ducked as the silver bullet flew by, snatched another potato and, without aim, threw it across the room. Then she threw another, then another, then another. Her guests responded in **kind.** Soon, foil-wrapped projectiles were flying back and forth across the room, smashing into people and the walls. It was such fun that I didn't even remember that Larry and I'd have to clean up the mess.

When all the ammunition had been expended and was squashed into the carpet, a large tray of pastries arrived. In a flash, Joey's manager was on it. He selected a huge piece of chocolate cake, stuffed the entire thing into his mouth, and started across the room, cake, icing and whipped cream oozing out of his mouth. An error in judgment brought him close to where Joey was sitting. She grabbed him, and smeared the gooey mess all over his face, into his nose and over his glasses. He stared at her a moment, turned and walked back to the pastry tray. Picking a cream-filled eclair, he heaved it in Joey's direction. Here we go again, the pastry round of the food fight was on.

As that phase wound down, something was happening on the far side of the room, drawing everyone except Joey away. She remained seated as it occurred to me that I might as well begin cleaning up. I picked the remains of a potato from the floor near where Joey was sitting. All being a little silly anyway, I stuck it under her cute little nose. "How 'bout a potato?'

"Not for me, thank you,?'she said, straight-faced.

I scooped a gob of butter from the carpet. It was a mess with strands of carpet and grit from the floor. "How 'bout some butter?'

Again, straight-faced, she said, "Not for me, thank you."

I tried the sour cream, putting it very close to her nose.

"Not for me, thank you." Her demeanor disclosed not the slightest bit of irritation.

Before I could find another offering, she jumped up, grabbed the half empty punch bowl and started looking for someone to dump it on. First, she made a move in my direction, then took after one of her musicians. Considering her beauty, I don't suppose that men often made an effort to keep away from her, but everyone in the room gave her plenty of space as she ran with the red liquid splashing all over her and the floor.

Someone suggested that her manager put on a show. With some persuasion, he agreed, but said he needed a prop. He left the room, saying he would be right back. While we waited, Joey decided to clean off the **canapé** table. In short order, the food fight moved into the canape phase.

By the time that ended, her manager was back, and the announcement was made that he was going to put on a strip show. Before long, word had spread through the entire building, and everyone left in the place was in attendance. The room was an absolute wreck.

As everyone settled into place, the folding doors at the end of the room slid apart just wide enough to reveal the manager's bare behind in the center of the opening. Hoots and catcalls accompanied the show's opening. He moved into the room, using one of Joey's feather boas to put on a Gypsy Rose Lee-style strip dance. Cries of "Take it off, take it off," filled the building. The fact that he was awkward as hell broke everyone up as he paraded around the room, failing badly in his attempts to cover his bare body with the boa.

The mischief was not over. While he was dancing, some of the girls managed to find his clothes. They promptly took all his stuff downstairs to the dressing room. So, at the conclusion of his strip show, he discovered that the only choice he had was to race through the club, stark naked, to the delight of the few of us still there at 3:30 AM.

Life was no more boring at the new Beverly Hills than in the good old days. I ended up that **evening/morning** with Joey and several others at the top of the spiral stairs. After some conversation, Joey walked up to me, threw her arms around my neck and gave me a big hug and kiss. I have a long list of memories of my times at the Beverly Hills. Holding one of the world's most beautiful women in my arms is right at the top.

The Cabaret Showroom, 1977 just before the fire. (W. Dammert)

Chapter 8

B y the summer of 1974, the popularity of the new Beverly Hills Supper
Club had given Richard Schilling the wherewithal to bring his long
standing dream of a new, expanded showroom to fruition.

He called in his architect, told him he wanted a room that would accommodate 1000 patrons on the northeast corner of the building, and asked
him to draw up the plans. Several times during the early summer, as I
passed by Mr. Schilling's office, I'd see him and the architect pouring over
sketches. From what I could observe, Mr. Schilling did most of the talking.

On July 8, a building permit was issued for the new addition. Construction soon began. They pretty much tore out the existing showroom
and started over with it. Only later — too late — did we learn that because
the architect was not licensed to practice in Kentucky, the entire project
was in violation of state law.

Mr. Schilling left the name of the new room as The Cabaret Room. On
November 11, 1974, it opened to the public. It was a huge room, tiered
into four levels so that every one of the 1000 customers had a good view of
the centrally located stage. The facility was complete with two service
bars, dressing rooms for the performers and new rest rooms. Entrance to
the room was provided by a set of double doors from the main north-south
hallway which still ran the length of the building front to back. Doors,
leading outside, on each side of the stage would serve as emergency exits.
A new hallway, running perpendicular to the main hallway, between the
north end of the Viennese Room and the south side of the Cabaret Room
allowed employees' service access. This new corridor opened into the main
hallway, but the entrance was disguised so that the patrons would not notice it as they moved by on the way toward the more obvious entrance.

The new room was every bit as successful as had been expected. Almost every night, it was filled to capacity, and, at times, overfilled. Some of the acts were very popular, and the Schillings and the staff hated to turn anyone away and would not do so if it were at all possible to avoid.

Sometime during this period, on a very busy Saturday night, the Viennese Room and the adjacent restrooms filled with thick, black smoke. The word of fire in the building spread more rapidly than the smoke. I saw two of the Schillings and Paul, the kitchen manager, headed for the basement armed with fire extinguishers, so I grabbed a flashlight and followed to see if I could be of help.

Despite the smoke in the basement area under the Viennese Room, we plunged right in. "Anybody see the fire?' Rick Schilling yelled.

"Not over here," Paul shouted from one side of the room.

"No fire here, either," I said from my side.

We all converged on a pit in the center of the room. "What's in there?' Paul asked.

"The main air conditioning unit," Rick said.

"It seems to be the source of the smoke," Ron Schilling observed.

"I'll see," I said, dropping into the pit. With the aid of the flashlight, I saw the problem. "I've found it," I shouted up.

"What?' The three voices asked in unison.

"The pulley's frozen on the shaft," I said. "The motor's still running and it's caused the belts to bum up." I climbed out of the pit, bits of black soot clinging to my face, hands and clothing.

"Throw the switch," Rick shouted.

Ron jumped across the room and shut off the electrical power to the unit. When we opened the windows, the smoke immediately began to dissipate down there, although enough of the thick, burnt-rubber stuff had entered the air conditioning system that the party in the Viennese Room had to be ended. The remainder of the Club was not even aware of the problem, and so the fire department was not notified. Nor did anyone recall that we were supposed to be trained in fire prevention and fighting "as soon as the employment situation stabilized." We'd had no training of any kind and no fire drills. Evidently, the situation was not stable yet.

One evening, my friend Fred Cianciolo came upstairs during the orchestra's break between shows. As a measure of respect, we called him Mr. C. At the time of his visit, only one party, which happened to be composed of twenty-five beautiful women, remained in the Crystal Rooms. I was standing in the service hall with a left-over bottle of champagne in my hand when Mr. C. walked up. "What's **goin'** on, Wayne?'

"Not much," I replied. "The party's about over. They're going to the second show."

"It's a good one," he said. "The orchestra's in fine shape tonight."

I had an idea. Pouring a glass of the champagne, I said, "I've got to check on the party. I'll be right back." I walked into the room and called for the ladies' attention. "A friend from the orchestra was walking by the door," I announced. "He spotted a pretty girl in here and asked me to present her with a glass of champagne." The ladies twittered and giggled as I held the glass aloft.

To the applause of the rest of the group, I selected one of the women and gave her the glass. They were still chattering and giggling when I went

Mother's Day ad in <u>The Kentucky Post</u> *showing the great entertainment values at The Beverly Hills. (W. Dammert)*

back to where Mr. C. was standing, totally unaware of my joke. After we talked a few minutes, I went back into the room armed with the bottle. "Ladies," I said, "Mr. C. has decided that you all deserve a little drink."

I poured a little champagne for each of them into the coffee cups they hurriedly wiped clean. "This Mr. C. must be quite a guy," many of them remarked.

Back in the hall, I informed Mr. C. that there was someone I wanted him to meet. I ushered him into the room. When I introduced him, the ladies afforded him a standing ovation, complete with hugs and **kisses**. In the crowd of women surrounding him, Mr. C. looked askance at me, his face beet red with embarrassment. I never did explain why the women were so happy to see him.

"The what Room?'

Every new employee's reaction was always the same. The first time they heard the term "The Zebra Room," they didn't know where it was.

I don't remember when it started, but we usually referred to the storage room under the spiral stairs as the Zebra Room. This was the L-shaped area that had been the old dealer's break room. It had been utilized only for storage of various things since the Club reopened. The term was coined by one of the busboys when he stored some chairs in there. He thought that because the other areas were so elegant while this room was such a complete nothing, Zebra would be a good name for it. We all thought it was a fine example of esoteric humor, and so the name stuck. The standard answer to "Where can I find ..." was, "Check the Zebra Room." Late in 1975, under pressure, yet again, for more dining space, Mr. Schilling decided to **spiff** up the room and use it for another dining area.

With such names as the Empire Room and the Crystal Rooms, I thought some more prestigious name would be in order, **thinking** he'd dub it something like "The President's Room." But, no. The Zebra Room it remained.

The area was small and so added little to the Club's overall capacity, but Mr. Schilling furnished it such that it became one of the more elegant banquet rooms in the Club. Entry was provided by a set of double doors from the main bar. Upon entering, the opulence was obvious. One was faced with a wall full of mirrors; a massive marble fireplace in the center of the wall. The other walls were finished with rosewood paneling. The carpet underfoot was thick and lush while the overhead sparkled from the recessed lighting refracted through the crystal chandeliers. Not obvious was the fact that Mr. Schilling had designed and built the room without the benefit of any professional help, had obtained no building permit, or that the construction had undergone no inspections of any kind. Fate held a dark role for this room. Again, we did not learn until too late that the uninspected electrical wiring was flawed. These factors, in conjunction

FRANKIE VALLI·THE FOUR SEASONS

Topperformers were commonly found at the Beverly Hills. (W. Dammert)

with the physical location of the Zebra Room — under the unenclosed stairway and next to the main hallway — produced a true prescription for disaster.

Crowds poured into the Beverly Hills. Every night, the place was packed with people of all descriptions. Governors, senators, bankers, salesmen, families and construction workers all flocked to the Club. Most of the time, the Schillings provided a dinner-and-show for one price deal, a popular attraction. Many others came just for dinner, and the number of banquets held there was phenomenal. Additionally, Mr. Schilling had installed the beautiful garden area at the rear of the building. Rock pathways, lined by flowers and scrubs, wandered by ponds and fountains, over bridges and around a large, lovely gazebo. At the rear of the garden stood a chapel, capable of seating more than 100 people on white pews. Inside, the chapel was exquisite, complete with a pipe organ and stained glass windows. Throughout the good weather portion of the year, the garden witnessed several weddings each week. The wedding party, of course, was treated to a reception at the Club.

Entertainment in the Cabaret Room was, however, the main attraction. And understandably so — the acts were fabulous. One Saturday evening, Frankie Valli, one of the most popular entertainers, was appearing. The early show was sold out, and long before it was finished, a line began to form for the late show. A full hour before the second show was to begin, the line extended from the entrance to the Cabaret Room, all the way down the hall, through the Hall of Mirrors, and into the main bar area. When the group starting getting unruly, I looked for one of the Schillings, but finding no one, I decided to direct the human traffic myself. Before I managed to get the situation organized, the line was wound around itself, serpentine fashion, in the bar. Tempers were flaring.

I managed to get the queue of people, who were four or five deep by this time, wound through the foyer and out the front door. Fortunately, the weather was good. Outside, I started telling people that they could not enter the building until the first show had ended. Before it did, the line extended out the front door and 50 feet down the drive. I saw no way that all of those in line would ever fit into the Cabaret Room.

At length, the first show did end, and the room eventually emptied. Much to my surprise, the people in the line did not push or shove, but it seemed that they surged into the Cabaret Room in a few seconds. The seating arrangements in the showroom were beyond my purview, so I have no idea how they managed it, but everyone in the line went in the Cabaret Room. As far as I know, that show went off without a hitch. This kind of thing was not abnormal; the showroom — as well as the rest of the Club — was usually packed.

In the spring of 1976, Mr. Schilling decided to expand the Club once again. This time, the plan was to expand the Garden Room area on the back of the existing building, more than doubling its size. Once again, Mr. Schilling called on his architect — who was still unlicensed for Kentucky — and told him what he wanted. In short order, plans and drawing were delivered and construction began.

A critical factor in this new addition was fairly obvious. A door at the north end of the north-south corridor provided direct access outside only a few feet from the Cabaret Room. This exit was clearly the best way out of the showroom in the event of emergency. Extending the building 50 feet north, as called for by the plans, would cause the Cabaret Room to lose this means of egress. But, if we noticed, we did not talk about it. After all, the building inspector and the fire marshal were in the Club all the time. They had their problems and we had ours. Among theirs, unknown to me, was the fact that the Cabaret Room was, by law, already short one required exit.

By fall, the Garden Room was complete and it was fabulous. Actually, it was four rooms. Like many of the other rooms, it could be divided by folding partitions, or used as one large, open area. Each of the four had different tiers and decor, but nonetheless, it could be, and, on many occasions, was so utilized. The entire back wall was glass, so that one could view the garden — chapel, ponds and all — from inside the club. Being in the room was like being outside, but in indoor comfort. At the base of the back wall, lighted flower beds provided a beautiful transition for the **inside/outside** effect.

The ceiling worked in the same way. A large portion of the roof was also glass, allowing one to view the stars from a dining table. Other areas of the ceiling were adorned with mirrors and hanging plants, enhancing the ambiance of the room. In the center of the room, a huge chandelier, purchased at an auction when an old Cincinnati hotel closed, provided a nostalgic centerpiece for the large, open area. Like all the other improvements Mr. Schilling had made, this area was a hit with the public and quickly became one of our most popular dining areas.

Mr. Schilling was well on the way to fulfilling his ambition to make the

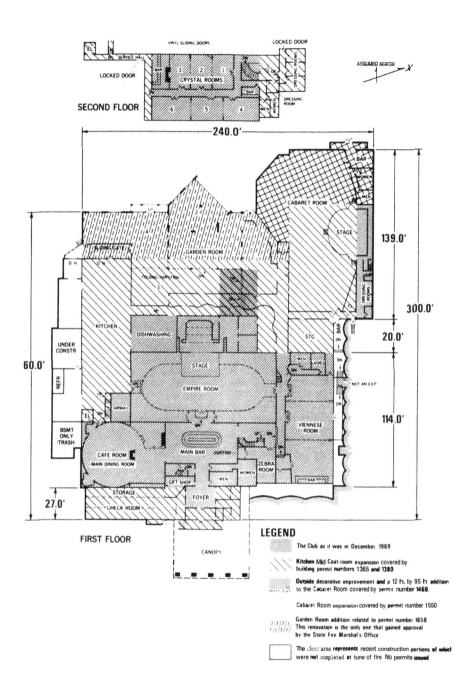

The Beverly Hills' floor plans. (National Fire Protection Agency)

Beverly Hills Supper Club "The Show Place of the Nation." One may have thought that he'd taken the place about as far as it would go, but not Mr. Schilling. He had many more ideas about what he was going to do — his plans included a motel, a disco and a convention center — but they were not to be.

December 31, 1976 was the most hectic night we ever had up to that time. The Van-Dells, a popular singing group, were to appear twice that evening: one show in the Cabaret Room and later in the Empire Room. Some 900 reservations were booked for the first show and about 800 for the late show. Additionally, large crowds were expected for dinner only.

The Van-Dells shows were in the context of one of Mr. Schilling's one-price deals. We had it arranged so that dinner for all the 1700 expected guests would be served buffet-style in the Viennese Room. All began well, but the situation soon got out of hand. So many people were at the buffet tables that we simply could not keep it stocked with clean dishes and food. It was such a mad-house that I suspected that many people just wandered in off the street and took advantage of a free meal. I do know for sure that every time I ventured into the room, I was mobbed by patrons with de-mands for more dishes, more food and drinks.

During this mess, I decided to take a quick break. I was standing in the hall, licking my wounds and catching my breath when I saw a friend in line for the show. Spotting me, he ran to where I stood.

"How you **doin'**?" I greeted him.

"I'm not happy with the seats we got for the show!" was his reply.

I could see this was not going to be a good night for me. "I can't help you with that," I said, "but, I can make sure you get plenty of food and drinks."

Disappointment was obvious in his face. "Well, if that's all you can do … " He walked away.

I knew that Mr. Schilling did not like to disappoint a customer about anything, so I got a bottle of champagne to take to my friend and his party. There were so many people in the building that I had to detour through the main bar to get to him. As I passed through the a room, a beautiful woman seated at the bar caught my eye. For some reason, I decided that she had just come in from outside, and with so many people in there, I knew she'd have difficulty getting served. So, I walked over to where she sat. "Would you like some champagne?' I asked, flourishing the bottle.

"Sure." She flashed a gorgeous smile on me.

I got a glass, and making a great show of it, I opened the bottle and poured her a drink. She accepted the glass, still smiling. As I pondered my next move, a guy twice my size showed up and made it clear he was her escort. "Hello," he said to me, unsmiling. He squeezed in next to her.

I took a good look at this large man. "Good-bye." I continued on my original mission and got back to the work I was being paid to do.

My next trip to check on the buffet was so bad that I concluded to just stay out of there. I stationed myself in a service hall and began to wipe steaming hot plates fresh from the dishwasher dry as fast as I could. In the midst of that activity a woman, accompanied by her husband, showed up in the hallway. The man was clearly very ill. In fact, I seriously thought he was dying. "Can you help me?" she cried.

"What's the problem," I asked, alarmed.

"My husband's a diabetic," she shrieked. "I think he's in insulin shock."

Dottie, one of the waitresses, happened by. "Call the emergency squad," I yelled. She did, but by the time they arrived, the man had recovered somewhat, and refused to have any dealings with them. In fact, he was quite indignant about having his evening interrupted. As I recall, the fire department's rescue squad was called five times that night.

The first show, in the Cabaret Room, was late starting. I suppose the crowd must have been mad and therefore unruly. I can tell you for sure that when the first show ended, the Van-Dells were not a happy group. Because the first show was late, the second show would be, too. The crowd was getting anxious. Chants of "Start the show!" were pouring out of the Empire Room. I went to the dressing room to see what the hold-up was. "Come in," answered my knock on the door.

"Hi, guys." I tried to sound cheerful. Some of the group mumbled a

The Chapel found in the garden area of club and just behind Cabaret Room's rear fire exit. (W. Dammert)

greeting. They were in costume and appeared ready to perform. "You ready for the second show?'

"I guess," the leader of the group sighed. He motioned to the group to get up. They followed me, somewhat reluctantly I thought, to the backstage area of the Empire Room. The leader peeked through the curtain and turned to me. A look of disgust on his face, he announced, 'We ain't goin' out there with that mob!"

Panic set in. The crowd that had been waiting for hours would tear the building down if they did not perform. "Wait right here!" I shouted as I dashed off to locate one of the Schillings. I found Rick in a hall. "The Van-Dells say they aren't going to go on," I told him, my voice shaking.

"Where are they?" He seemed fairly calm.

"Back stage," I said as he headed off in that direction.

I have no idea of the conversation Rick had with them, but they did perform the second show. I didn't see the show, so I don't know what happened, but as it ended, someone threw a beer bottle at the performers. The ensuing minor fight provided an appropriate ending to a less-than-perfect New Year's eve. At the time, I thought that Murphy's Law had been fulfilled — everything that could go wrong at the Beverly Hills had done so on this evening. I was sadly mistaken.

In the Viennese Room with an unknown customer, 1976. (W Dammert)

Fellow Banquet Captian Larry Wettenkamp and me near main entrance to the Cabaret Room. 1977. Larry worked for many years for the Schillings both at the Lookout House and at Beverly Hills. (W Dammert)

Part Three

FIRE AT THE BEVERLY HILLS!

John Davidson, who was to perform on the night of the fire, is shown here on stage at Riverfront Colliseum fall of 1977 for a benefit for victims' children, staged by former club employees - also known as memorial fund benefit. (W. Dammert)

Chapter 9

As evenings at a supper club go, Friday, May 27, 1977 was one to remember. Nature could not have provided a more perfect evening to begin the Memorial day weekend. The Schillings had a bunch of promotions going on, and John Davidson, one of the most popular singers ever to perform at the Beverly Hills, was appearing in the Cabaret Room. We expected huge crowds, and we were not to be disappointed.

I reported for work early in anticipation of a busy evening, enjoying the spring weather on the drive. My expectations were fully met and exceeded. The place was jam-packed with people from the moment the doors opened. Every square inch of space was filled with dining tables?portable bars and food-laden carts. I even had difficulty **making** my way from one room to another due to the people, tables and confusion.

As time for the second show approached, a long line had formed from the entrance to the Cabaret Room down the main corridor. The situation was in hand? however, and I didn't have to direct traffic this time. As the line lengthened? it became apparent to me that all these people would not get in to see the show. Passing down the hallway? I spotted a friend, Carol Jean Ockerman, with another lady. Carol was the Pendleton County clerk.

"Hi, Carol," I said, stopping where they stood. **"You** certainly do look nice." They were both dressed to the nines for the occasion and clearly looking forward to their evening.

"Hello, Wayne," she greeted me and introduced her friend.

"You having fun?"

In answer to my question, she said?"**I've** had better times than standing in this line.??Her giggle barely covered the impatience.

"A lot of folks here for the **show**," I observed.

"Yeah," Carol agreed. **"Do** you think **we'll** get in? **I'll** die if we don't get to see the show."

"Well," I tried to sound reassuring. "Not all these people are here for the show, some just come for dinner, you know."

"If you can help, I'd appreciate it," she said.

The showroom arrangements were still beyond my purview, so I didn't know if I could help. "Hang on a minute and I'll see what I can do," I told them. I walked down the hall, slipped into the hidden entrance to the service hall and into the Cabaret Room. The regular seating was in place. Although show time was still some time off, nearly every table was filled. I found a table for four with only two seats taken. "Would you folks mind some company?' I asked.

The man and woman eyed me a moment, then he said, "No problem." They knew as well as I did that the hostess would soon seat someone there anyway.

"Don't let anyone have these seats before I get back," I said.

"We'll hold 'em," he said with a smile.

Back in the service hall, I ran into John Davidson, who I knew from all the previous times he'd appeared at the Beverly. He had a cassette tape in his hand. "Where you **goin'**?" I asked.

"I need to get this tape to my sound man so he can record tonight's show," he replied. "He's out in the showroom, I think." He was moving toward the main hallway.

"You don't want to go out there, John," I warned. "It's a mad-house. If you go out in that hall, they'll mob you."

He hesitated. "Well, I guess you're right."

"Shall I deliver the tape for you?'

With a sly grin, he said, "Now why didn't I think of that?' He handed over the tape and gave me spec c instructions to pass along to the sound man. I suppose it must have been important to him. Before I left, he made me repeat what I was to say when I got to the sound man. I passed his inspection, delivered the tape and made my way back to my friends in the hall.

"We were beginning to think you got lost," Carol said.

"A busy night." I noticed that many of the other people in line where watching us. Not wanting them to think I was giving my friends any special treatment, I said, "You ladies come with me. I want to show you something." I took them through the service hallway, into the Cabaret Room and showed them the table, the two seats still empty. I thanked the couple at the table and ordered a round of drinks sent to all four of them.

Turning to view the room, I saw many people just milling around. I don't know how they got by the doorman, but they were in there with nowhere to sit. To say that they were angry would be an understatement. I asked all those I saw to be patient, that I'd look after them. I went to the **kitchen** to get help.

In the **kitchen,** I found a couple of the banquet waitresses on break.

"You girls get up to the Cabaret Room," I ordered. "There's a bunch of people up there with no place to sit."

"We're on break," they protested.

"I don't care. There's problems in the showroom. Get up there and do whatever you can to help out." They left. I cannot say happily, but they went.

I grabbed a couple of busboys. "Come with me," I ordered. They followed me to a storage area where the three of us loaded up all the chairs we could carry. We took them to the showroom. The waitresses had gotten the drink orders — most of those standing now had glasses in their hands. We lined the chairs along the ramp to the right of the stage. "You can sit here," I said.

"First class accommodations," a man grumbled.

"We're doing the best we can," I replied. "I'll tell you what. Because you don't have a table, there'll be no cover charge."

"That's more like it," he said. At least I'd made a few of the patrons happy.

Some, but not all. As I passed down the ramp, I heard someone sitting along the wall say, "I'll bet a dollar the fire marshal would frown on these seating arrangements."

Out in the hall, I encountered Rick Schilling. "How's it going, Wayne?" he asked.

"It's bedlam," I told him. "There's people in every available space in there, and maybe 50 people standing."

"A real dilemma," he said, shaking his head. "You let 'em in and somebody complains about fire safety; you tell 'em no and they complain that you're not being fair."

"The price you pay for having such a popular night spot," I reminded. "A real no-win situation."

"Yes," he agreed. After a moment's thought, he said, "Don't let 'em push the limits too far. We have to draw the line somewhere."

"Yes, sir," I said as he walked toward the office.

We got through the evening somehow. For my part, I stayed away from the showroom and let those whose job it was worry about the situation in there.

Among my own responsibilities early that evening was a party of about thirty women. They were to have dinner in one of the small rooms and then see John Davidson's first show. While they were **drinking** and having a good time, I decided to play a little joke on them. I casually strolled into the room and called for their attention. "Ladies," I said, "I have an announcement." All heads turned to me as the conversation died out. "I have just spoken with John **Davidson.** I told him that you ladies were here for the show and were quite eager to see him." I paused for effect. I had their attention, all right. All eyes were on me as they waited for what I was going to say next. The looks on their faces should have told me I was already in trouble. "John's always happy to greet his fans. He said," I continued, "that if any of you would like to meet him, I could bring you up to his dressing room."

They went wild. Now I knew for sure that I'd made a mistake. As they mobbed me clamoring to go, I was thinking fast. "Calm down," I shouted. "Let me go make sure it's OK, then I'll be back." I got out of the room as quickly as possible, knowing damned well it was not OK. John Davidson didn't want anyone in his dressing room.

I killed enough time to let them think I'd been to John's dressing room, then went back into the banquet room. I was mobbed again at the door. "I'm sorry, ladies, "I announced. "John's running a little late and won't be able to see anyone this evening." Groans of disappointment filled the room. "Disappointment" may be a weak description for their emotion— in fact, they were angry. Thinking of some way to redeem myself, I said, "I can, however, get you autographed pictures." This cheered them up. In a moment, I was on my way up the hall, the ladies' names in my hand. I knew they kept some publicity pictures of the stars who appeared at the club in the front office, and surely they'd have some of John. Wouldn't you know there was only one picture left? I choose one of the lady's names at random and had the girl in the office sign John Davidson's name on the only picture, personalized to that woman. Wishing I hadn't got myself into this, I took the picture back. Again, they were disappointed. Except for the one who had the autographed picture — she was all smiles. I thought I owed them something for my deception, so I made sure they had everything they needed for dinner. I paid special attention to ensure that they enjoyed as perfect an evening as the Beverly Hills could provide. When they finished eating , I confessed my little joke and accompanied them to the show room to do what I could to help them get good seats.

I was in a mischievous mood. Another of my parties was a group of high school senior girls upstairs in one of the Crystal Rooms. I'd teased them in a similar way, so I obtained a picture of John autographed to the class (yes, girls, it's a genuine signature.) They were so thrilled that I had another prank idea. One of the waiters **working** that evening was a nice **looking** young man who slightly resembled John Davidson. I conspired with him, then announced to the girls that he was John's younger bother, Bob.

"If you're John Davidson's brother, why are you **working** as a waiter?' one of the young ladies demanded.

"Uh, John wants me to learn the business from the ground up," Bob replied. "I travel around with him and work at some different job wherever he appears."

Needless to say, they were skeptical, but we kept up the deception. They all asked for, and received, **Bob's** autograph before the evening was over.

I did not indulge in such pranks every night. I choose parties who I thought would not be angry when they found out. Mr. Schilling encouraged his employees to make the customers feel that they were a part of the Beverly Hills, and such pranks were just my way of showing a little personal attention.

When John **Davidson's** show ended, the hallway was jammed with people leaving the building. In the years since, **I've** often wondered if I gave any thought to how long it took for all those people to exit that evening. The showroom was packed that night. At the end of his show, John Davidson usually left the stage to sing among the audience. I didn't see the show, but I understand that he did not do that this time due to the large number of people crammed around the stage. I do know that the hallway was packed when the show ended, and all those people did not get out of the building very quickly. I don't remember what, if anything, I actually thought about it, but, retrospect always gives one a better view.

Late in the evening, I was passing through the bar on my way out, thankful my job was done for the day. "Hey! Wayne," someone yelled.

I turned to see a friend, Don **Fangman,** sitting at the bar. Don's wife, Pam, was a hostess at the Club. I supposed he was waiting for her to finish up so they could go home. I walked over and we chatted a few minutes. While Don and I were talking, I noticed Ron Schilling in animated conversation with a beautiful woman on the other side of the room. The hour was late, the room was nearly empty, so we could see and hear pretty well. She was a very nice looking lady, dressed in an exquisite white lace dress. Although we could hear their voices, we could not make out what they were saying, but it was apparent that she was quite upset. Suddenly, she placed both of her hands on Ron's face and appeared ready to dig her fingernails in. I started in that direction, but fortunately for all, she quickly backed off. Ron said something to her and left the room.

She snatched a beer bottle from the surface of the bar and threw it after him. That did it for me. Approaching her, I said, "We will not tolerate that **kind** of behavior in here."

The lady stared at me as if I'd spoken an alien language to her. She'd had a few too many drinks. "I'll have you know **I'm** a personal friend of Ron Schilling's," she slurred.

I'd had a rough evening, too. "I **don't** care whose friend you are, you pull another stunt like that and you're going right out the front door." I'm sure my voice was not **kind.** She began to cry, which didn't make me feel any better. "He took my girlfriend backstage to meet John Davidson and didn't take me," she blubbered, along with some unintelligible speech. Finally, she blurted out, "I want to call my ex-husband."

She grabbed the phone on the reception desk, but was too drunk to manage a phone call. While she fumbled with it, Ron Schilling returned. Clearly unhappy that she was still there, he took the phone from her, saying, "Get off my phone. If you want to make a call, you can use the pay phone in the foyer." While this melodrama was being played out, the band in the bar sounded "taps" for her.

Some sympathy for her had welled up in me. "Come with me," I said. She followed me to the front office. Positioning her at Rick Schilling's desk, I said, "What's the number you want to call?' I dialed the number she gave me, her ex-husband's, I guess. When he answered, she said a few words, then violently slammed the receiver down. "Son of a bitch hung up on me," she cried, redialing the number. She had better luck with the phone this time, but he evidently hung up on her again. If she was upset before, she was fuming now.

As fate would have it, the first object her eye fell on was a birthday cake someone had left on the desk for Rick Schilling. With a shriek of rage, she swept everything from the surface of the desk, phone, blotter, pen set, cake and all. As these objects struck the floor, I made a grab for her before she could inflict more damage. The red icing from the cake had splattered on her white dress. The dress was ruined, I'm sure, but that was the least of my worries at the moment. She was screaming, kicking at me and flailing the air with her arms. I managed to get behind her. With my hands locked around her waist, I attempted to pull her from the room. She continued to kick, flail and hang on to anything which fell to hand to prevent my dragging her out. She swatted at a color television set perched on a shelf. I let go of her long enough to rescue the television before it fell.

Finally, I managed to haul her into the foyer, her kicking and screaming every inch of the way. I made her sit down on the floor. "Don't you move until you calm down," I ordered.

She glared at me, but said nothing. I guess the anger or liquor or whatever got the best of her at this point, she began to sob quietly. Ron Schilling happened to spot us from the bar. He came into the foyer. "What the hell happened?' he asked, observing her disheveled condition.

"Well," I began, "it's quite a story." I told him how I'd let her use the phone in the office. "She just went ballistic on me," I said.

"All right, Wayne," he said. "I'll take it from here. You go on home."

I did not argue. It'd been a hellish night at the Beverly Hills. I walked through the foyer and out the front door. Outside, the air was fresh and cool. I stopped a minute, just to catch a breath from the night's work. The early morning spring air was soft and sweet. It was only Friday — Saturday morning now. The Memorial day weekend had another night to go. As I steered the car down the winding drive, I had no reason to suspect that Saturday night would be any different.

BEVERLY HILLS COUNTRY CLUB
SPECIAL PARTY MENU

DATE __**Saturday May 28, 1977**_____ NATURE OF FUNCTION _____

NAME OF PARTY __**Cincinnati Chorus   a   Tea Room Modeling**__

SPONSORED BY __**Charlene Mathews**__

TIME __~~6:00~~ *7:00*_____ ROOM __**UP 1-2-3**__

NO. PLATES __**100 - ~~120~~** *Set 115*__

TAKEN BY _____ PHONE __**281-9671**__

BILL TO __**Paying by certified check that night**__

ROOM INFORMATION	MENU	BAR INFORMATION
Rounds of 10	SERVING TIME **7:30**	**7:00 - 2:30**
No head table		
Dance floor		Cash Bar
Podium/floor for fashion show	Tomato Juice	
Fashion show 8:30 - 10:00 *Tea Room modeling*	Broiled Chicken	
6 piece band & dancing 10:30 - 2:30	Baked Potato/Sour Cream	
	Toss/House	
2 - 4ft tables for speakers for band & ~~6 4ft tables for band~~	Parfait	
2 brides rooms / small one & 1 regular one	$100.00 deposit recieved 3/16/77	
6:00 Models , committee & band eating same menu early	*3 Chopped Sirloin*	
	6:00 *27 models eating Br. Chicken in Up 1-2-3*	

MANAGER

Work sheet for a party: each party at the club had a work sheet like this one.
Please note that the party was sponsored by Sharlene Matthews, a hero of the fire
and the last person to be pulled from the wreckage. (W. Dammert)

Chapter 10

O h, but was Saturday different! May 28, 1977 was to prove to be the most fateful night of my life. I was due at the Beverly Hills at **6:00** PM, a little later than normal, so I kissed my wife and **kids,** as usual, and left home about **5:40** for the fifteen minute drive. Once again, I enjoyed the perfect spring weather on the way. Memories of the previous evening's bedlam and anticipation of more of the same occupied my thoughts as I turned into the steep, winding driveway.

Although it was early yet, many cars were in the drive. If I'd had any doubts of another hectic night, they were put to rest **now—clearly,** the club was going to be packed again tonight. Eventually, I made it to the **parking** lot. I parked the car and made my way into the front office to check the schedule. I found that I was assigned to two parties, both upstairs in the Crystal Rooms. The Afghan Hound Club of Southwestern Ohio had a party of 90 booked for Crystal Rooms 4, 5, and 6, on the side of the upstairs hall toward the back of the building; The Greater Cincinnati Choral Union, with about 100 people, would occupy Crystal Rooms 1, 2, and 3, on the opposite side. The Choral group number was a bit of a surprise, we'd set the room for the maximum it was designed to hold, 120, as that had been the expected number. Well, it would not be too crowded tonight. I took only casual note of the doctor's party to be held in a comer of the Viennese Room and a small wedding party scheduled for the Zebra Room. I wasn't working either, so they meant little to me.

The Choral group was scheduled to eat at **7:00.** A handful of them who were to put on a style show were to be fed at **6:00.** I quickly went up the spiral stairway to check on the rooms. I already knew that all was in order — we'd set it up the night before. For these large parties, the rooms were in the undivided mode, that is, the folding doors were pushed against the wall so that each room was one open area.

At the top of the stairs, I moved to my right to check each of the four dressing rooms. Before the Cabaret Room dressing area was built, the stars appearing in the showrooms used these upstairs dressing rooms. Now, they were used by the performers when they had a large troupe and needed the space. For the most part, they were utilized by brides, but tonight, the style show models would change in there. On the way to the party rooms, I checked the restrooms. Everything appeared to be in order.

Seeing that the party rooms were ready, I moved down the hall and turned into the L-shaped service hallway which ran perpendicular to the main hall. Turning right, I walked to the end of the hall and made the 90 degree left turn. I walked by the locked door which led out onto the roof and the service elevator to where a set of wooden stairs led to the **kitchen** on the first floor. I may have noted that the doorway onto the roof had been covered by a sheet of plywood held in place by a hasp with a padlock. I descended the steps to the kitchen to check on the food.

Everything was ready down there, so I went back upstairs to meet the crew. I was in charge of four waitresses, one waiter, two busboys, three bartenders, and two cashiers who would be **working** with me tonight. I'd only arrived when a lady approached me. "I'm in charge of this group," she said.

"Hi," I said with my best smile. "My name's Wayne. Welcome to the Beverly Hills." I extended my hand.

Shaking my hand, she returned my smile. "Sharlene Matthews."

"I'm here to help with anything you need."

"As a matter of fact," she said, "we do need some help with the band."

I gathered the two busboys and the three of us helped the band get set up in the rear of the room. Soon after we finished that, the twenty-five style show people arrived. We fed them, as scheduled. Once again, Ms. **Matthews** approached me.

"Can you take some of these tables out?" she asked.

"You don't think you're going to need them?"

"No," she said. "We're only expecting about 100, and there's not enough room for the style show."

"OK. I'll get them out." We'd over set the room anyway.

I was helping the busboys remove three tables when a man, seated near where we were **working** said, "Don't take that table out, we're going to need it."

"I don't think so, sir," I replied. "We had too many place settings in the first place and Sharlene wanted more space for the style show."

"Well, we're going to need those tables," he grumbled.

He was right. No more had we removed the tables when a bunch of additional guests showed up, ready for their dinner. We brought the tables back and reset everything. My expectations for a hectic night were being met, and I'd only been at work a little over an hour! We started serving the entire group dinner about 7:40.

Across the hall, we were to serve a buffet-style dinner at **8:30.** I could see that the two dinners were going to overlap, meaning that we'd have trouble keeping up with both parties at once. I tracked down the man in charge of the Afghan Hound group.

"Sir," I said, "we're running a little behind, would you be upset if we served your dinner a bit late?'

Not many of his group had arrived yet. "No problem," he said with a smile. "Make it **8:45.**"

"Thanks," I returned his smile. "That'll help a lot." Actually, it would help a little, and I knew we would actually serve them closer to **9:00.**

I ran down to the salad department to see if they were ready for the Afghan Hound group. They were, so I dashed back up the wooden service stairs to begin setting up for the buffet. I checked my watch on the way up — **8:25.** We were pretty close to schedule. I was working on the buffet table when someone called, "Wayne?'

I turned to see Shirley Baker, a waitress, standing there "Hi, Shirley. What are you doing up here?'

"I'm **working** the party in the Zebra Room," she said. "It's almost over and I need someone to make up the bill."

I had two parties going on. I started to tell her that I was busy, so she should get one of the Schillings to do it. Shirley was a sweet person, and I liked her, so I said, "OK. I'll do it as soon as I have time."

"Thanks," she said with a relieved smile. "I need it right away. They're about finished and the guy is waiting for the bill."

I turned what I was doing over to the waiter **working** with me and headed for the **kitchen** to get a blank check from the cashier **working** there. My legs felt like this was about 500 trips down the service stairs. Blank check in hand, I took a short cut for the front office, through the Empire Room. The Savings and Loan League of Southwestern Ohio and Northern Kentucky was holding an awards banquet in there. They had just finished their meal and appeared ready to begin the awards ceremony as the trophies were standing on a table at the front of the room. This room was crowded, as I supposed all the others were, with maybe 400 people in there.

Moving into the main bar, I was surprised to see it fairly empty. "Sparse tonight?' I called to the bartender.

"Not hardly," he laughed. "Everybody just left for John **Davidson's** first show. The late crowd will be pouring in here soon."

"Have a good time," I said, **walking** on toward the office. I knew he was right, the bar would soon be packed.

In the front office, I obtained the party sheet for the Zebra Room. It was for a wedding party of twenty-five. I made up the bill and headed down the hall for the Zebra Room. The double doors were closed. Pushing

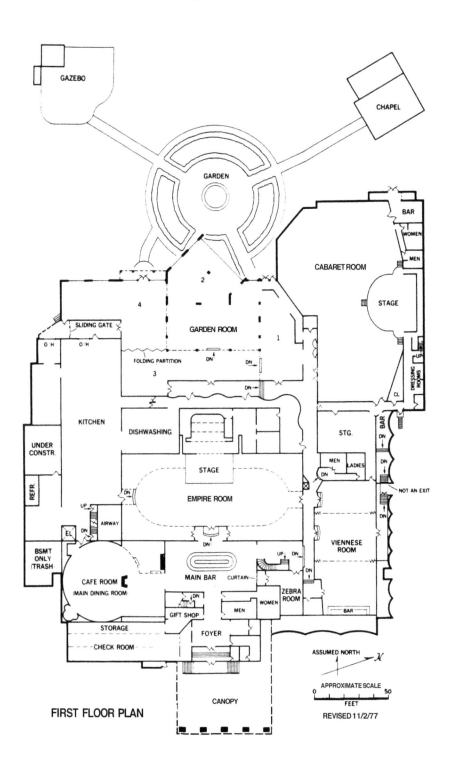

FIRST FLOOR PLAN

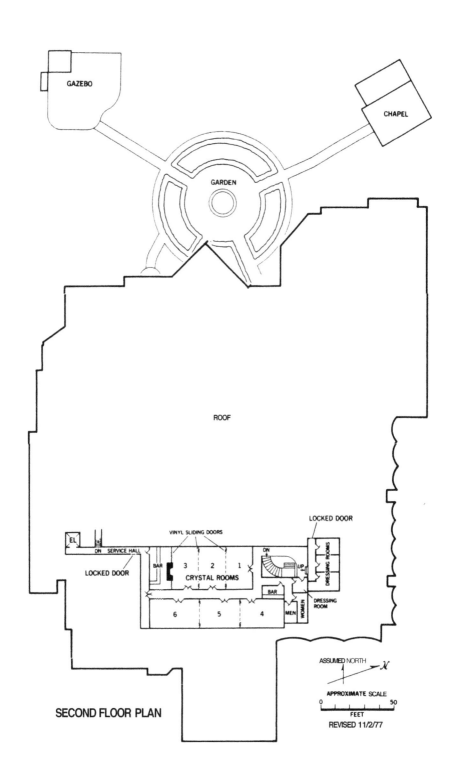

GAZEBO

CHAPEL

GARDEN

ROOF

LOCKED DOOR

EL

ON   SERVICE HALL

LOCKED DOOR

VINYL SLIDING DOORS

BAR

3   2   1

CRYSTAL ROOMS

ON

UP

DRESSING ROOMS

6   5   4

BAR

MEN   WOMEN

DRESSING ROOM

SECOND FLOOR PLAN

ASSUMED NORTH   X

APPROXIMATE SCALE

0   50

FEET

REVISED 11/2/77

them open, I saw Shirley on one side of the room and a couple of men on the other. I approached the men. "Everything all right with your party?"

"Just fine," he said.

I presented the bill. "This is for you."

"No, no. That guy over there gets that," he said with a laugh. "I'm just here to party, that's all."

I turned to the other man. "No, not me." He was **joking,** too.

I could see that they were in a jovial mood, but I didn't have time for it. Because it was Shirley's responsibility to collect, I gave the bill to her.

"**Thanks,** Wayne," she said, accepting the slip.

"Hey," one of the men yelled. "Did you get the air conditioning turned down?"

"What's that about?" I asked.

"Oh," Shirley answered, "they were complaining about it being hot in here earlier."

"Seems fine to me," I commented.

"Well, they were complaining." Apparently, she was having a bad night, too. It was about to get a lot worse.

Knowing my party upstairs was running late, I checked my watch once again. It showed **8:35.** I was worried about the time, so, "Shirley, what time do you have?"

She pushed her hair back and lifted her wrist. "**8:35.**"

I didn't know it, of course, but at that very minute, a fire was smoldering in the paneling a few feet from where Shirley and I were standing. I made no notice of the temperature being elevated and no one complained to me. I saw no smoke or any clue of any **kind** that the fire was starting. I left the room totally unaware. In just a few minutes, we'd all know about it.

I made my way back through the Club to the **kitchen.** They had the buffet items ready, so I loaded some things onto a cart and took it to the service elevator. By the time I arrived back upstairs with the cart, the time was about **8:50,** and the Afghan Hound folks were ready to eat. As I moved to the buffet line with the cart, no one made any notice of me, so I assumed they were not too angry.

When all the things I'd brought were in place, I took the cart back to the **kitchen.** The last item I needed for the buffet was the salad, and I planned to bring it back up on this trip. Just as the elevator opened at the bottom, I checked my watch yet again. **8:55.** The patrons upstairs would be about at the end of their patience! I entered the walk-in cooler where the salad should have been. No salad.

"**Toni,**" I shouted for the lady in charge of the salad department. "Where the hell's my salad?"

"Look behind the storage rack in there," she yelled back.

Behind the rack, I found the large salad bowl for the buffet. I offered a small prayer of thanks. Now all I had to do was get this bowl upstairs so they could begin their dinner. I grabbed the bowl and started out. "How's it **goin'**, Wayne?' Curtis, one of the chefs was putting on his clean white coat.

"A bit hectic, but OK," I said. "You working our party?'

"Yes," he replied, donning his tall, white chef's hat. "I'll be up to serve the ham and beef in a few minutes."

"They'll be ready by the time you get there," I said, starting up. Years later, Curtis told me that just after I left, he'd gone to the basement to get a clean uniform. While he was down there, he thought he'd heard some crackling noises overhead. The area where he would have been was directly under the Zebra Room.

My watch showed exactly 9:00 PM when I entered the hallway upstairs through the double doors. Fran Oaks, one of the waitresses was standing just inside the doors, her face showing excitement. "There's a fire in the Zebra Room," she announced.

I cannot recall my emotions of that moment. "How do you know?'

"Somebody sent word from downstairs," she said.

"I was just in there a minute ago, and I didn't see any fire," I said.

"Well, it's sure as hell there now," Fran observed. There was a sense of urgency, but no panic in her voice. "Look!" She pointed down the hall. At the far end of the hall, the end closest to the spiral stairs, a few strands of wispy, gray smoke were floating in mid-air.

"You're right," I said. As a captain, I considered it my responsibility to get to the problem as quickly as possible and see what I could do. "Take care of things up here," I told Fran.

I still had the salad bowl in my hands. I dashed about 10 feet into the Crystal Room, put the salad bowl down, and returned to where Fran was standing. The instant I stepped back out into the hall, my heart nearly stopped beating. I feel sure that I hadn't been gone more than 5 seconds. In that brief time, the wispy, gray smoke strands had been replaced by thick, black stuff rolling around the "L" at the far end of the hall. I knew that the fire was unquestionably serious. The look on Fran's face said that she knew it, too.

My mind raced. All thoughts of going to the Zebra Room were gone — I had bigger things to worry about. There were some 200 people up here, and my responsibility now was to get them out. The thick, **oily-look**ing smoke rolling down the hall toward us made it clear that nobody was going to get down the spiral stairs. That fact was not of major concern to me, I knew we could get down the service stairs at the other end of the building. But, the patrons were unaware of its existence. Every one of them would try to take the only way out they knew — the spiral stairs by which they'd come up. I couldn't let them try to get through that way!

Although my mind was on getting these people out, I had a fleeting thought about the Club. There was so much smoke up here already that even if the fire was extinguished quickly, we'd have to evacuate the building. The parties ruined, the show canceled. I dashed into the Crystal Rooms on the front side of the building, with the intent of checking the double doors at the other end of the room. These doors opened into the hallway after it had made the **90** degree turn. A couple of long strides brought me close enough to see that the heavy, black smoke was oozing under and between these doors. It was seeping under the doors and crawling along the floor toward me. Undulating as it moved into the room like a sea wave rolling to shore, it appeared to have a life of its own; some kind of living, breathing, reptilian monster whose goal was to choke the life from me to sustain itself.

Two facts were now apparent: the fire was serious, and we weren't going out via the spiral stairs. Obviously, then, the only way out was down the service stairs at the rear, through the kitchen and then outside. I moved into the center of the room and yelled, "Everybody out the back! Out the back! Everybody!" At this point, the smoke was so thick that I began to have difficulty breathing.

Of the perhaps **90** people in the room, (I later learned that some patrons had chanced to be standing at the top of the spiral stairs when the smoke first appeared, so they went on down at that time and hence were already out) no one said anything. They simply started toward where I was pointing, the double doors at the rear of the room. The apparent lack of concern was amazing, especially because I was sending them in the opposite direction from the only exit they knew. I went to the other end of the room, making sure everyone was going out. Thank God, Fran Oaks had remained in the hallway. She was indicating the way into the service hallway through the doors in the hall. I reversed direction to follow the patrons into the hall. A man in front of me stooped to pick up something he had dropped, his jacket, I think. "Get out," I yelled at him. He continued to fumble around, trying to pick it up. "Get the hell out!" I screamed and moved to push him toward the rear of the room. Just as I put my hands on him, a huge volume of smoke, riding a wave of super-heated air, roared into the room. As the wave swept past us, the man required no additional coaxing to move; we both ran for the rear door.

I was the last one out of the room. All those patrons had moved into the service hallway, at **Fran's** direction. Her face now showed terror. The oily, black smoke had almost totally filled the hall, the black stuff seeming to have piled up in layers on itself so that we could not see into it, although it was a little thinner at our end. Fran and I both were having difficulty breathing and the temperature was quite high. "What do you want me to do now?" Fran shrieked. Beads of perspiration appeared on her forehead.

"Get out," I yelled. I was sweating, too, partly from the heat, partly from anxiety.

She stared mutely at me for a moment. "Get the hell out," I repeated and shoved her through the door into the service hall.

My next thought was to ensure that all the patrons were out of the rooms on the other side of the hall, so I ran into Crystal Rooms 1,2 and 3. In there, the smoke was not quite as thick, probably because the doors to this room were a little more remote from the stairway where the smoke was boiling upstairs. I think this was what caused me to think about the location of the fire. If it was burning in the Zebra Room, directly under the stairs, the smoke and flames had an unobstructed path to this part of the building. Although the smoke was not as thick as on the other side of the hall, there was enough in this room to cause difficulty not only breathing, but seeing as well. Additionally, the smoke was beginning to bum my eyes. I could see no one in the room. There was no response to my shouts of, "Anybody in here?' I supposed that they'd mingled with the people from the other side and were going down the service stairs now. I was to later learn that some of this group had been in the hallway when the smoke first started coming up. They had alerted their friends on this side, and so some of them had exited down the spiral stairs and out the front.

Now, my thoughts turned to the dressing rooms where the style show models had been changing clothes. Had they gotten out? To get there to see, I'd have to go out the doors at the opposite end of the room — some 100 feet way — and across the landing at the top of the stairs. I crossed the room, with difficulty, and approached the double doors that opened into the hall. I grasped the handles and pulled the doors toward me. When they opened about six inches, an incredible blast of heat roared through the gap between the edges of the doors, driving me, physically, back. Whatever I wanted to do, I now had no choice — anyone who was in those dressing rooms would just have to find their own way out.

I ran back toward the rear of the room. My breathing was now labored as the smoke was quite thick. If I'd had any question about the seriousness of the fire, it was gone now. The Beverly Hills was in deep trouble. So was I. I stumbled over a table obscured by the smoke. Cussing, I fell to the floor. Actually, falling was a fortunate accident. On the floor, I noticed that the air was clearer — breathing was a little easier. A couple of deep gulps of the air cleared my head. Clearly, the fire, starting in the Zebra Room, was roaring up the spiral stairs, **blocking** that exit. The service stairs, leading to the **kitchen** on the opposite side and opposite end of the building, were the right choice.

There's no way for me to say how much time had passed since I'd ushered the patrons and Fran into the service hallway. Probably not too long, but they should be out of the building by now. At least, they should be passing through the kitchen which had an outside exit. I got up, went out the doors at the end of the room, and into the service hallway, expecting everyone to be gone. Twenty feet into the hall, where it made a left hand turn, everyone was just standing there! What the hell's wrong? Why weren't they moving?

Much to my surprise, these people, maybe about 75 of them, were just calmly standing there. No panic and no conversation despite the acrid smoke now filling this part of the building. "What's the hold up?' I shouted as I moved by them, heading for the opening at the top of the service stairs. No one answered my question.

The area was so dark with smoke that I just felt my way along by the people lined against the wall. "What's the problem?' I kept yelling. I think I threw in a few shouts of, "We've got to get the hell out of here!" along the way. No one responded. In the darkened atmosphere, I went right past the top of the service stairs and ended up fifteen feet beyond, where the hall ended at the steel doors to the service elevator. A group of the patrons were trying to force those doors open. "What are you **doing?**" I shouted.

"The damned doors are locked," a man said.

And thank God they were. If they'd managed to get them open and the elevator car had been on the lower level, they'd have fallen to their deaths. I had a quick vision of people blindly following each other into the vacant elevator shaft. Even if the car had happened to be on the upper level, I feel sure anyone who entered it would have died in there. The mental picture of a small elevator cubicle full of people inhaling toxic gases as the car descended into thicker smoke was not pleasant, either. But, by the grace of God, the doors were locked, saving us from that fate.

I turned to go back down the hall to where the top of the service stairs entered. By now, the smoke was very thick and the heat was reaching an unbearable temperature. Sounds of hacking coughs now mixed with the smoke filling the lung-scorching air. Feeling my way along the wall, my hands detected a difference in the texture of the surface. The door — the hole in the wall I'd seen open to the breeze years before! It was right here! The opening was filled with no more than a sheet of three-quarter inch plywood, held in place by a hasp secured with a padlock. It was not an exit — I'd seen it standing open many times when we wanted air circulation up there — and I knew it only led onto the roof of the front part of the Club. If we got out there, we'd still be stranded some 20 feet above the ground, but at least we'd be able to breathe. Maybe someone could get a ladder up to us — surely the fire department had been notified. I hoped with all my heart that the call, "Fire at the Beverly Hills!" had gone out by now so that help was on the way. Even so, there was no help for those of us up here right now. We had to help ourselves. Two hefty patrons were beside me. "Knock that thing **out!**" I screamed. "Knock the damned door out!"

The two men instantly recognized what I had in mind. They moved to the far side of the hall to gather as much momentum as possible. In unison, they flew across the short span of the hall and slammed their combined weight against the flimsy door. It vibrated, but did not open. "Again!" I yelled. "Hit it again."

The two men slowly gathered their strength, moved back across the hall and repeated the procedure. The result was no better — the door, insubstantial as it was, did not budge. "Again! Knock the son of a bitch out!" I cried. In the heat and smoke, even more slowly, they tried again. No luck. That door would not open.

I was near panic myself and I expected it from the patrons at any moment. The acridness of the air and the temperature were nearing the point that I felt would no longer support life. An icy hand of fear gripped my spine, and I couldn't imagine what the others must be thinking. At that moment, the lights went out, plunging us into total darkness and unspeakable terror.

Chapter 11

If the situation upstairs was terrorizing — and it was — I can't even think of a term to describe what some of those downstairs must have been enduring at that time.

To say that there's such thing as a good time for a major fire to strike a crowded building would be an oxymoron, but **9:00** PM on a holiday week-end Saturday has to be one of the worst times and a nightclub one of the worst places. At the time the smoke was discovered, the first show had just begun in the Cabaret Room. That room was crowded, probably not much different from the previous evening — I've seen estimates ranging from 900 to 1350 occupants of the showroom. The actual figure may have been around 1000, but whatever the number was, all agree that the room was packed, and as remote from the Zebra Room as any part of the building. Additionally, at least 1300 other persons were scattered throughout the building. Right up until the last minute, all were having a good time, dining, drinking and enjoying the show. For many of the diners, it would be their last meal.

A short time after I handed the bill to Shirley Baker and went back upstairs, the last of the wedding party left the Zebra Room. Shirley and a busboy cleaned the room, leaving the dirty dishes on trays to be picked up later. About **8:45** PM, these two blew out the wedding candles, then went on to other duties.

A couple of minutes before **9:00** PM, waitresses Roberta **Vanover** and her sister, Marsha, went into the Zebra Room to get some additional tray stands for the party they were working in the Viennese Room. Opening the doors, they discovered dense, black smoke hanging near the ceiling of the room. Neither woman saw any flames, but they both instantly knew that something serious was happening. One of these ladies closed the doors to contain the smoke while the other ran to locate the Schillings. Thinking they might be in the kitchen, she ran in that direction, notifying other employees of "fire in the Zebra Room" along the way.

Soon, Rick Schilling arrived at the Zebra Room, accompanied by a busboy, Dave Brock. They were hurrying so much that when Rick opened the doors to the Zebra Room, he was nearly sucked into the room by the force of the draft drawing oxygen to the fire. He immediately closed the doors, hoping to contain the smoke. I'm sure that he had little hope that the fire would remain confined to the small room for very long. He ordered receptionist, Eileen Druckman, who was in the small area we called the "cubbyhole," between the main bar and the Zebra Room, to call the fire department. Included in the great amount of speculation following the fire, is the fact that so many lives were lost due to failure to promptly notify the fire department. The fact is that the Campbell County Dispatch Center log shows that the call arrived at **9:01** PM — within **60** seconds of the time I became aware of it upstairs, which was probably less than two minutes after the smoke was first discovered.

Rick also ordered everyone he could find to "get everyone out of the building, promptly." Then, knowing that the fire department would soon be on the scene, he went out the front door, heading around the building to unlock the door on the east side of the building. Rick thought that this door, which opened into the Viennese Room, would allow the firemen the most direct access to the Zebra Room. On the steps out front, he encountered patrons who had already evacuated the building milling around and cars still arriving. Knowing that both of these activities would interfere with the fire department, he shouted, "Get further away from the building!" Then, he located the man in charge of valet parking. "Get everybody away from the building. Fire trucks are going to be here any minute, and I don't want people in the way when they get here." He also told the man to direct the firemen to the door he was on the way to open, and continued on his mission.

In the meanwhile, Ron Schilling arrived at the Zebra Room with the youngest Schilling brother, Scott, and a bartender close on his heels. Each was armed with a fire extinguisher. They had all been delayed somewhat because, as the alarm had spread, many patrons were making their way out the front door from the Empire Room, the Viennese Room and the Main bar. When this trio got there, the doors were slightly open and smoke was pouring out, although flame was still not visible. They spotted a red glow on the east wall, to the left of the entrance. This glow may have been the fire, or it may have been reflected lighting. Assuming the glow was the fire, they moved as far into the room as possible, stooping low, and emptied the fire extinguishers in that direction. This action had little effect, if any, on the fire that was producing the smoke now boiling out of the room.

The first fireman arrived at the Beverly Hills at **9:04** PM — three **min-**

Teeter and McDonald: Comedy team that was on stage when the fire began. (W. Dammert)

utes after the call was received. The short time span is explained by the fact that the fire fighter happened to be driving by in his own truck when he heard the alarm on the radio. By then, smoke was leaking out of the eaves of the building along the roof line. Many people were gathered on the landing of the front steps and milling about the front of the building. Given these scenes as a greeting, the experienced firefighter knew that they were in for a major battle.

Such events as lighted cigarettes starting fires in paper towel bins in the restroom were a frequent occurrence at the Beverly Hills. Coupled with the fact that no one had, as yet, seen any flames caused some to think that this fire was not serious. Therefore, the patrons in the Cabaret Room, at the far end of the long hallway from the Zebra Room, were still unaware of the problem. There may have been some smoke in the showroom at this time, but the room was full of cigarette smoke anyway and, if the atmosphere was abnormal, no one noticed. The comedy team of Jim Teeter and Jim McDonald were performing their act on stage, opening the show entertainment for the star, John Davidson. The handsome, dashing young singer was in his dressing room, waiting.

Just after Rick Schilling had departed the Zebra Room for outside, a teenage busboy, Walter Bailey, had become aware of the fire. He moved down the hallway, shouted a warning into the bar and continued on toward the Cabaret Room. Passing the Viennese Room, he shouted a warning to another teenager, Jay Neace, to get those people out. Jay quickly led those people to safety.

As Walter neared the Cabaret Room, he encountered some people already forming a line in the hall for the second show. He informed them that there was a fire in the building and directed them to exit via the adjacent Garden Room which had two exits leading directly outside. As they heeded his warning and filed away, he then entered the showroom where the comedy act was in progress. Thanks to his — among other's — actions, many of the patrons were already alerted and out, or on the way out, of the building.

He approached Pauline Smith, the showroom hostess and told her about the fire. Perhaps with some hesitation, this 18 year-old young man made a decision. He walked into the room, went onto the stage, took a microphone from one of the comedians and informed the audience that there was "a small fire on the other side of the building." Walter was very unruffled: in a quiet voice, he instructed the patrons to remain calm, but to exit the room immediately, and pointed out the exits on each side of the stage and the one at the rear of the room. Several sources document the time as 9:08 PM, so if Walter did hesitate, he did not do so for long.

In the aftermath of the tragedy, some accounts contend that Walter did this only because one of the Schillings had so ordered, while other accounts said that he did it of his own volition. My personal opinion is that he did it of his own accord, but it really does not matter — the unquestionable fact is that the actions of this boy saved many hundreds of lives. Walter was also taken to task in the press because he said that the fire was "small," and "on the other side of the building." I know, in my heart, that he was merely trying to avoid panic, and it seems to me that the critics overlook the fact that what he said happened to be exactly true. In my eyes, anyway, Walter Bailey demonstrated great courage, and is a hero.

Unfortunately, not too many of the patrons took Walter's warning seriously. Some may have thought that he was part of the comedy act, and that his warning was a joke. The temperature in the room was normal, and the amount of smoke was not beyond the ordinary. Many started toward the exits; many others remained seated, drinking their cocktails and waiting.

Through the evolution of remodeling and additions to the building, the Cabaret Room had ended up with three exits, — one less than fire codes required — and none of the three was ideal. The one at the rear of the room opened into the main hallway. For the patrons to exit the way they came in required going out the door, then a left turn, then a walk all the way to the front of the building, past the Zebra Room, through the Main Bar, then the foyer, and finally, out the front door. If this avenue was

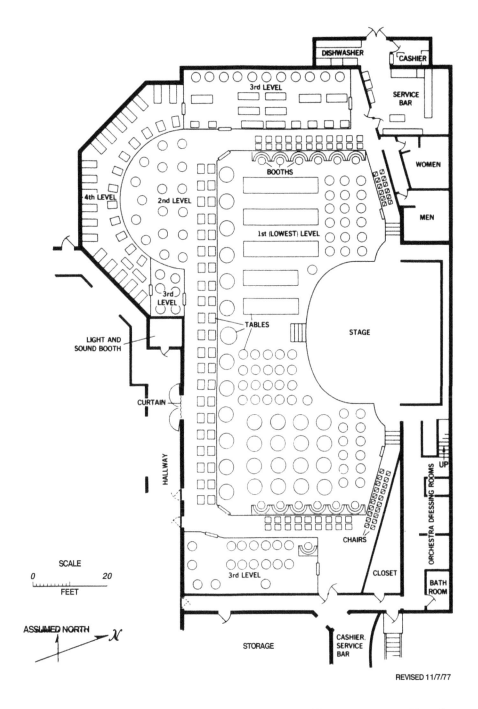

Cabaret Room hostess' seating chart showing May 28 arrangements. Note the packed table placement and chairs on stage access ramps. (National Fire Protection Agency)

available when Walter made his announcement, it would not remain so for long. One could turn right — toward the rear of the building — after leaving the Cabaret Room via that door and exit down the hall that way or through the Garden Rooms, but the patrons probably were not aware of that and would do so only if directed by employees.

As you faced the stage in the Cabaret Room, the exit on the right was the shortest path from there to outside, but it was not a direct path. Going that way required that you make a right angle left turn, go a short distance down the service hall, (this was the hall that had the hidden entrance, at the other end, into the main hallway) then turn left through a door which put you outside on a small landing some eight feet above the ground. A set of steep, wooden steps led down from the landing to the ground. There was no sidewalk or drive on this side of the building, just a path on the narrow strip of earth next to the building. Beyond the path was a sharp drop-off in the terrain.

The door on the left of the stage provided a slightly more direct exit. It led into a service bar area, with the bar extending across most of the back of the room. One had but to go through the door, make a left turn, walk through some service areas, then outside.

Of these four evacuation options, at least three were open when Walter made his announcement.

But not for long. "Flashover" is the term professionals use to describe the event which takes place when all combustible materials in an area reach a sufficient temperature to ignite simultaneously. The time is not definitely fixed, but when flashover occurred in the Zebra Room, many of the patrons were still in the Cabaret Room, while the remainder of the downstairs area was pretty well evacuated. The fire, which had been confined to the small room up to this time, now roared, literally, through the double doors and into the Hallway of Mirrors.

Again, there was a wealth of post-fact speculation about the materials in the room when flashover occurred. It is my understanding that the fire began in a concealed space either at the top of a wall or above the ceiling. After smoldering for a time in the confines of the wall or ceiling, the temperature in the confined space reached the point to allow the highly varnished paneling to ignite and it began to bum. In the Zebra Room, two kinds of chairs were to be found. The two looked identical, but some were newer than others. The newer ones were properly fireproofed, but the older ones used a foam rubber padding which was highly combustible. I understand that five of these older chairs were lined against the wall where the fire began. I further understand that had someone been aware of this situation, each chair could have been fireproofed for approximately **twenty-**five cents. When the paneling began to bum, hot embers and/or flames reached the chairs and they shot off like rocket fuel. At that point, the fire was out of control, those in the vicinity of the Zebra Room had to run for their lives, and the building was doomed. Ron and Scott Schilling, along with Dave Brock were still there, attempting to battle the blaze. The tremendous release of energy literally blasted the three of them out of its way as it roared out of the room. They dispersed, now telling everyone they saw to "get the hell out!"

Once out of the Zebra Room, the smoke, flames and toxic fumes divided into three parts. One took the path of least resistance, up the unobstructed spiral stairway. I suppose this accounts for the difference I noted in the condition of the hallway in the short span of time it took for me to set the salad bowl down in the Crystal Rooms upstairs. It certainly accounts for the terrible condition we were in up there. Another part of the inferno headed down the Hallway of Mirrors toward the main bar, while the third — the most disastrous — roared into the main hallway, moving toward the Cabaret Room.

Most people had cleared the front part of the building by now. Upstairs, I didn't know it, of course, but the hold-up we were experiencing was caused by so many people from downstairs exiting through the **kitchen,** now that the front door was no longer an option. A factor in the congestion was that the door leading outside from the **kitchen** opened onto a loading dock, requiring those going out that way to descend some steps. These steps provided a bottleneck, resulting in the concentration of people in the kitchen that prevented us from descending the service stairs.

The danger in the Cabaret Room had now reached an epic dimension. Smoke, flames and toxic fumes were roaring down the unobstructed main hallway toward the showroom, fed by the combustible materials in the ceiling, on the floor, and lining the walls. Some accounts say that the fire was moving faster than one could run away from it, others likened its progress to a "speeding train." There was now no more time for those people to wait — those who were going to survive had to get out of there now.

The comedians were still on stage, not entertaining, but urging the patrons to remain calm, but to get out. The mass exodus had begun, but with no sense of urgency. Conditions were still normal in the room, not one person in there had seen any smoke or fire, and, in an effort to avert panic, they had been told that the show would resume as soon as it was safe.

The showroom crowd had divided into three parts, one headed for each of the exits. At the rear door, in the main hallway, employees were stationed directing those who chose that exit toward the back of the building. Unfortunately, the outside door at the back end of the hall was locked — egress in this direction was provided only through the doors on the east side of the Garden Room. Pam Browning, who was a sister of Roberta and

Marsha **Vanover,** as well as Cindy Schilly who also worked at the Beverly, and bartender Jerry Walker were at this exit directing people out into the garden. This exit was not of sufficient width to accommodate all trying to use it, and those outside were not moving away from the building. Another bottleneck!

Another portion of the Cabaret Room crowd was moving toward the exit on the right of the stage. Despite the two right angle turns required, the flow out this way was smooth, and hampered only by the steps that had to be negotiated to reach the ground from the outside landing.

The largest part of the patrons had chosen the exit to the left of the stage, leading through the service bar in the north-east corner of the building. William Snow, the head dishwasher, Joe Kennedy, a bartender, Scott Schilling, and other employees were in this area directing traffic out that way, but still, there was no sense of urgency in the crowd. In fact, they were jovial. Calls of, "Hey! Gimme a rum and coke to go," were heard as they moved through the service bar area.

My old friend, Fred Cianciolo — "Mr. C." — was in the orchestra playing in the showroom that night. About this time, as he started out of the room, Douglas Herro, John **Davidson's** music director, yelled, "Hey, Fred! Help me gather up the music." At first, Mr. C. snatched some of the sheets from the stands, but soon realized that there was no time for such activity.

"Let's get out of here, Doug." he shouted, and headed out the exit on the right of the stage. He was able to make his way outside, and stumbled on the stairs leading to the ground. As he tripped and started to fall, he was caught by none other than John Davidson.

"Have you seen Doug?" John asked.

"Yes," Mr. C. replied, "he's right behind me." Sadly, Mr. C. was wrong. Doug Herro had not followed Mr. C. out, but rather had gone — along with four of Mr. C.'s orchestra friends into a storage area to try to save some instruments. The five of them saved neither the instruments nor themselves.

Suddenly, the fire coming down the main corridor gained lethal intensity. It now overcame the air handling system, allowing the smoke and toxic gases to enter the air ducts, thereby gaining access to the showroom. At about the same time, the horrible thick, black stuff rolled down the hall and began to enter the Cabaret Room via the doors, driving those who chanced to be in the hall before it. Extreme elevations of air temperature accompanied the smoke and deadly vapors. The lowest level of the room, the "pit," soon filled with noxious fumes, and in what seemed seconds to the occupants, the entire room filled with oily, black smoke, super-heated air, and hot gases. The long lines of people trying to get to the exits at the sides of the stage got longer as those driven in from the hall joined. Those still in the Cabaret Room now had the sense of urgency, but those in the service hallway on one side, and the service bar on the other did not. These people were unaware of the seriousness of the situation behind them, and they were between those who did know about it and the outside door. The panic was at hand.

If that state of alarm needed any further impetus, it soon arrived in the form of a fireball. The flames had now transversed the entire length of the hallway, and blasted into the showroom, shooting a flaming orb of **orange**-colored death 15 feet or so past the doorway.

At that point, two things happened. Some of the decorative panels in the room covered with a polyvinyl chloride material ignited, adding deadly hydrogen chloride gas to the already lethal atmosphere in the room. Inhaling a small amount of this gas causes one to become disoriented — a fact which, no doubt, cost some lives. Ingesting larger amounts will — and surely did — cause death. The people in the room were, of course, unaware of that peril.

The other event was just as deadly. The basic human instinct for self-preservation came into play. In the smoky, dark, unbearably hot room, with breathing nearly impossible, most of the people still in there must have come to the terrible realization that not all of them were going to get out. As the fireball shot into the room, panic took control. Suddenly, people were screaming, crying and pushing toward the exits with all their combined might. Some threw chairs and tables out of their path without regard to obstructing someone else's progress. Some climbed on the booths and hopped from one to another in an effort to gain an advantage on those moving along the floor.

The panic effected both comers of the room. On the left of the stage, where the doors led through the service bar, the employees there tried to maintain some order, but the crowd — a mob now — was beyond control. These people, engulfed in smoke and fumes with fire nipping at their backs, made every possible effort to push their way on through. Earlier, anyone who stumbled or otherwise needed assistance received it from someone, but not now. Anyone who impeded progress was either shoved ahead with the surge or trampled. The doors were too narrow for the volume of bodies trying to press through, so, at times, the doorway was jammed with humanity. Perhaps under the influence of the disorienting gas, perhaps just from the panic, or maybe under the influence of the alcohol they'd consumed, many people moved in the wrong direction in the small room and wound up behind the service bar at the rear. They were still there the next morning.

Atrocious as that situation was, the predicament of those on the other side may have been worse. The camouflaged door at the end of the service hallway had protected that area from the smoke and flames up to this time.

Suddenly, the door burned through, and the fire, smoke and fumes roared into the hall toward those who were already out of the Cabaret Room, but not yet out of the building. This event heightened the panic and had consequences not only for those in the hall, but those on the outside landing as well. The influx of the new threat caused those in the hall, who may have relaxed a bit at being out of the showroom, to renew the pushing, resulting in some people being forced off the landing. For anyone so unfortunate, a fall of eight feet or so to the ground was the outcome.

One aspect at this exit was the same as on the other side — the door was not wide enough for the crush of people. The doorway could accommodate, perhaps, two bodies at once. Now, as many as seven or eight were trying to press through simultaneously. Very soon, here, too, the opening would be crammed with bodies.

The Southgate Fire Department, and perhaps fire fighters from other stations were on the grounds by now, and firemen were at this exit where people were being propelled off the landing by those behind them. The fire fighters could assist those outside, but realized that any attempt on their part to enter the building would, at this point, simply hamper the escape efforts. So, these professionals had to be content to help those whom they could, try to keep the exits clear, and wait.

Additionally, many of the people who were outside had friends, loved ones and relatives for which they could not account. In a given case, a wife or a husband, or a friend, or a brother or a sister, or even a child, may have been outside, unlocated on another part of the grounds, or still inside. If inside, the party may have been alive, maybe already dead. Wondering and praying, those people waiting hung around the exits, despite the firemen's shouted orders for them to move away from the building, and further impeded the egress.

I don't know the time, maybe the clock had reached 9:30 PM by now. It's for sure that in less than 30 minutes the fire at the Beverly Hills had, from every possible aspect, become a true disaster.

Chapter 12

When the lights went out in the upstairs portion of the Beverly Hills, my heart leapt into my throat. At the end of May, complete dark would not have come outside yet at 9:00 PM, but up there, in thick smoke, we were engulfed in pitch black. In the smoke and gases, breathing had become difficult anyway, but now I felt sure that my heart was blocking my windpipe, and the most fundamental act of life required extreme effort.

In truth, until now, I'd simply been too busy to be frightened, but when the lights went out, I was scared. Simple, unmitigated fear gripped me. I was in a hallway, jammed with people who knew the downstairs was on fire. We all knew the fire was rushing towards us. What these people did not know was the way out, I was the only person there who knew the physical layout. They were only in this hallway because Fran and I had herded them in. I had no idea where Fran might be, so it was up to me to get us all out of there.

All was quiet in the hall. Someone was saying, "Keep calm, keep calm!" in a low voice. Although the air was full of smoke and fumes, there was no screaming. The smell of panic was mixed in the atmosphere, as well. Some men, of their own accord, tried to knock the plywood door out again, but the damned, flimsy thing would not open. They soon abandoned the effort.

Suddenly, the lights flickered back on. Our hopes soared on the brightness, but our eyes had not yet adjusted to the light when it went off again. This time for good. Plunged into total darkness again, time seemed to stand still. I don't know about anyone else, but I began to consider the possibility that we were all going to die in this place at this time. In the midst of that horrible complementation, — and I swear this is true — a picture of my wife and kids flashed before me. A large, clear, color family portrait. I could perfectly see Betty's hair and eye

This is a view of the fire from down the steep slope as seen from U.S. 27. Victims at the Beverly Hills Supper Club would die because the fire spread throughout the building before they were able to get out to safety. (Joe Ruh, The Courier-Journal)

color, and the slightly amused raised corners of the children's mouths. I had not had a thought of myself or my family up to this time. Surely no more than five minutes had passed since I was standing there with the salad bowl when Fran had told me there was a fire, and my mind had been occupied every second of that time.

In the intervening years, I've often thought of that moment, trying to determine what God was trying to tell me. I remember thinking that I'd done all I could do for those in there with me — it was time to just save myself for my family. I also remember realizing that I was at the end of the line and that if these people panicked, none of us were going to survive.

I don't know how long I remained in this reverie. Probably not more than a few seconds, but I then decided that I had to get to the stairs to the **kitchen** and get us the hell out of there, if possible. I was unaware, of course, of the concentration of people in the **kitchen** below.

At this time, I was against the front wall; the opening for the stairs was in the opposite wall. If I could get to the opening, perhaps I could work my way down the stairs and locate whatever the hold-up was. I assumed the stairwell was full of people, too, but if I could just get there … I eased myself across the narrow hall and forced my body against the wall. I was **taking** no chances on accidentally passing by the opening again. The air was unbreathable, hot and full of smoke and fumes. The memory of the fresher air near the floor when I'd stumbled earlier returned. "Get down," I screamed. "On the floor. Crawl!"

The stairs were some twenty feet distant. Every step of the way, I bumped into someone. "I'm an employee. I know the way out. I'll get us out of here," was all I said to each one. I tried to keep myself calm, hoping I sounded reassuring. In what seemed an eternity, my fingers detected the opening. I'd made it!

Feeling for the opposite side of the door frame, I moved into the opening in the wall. I had had my eyes closed all the time, to protect them from the smoke. Vision was not possible, anyway. Now, I had to gather all my mental fortitude to force them open. If I saw light down the stairwell, we could get out and would be saved. If all I saw was orange flames, we were doomed. Even with all the smoke, I felt sure that if there was light in the **kitchen,** I'd be able to see it. As I forced my eyelids up, I prayed, "Oh, God, let there be light. Please, let there be light."

Even after my eyes opened, a few seconds passed before I could see. I suppose the smoke had effected my eyes. As my vision cleared, I saw light. Blurry at first, but light! Thank God, I saw light! A wave of relief covered me. I opened my mouth to shout that we were saved, that we could get out, but before I made a sound, people started moving past me down the stairs. Evidently, the crowd of people in the **kitchen** — who were as unaware of us as we were them — must have cleared just as I got to the opening.

No one required any encouragement. People flew by me and down those stairs. Part of my feeling of relief was that I wouldn't have to descend the stairs to discover the problem. My intent was to be the last one down the stairs so I could ensure that everyone was out. The people rushing out took that choice away. Suddenly, I found myself in a crunch of bodies, being propelled down the stairs. At approximately the speed of light in a vacuum, I might add. Having the choice made for me did not upset me any — I was damned glad to be out of there, for one thing. For another, I felt sure that everyone upstairs would now rush down the steps without guidance.

The air in the **kitchen** was clear, no smoke at all. Obviously, the fire had not effected this part of the building yet. The electric lights were burning brightly, and it was glorious. The kitchen personnel were standing on the stainless steel tables shouting directions. "Out that way," they yelled, pointing toward the doors in the back wall. Apparently, almost everyone who had chosen to exit via this route was already out; only a short line was formed at the door. We, pouring down the stairs in a wave, were among the last to go out this way. I was swept along with the flow, out the **kitchen** door, and outside via the door onto the loading dock at the northwest corner of the building. A narrow set of steps led me to the service drive at the rear of the building. I later learned that some people were injured from falling, in their haste, from the dock.

Words cannot describe the wave of relief that swept over me, or how sweet the spring air smelled. I took a moment to drink in the joy of being alive. I felt, then and now, as if I had looked death eyeball to eyeball, and lived to tell about it. Never before, or since, have I been so keenly aware of my environment. Every nerve in my body was tingling and my senses were keen. The fact that I was alive to inhale the odor of the grass, see the spring blossoms and feel the softness of the air was a true gift from God.

This euphoria didn't last long. I was unaware of the seriousness of the fire, but I assumed that it was probably worse on the first floor than upstairs, so there were probably people in need of help. Without any sense of purpose, I ran around the back of the building, down the service road and into the **parking** lot. Had I known about the situation in the Cabaret Room, I would have gone there. At this time, the only facts I had were that the fire was in the Zebra Room, and that it had roared up the spiral stairs.

Rounding the comer, I saw a fire truck sitting under the canopy at the front entrance. There were a few people standing around and some firemen, but, to my surprise, no one was coming out of the building. I approached the front doors, which were wide open, and looked in. The smoke

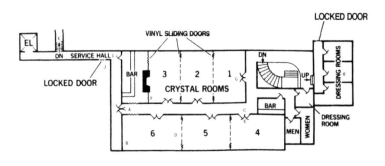

This is a diagram illustrating my movement from hearing of the fire through our escape.

A Area were Fran Oaks informed me about the fire in the Zebra Room. She stayed at those doors.
B Buffet table where I set the salad bowl down. I then proceeded back to spot A.
C Area where I first saw smoke coming around 'L'corner of hallway. This is also the area where I saw heavy smoke coming around the corner and knew that I could not go that way.
D Area where I yelled for the people to "Get out the back."
E Spot where I told man who was trying to pick up jacket to "Get the hell out of here."
F Yelled in this room to make sure everyone was out.
G Doors that I tried to open to get to dressing rooms to make sure everyone was out.
H Dressing rooms where Sharlene **Matthews** had gone to make sure every one was out. She got trapped with another woman and perished.
Z Hallway where I got trappped on my **escape from** the second floor.
J Service door that we tried to knock down.
K Stairs leading down into the kitchen.

was fairly light — compared to what I'd been in upstairs — and I could see about thirty feet into the foyer. I remember thinking that with the doors open at both ends of the building, the smoke had cleared out. Maybe the fire had been extinguished.

The next thought I had was to wonder if anyone was still on the second floor. I'd had no chance to ensure that everyone got out. If I could get on the roof, I could break the plywood door in and see if anyone was there. I grabbed an ax from the fire truck and turned to one of the men. "Can you help me get a ladder up to the roof?" I asked.

"No. The chief just gave me orders to go around to the side of the building."

"I've got to get upstairs," I said. "There may still be someone up there."

"Sorry," he said. Then, pointing down the drive, he added, "There's another truck coming up now. Maybe they'll help you." He disappeared around the corner.

As soon as that truck stopped rolling, I jumped on the running board. "Can you help me get a ladder up to the roof?"

"Sure," the driver said, opening the door. "What are you going to do?'

"I was upstairs," I replied. As we pulled a ladder from the truck, I said, "There may still be people up there."

"We'll see," he said as we moved the ladder into position on the front of the building. Without hesitation, I went up the rungs, holding the ax in my hand. The facade was about three feet higher than the roof, so I climbed over the brick and dropped to the roof. Turning back, I helped the fireman, who was right behind me, over. He was wearing a heavy fire coat and helmet and heavily laden with gear. He would have had trouble clearing the facade top without my help. "Where we **goin'**?" he asked, when he dropped to the roof beside me.

I pointed to the plywood door, about 60 feet to our left. "Over there!" We both ran in that direction. Twenty feet later, we encountered a wall, about four feet high. I scrambled over it, then helped him over. This portion of the roof was flat; we covered the distance to the door quickly.

"That ain't much of a door," he wheezed, gasping from the run.

It did look flimsy. Had we not tried so hard to knock the damned thing out, I would have agreed with him. "I'll tell you all about it sometime," I said, handing him the ax. He stuck the blade of the ax behind the edge of the door and gave it a jerk. To my amazement, it flew open. Perhaps our earlier efforts from inside had weakened it, which made me think that one more attempt might have gotten us out of there much sooner. At any rate, the door flew wide open, allowing thick, black smoke — the stuff we'd been breathing — to pour out into the darkened sky. We both stepped back to avoid inhaling the oily stuff. There was such a volume of smoke rolling out of the opening that we could not see into the building, and neither of us gave a thought to going in. In response to my questioning look, the fireman just shrugged. We did not speak, so I don't know what he was feeling, but I felt pretty helpless. Turning to walk back across the flat roof to the ladder, I saw Scott Schilling coming toward us. He looked beat. "Glad to see you got out, Wayne," he said. "Did you have any trouble?'

Thinking of what to say was not easy. Scott looked like he had enough problems without my adding any tales of woe. "A little," I finally replied.

"Is there anything we can do up here?' He peered into the opening in the wall.

The fireman answered. "Nah. We'll just have to wait for the smoke to clear out some. Probably won't take too long now that this door's open."

"Well, we might be able to be of some help somewhere else," Scott suggested. He and I walked back to the ladder and climbed to the ground. Some days later, the newspaper informed me that this fireman went down after Scott and I did, brought a hose back up there and battled the blaze from that post.

Once on the ground, Scott took off, leaving me to my own devices. I decided to go around the east side of the building. This was the side where only a narrow dirt path separated the Club from a steep cliff. My intent

Frontenac Room Matre' D Ray Howcroft directing patrons away from the fire and down the long driveway leading to U.S. 27. (Jack Klumpe Collection, The Cincinnati Post)

This picture was taken at approximately 9:15 PM. I am in the center and Scott Schilling on left. In my left hand is the axe used to open door leading into the upstairs service hall. Notice the dense black smoke that engulfed the entire building. (W. Dammert)

was to see what was going on at the Cabaret Room exit on this side. Just as I came to the front corner of the building, my eyes fell on a man standing on the grass, right next to the driveway. At his feet lay a motionless woman — unconscious, probably. Then the thought that she might be dead occurred. Incredibly, this was my first inkling that there might be casualties. I suppose that I must have thought that if we got out all right from upstairs, everyone else surely escaped, too.

As I started in that direction, an ambulance came screaming up the driveway and skidded to a halt. The attendant jumped out and looked at me. I pointed to the woman's body. There were no other bodies in the area, so he went over to her. I joined him. The sight before us on the ground saddened me beyond words. A beautiful young woman, tastefully dressed in a white gown, lay on the grass, not moving, with her eyes closed.
The man standing beside her cried, "Help her, she's got a heart condition!" When another attendant arrived, I helped them move her onto the stretcher, and we carried her to the ambulance. The attendant slammed the back door and started for the driver's seat.

"Where are you going?' I shouted.

Patrons are led away from a burning Beverly Hills Supper Club. (Jack Klumpe Collection, The Cincinnati Post)

Formally dressed patrons that survived the Beverly Hills Supper Club fire file down hill at the rear of the burning building. (Melinda Sheehy, The Courier-Journal)

He screwed up his face as if he didn't understand. "I'm **takin'** her to the hospital," he said.

"You'd better hang around," I told him. "I have a feeling there's lots more people needing help, and you're the only ambulance up here."

"I got no more room," he replied, moving to open the door.

At that instant some men carried a very heavy man stretched out on a wooden board up to the back of the ambulance. "Well, you better make some room."

We did. We slid the big man onto the floor in the back of the vehicle. At that point, the man got into the driver's seat, started the engine, and tried to move away. Tried because the driveway was almost totally blocked with fire trucks and police cars. If he needed further obstacles in getting out, we happened to be right next to the fire hydrant, and hoses covered the ground and pavement like a platter of spilled spaghetti. "I'll help you," I shouted to the driver.

Walking through open spots, I waved the ambulance through where I thought he could make it. There was not enough room for him to turn around, so he had to back all the way down the hill. We made it without too much difficulty, the only tense moment coming when another ambulance, coming up, passed in a very tight squeeze. Directing, I walked beside the ambulance all the way down.

On the way back up the hill, I thought about the lovely young woman and the man we'd loaded into that first ambulance. I never found out who either of them was, or if either survived.

The ambulance we had squeezed by on the way down happened to be from my home town, Alexandria. They quickly loaded all the people they could carry, and then I helped them down the drive in the same way I'd directed the first. Coming back up the hill this time, I met two busboys, Buddy Bethel and Mark Johnson, running down the hill carrying small metal cylinders. As we approached each other, I shouted, "Hey! Where are you guys going?'

"We've got to get more oxygen from the truck at the bottom of the hill," one of them replied.

As we passed, I could see that both of the boys were crying. Tear streaks down their cheeks glistened in the rays from the decorative lights. "Is it that bad up there?'

"It's terrible in the back," one of them said, running by. Over his shoulder, he added, "There's dead bodies laying all over the place back there."

My hopes were shattered. After helping load two ambulances, I'd thought perhaps that was the worst of it. At the top of the hill, I decided to go around back and see for myself. Dashing around the east side of the building, I ran along the narrow path. There was some kind of activity going on at the Cabaret Room exit, but I was determined to get around back, so I ignored it and ran right on. Full dark had descended by now, and the path being rough, I fell to the ground, skinning my knee. My lungs were aching and my eyes burned, but a skinned knee was to be my worst injury of this hellish night. I picked myself up, rounded the corner of the building, and walked into the nightmarish scene in the garden area.

The ground was littered with firemen who appeared to have been overcome by smoke, as well as many other bodies, some sitting and others lying. Many of them were yelling for oxygen; the need seemed to be as urgent as the busboys had indicated, so I turned and ran back toward the front of the building, hoping to inform someone of the problem. Just before I came to the Cabaret Room exit on the east side of the building, I bumped into Sonny **Carmack,** the mayor of Alexandria. Being so worked up, I did not even think to ask what he was doing here. "Sonny," I cried, "they need oxygen around back!"

"How bad is it?'

"Damned bad. The need is urgent. Please do something to get some oxygen back there. People are dying!"

He took my comment as seriously as I'd intended. "I'll see what I can do," he said, turning for the front of the building.

Returning to the garden area, I stumbled across the lady on the grass with her husband weeping beside her and so began the most hellish part of

Patrons that escaped the Beverly Hills Country Club fire stand at a distance and watch the landmark bum. (Jack Klumpe Collection, The Cincinnati Post)

Fireman battle the blaze in the Cabaret Room of the Beverly Hills Supper Club as bodies of victims lie in mute testimony. (Jack Klumpe Collection, The Cincinnati Post)

a hellish evening. After helping move a few bodies to the rear of the garden area, I began my chore of administering a kind of last rites to some of the victims. Another employee observed what I was doing and proceeded to do the same. Chef Charles Chandler later told me that the full impact of the tragedy did not occur to him until he observed us in this gruesome activity.

When we'd finished with all the bodies we could find, I went to the service bar exit on the back corner of the Cabaret Room. The double doors at the rear of the Cabaret Room were a mere twenty feet from where I was standing. The distance could just as well have been five miles for all the good we could do. The firemen had set up portable spotlights aimed directly into the opening. Not even these powerful beams of light could penetrate the darkness inside the hallway. No smoke was coming out the door. It simply hung, stagnant, in the interior, as solid as packed, wet, black sand. I could see nothing in there, not even any flame. Several firemen were squatting at the door, peering in. No one was saying a word. The situation was so staggering, and I know we all felt so impotent, that there was no need for conversation. We would have felt even more helpless had we been aware that the doorway we were trying to see was packed, from the floor to the top of the door jam, with dead bodies. Only later did we learn that as people were overcome by the smoke and fumes, they collapsed in the jammed exit. As others attempted to crawl over the stack, they, in turn, succumbed to the vapors, heightening the pile. Before the drama was over, the doorway was packed solid with humanity. One could only hope that they were all dead — the idea of being trapped alive in such an environment is beyond comprehension.

Behind me, in the garden, I noticed a group of employees surrounding a body wrapped in a clean, white tablecloth. Approaching, I asked, "Who is it?'

Through her tears, one of the waitresses, sobbed, "Terri Rose."

Tears instantly spurted from my eyes. Terri was a beautiful young woman, admired by every Beverly Hills employee for her attitude. No matter the problems, Terri always had a smile for everyone she saw. Now, what was left of her was wrapped in a tablecloth. "She didn't get out?' I stated the obvious.

"She was helping direct the patrons out," a quiet voice said. "She just stayed too long. Willie Snow pulled her out a few minutes ago." We all wept, not only for Terri, but for the others, and for ourselves, too, I suppose.

As I stared at the lump of white lying on the ground before me, I remembered the time Terri and I had stood, side by side in the showroom listening to Ray Charles tell a sad story about how the girl next door had moved away when he was a child. Ray said that it was a very sad moment

Some of the 167 victims of the Beverly Hills Supper Club fire in Southgate, KY. (Melinda Sheehy, The Courier-Journal)

for him, and then he sang, "It's crying time again, you're gonna leave me." As we listened to Mr. Charles, featuring the distinctive cry in his voice, Terri and I both had tears in our eyes. It was surely crying time now.

The incident of the police arresting the man riffling the pockets of the dead occurred at this time, so I assigned myself to watching over the bodies from the rock wall in the garden. My watch now showed **10:30.**

About **10:45,** there appeared to be enough policemen on the scene to handle the chore without me. At last, the idea of notifying my wife and family occurred to me. Surely, the Beverly Hills story was filling the radio and television waves, and I knew that Betty and the kids would be worried. I'd done all I could here, it was time to go home. Walking toward the front of the building, I stopped to talk to a policeman. After we'd chatted a minute about the horror, I asked, "Do you know how many are dead?"

"Not for sure," he said. "I've heard it's at least **150.**"

I could think of no reply, so I simply walked away. Behind the **kitchen,** where I'd exited the building what seemed years before, a rescue squad was passing out drinks. Someone handed me a paper cup. The cool liquid was a taste of ambrosia for my parched throat. While I was resting and **drinking,** a radio newsman approached me. "Do you work here?'

I really didn't want to talk to him, but I thought that perhaps my wife might hear it if he interviewed me, and so get the news that I was all right that much sooner. "Yes," I said.

The idea of interviewing someone who worked at the Beverly Hills excited him. He quickly geared up for a live link and started **asking** me questions. Other than my name, which I gave for Betty's benefit, I couldn't tell you what I said.

Finally reaching the front of the building, I couldn't believe the number of vehicles. In addition to numerous fire departments, the Cincinnati police, the Kentucky State police, and the Kentucky National Guard were all in evidence.

At long last, I arrived at the **parking** lot. There was little hope that I'd be able to get my car out, but at least I could lock it and take the keys with me. The lot was, as I'd expected, jammed. Not only 1000 or so cars were there, but busses and trucks were strewn all over. I locked my car and walked back to the front of the building.

Now, as if I hadn't witnessed enough horror, I saw the National Guardsmen in the process of loading bodies into their vehicles. I didn't know it then, but a temporary morgue had been set up at the Fort Thomas armory. The Guard and the police were in charge of transporting bodies there for identification. My tears began anew.

Through the blur in my eyes, I noticed a police car turning around in the drive. I ran to the driver's window. "**Are** you leaving," I sobbed.

"Yeah. Need a ride?"

"Yes," I said. He leaned across the front seat and opened the passenger side door. I collapsed into the car.

Due to the congestion, we had difficulty getting down the driveway. When we reached the highway, the policeman said, "Where do you want to go?"

My first impulse was to say, "I don't care, just get me the hell away from here." My feeling struck me as ironic — most people are fascinated by a fire or wreck, but I loved the Beverly Hills, and I hated to watch the place go up in smoke. Not to mention the fact that I'd seen enough death and destruction to last a life time. **"Wherever** you're going, " I finally managed.

The highway was lined with television trucks and emergency vehicles of every description. Flashing red and blue lights illuminated the grim face of my driver as we gathered speed. "I'm going to the **Newport** police station," he said. "I've got to pick up some equipment."

"Good enough for me," I mumbled. I really didn't care.

About a mile down the road, I saw three women I recognized to be Cabaret Room waitresses walking along. I asked the driver to stop.

"Do you all need a ride?" I asked.

"No," one of them answered. "We called and someone is coming to meet us."

"OK," I said. Then, I inquired, "Have you heard about Terri Rose?"

"No. What's happened to her?" Her voice was edged with dread.

I began crying all over again. "She didn't make it," I choked out. "She was helping people out of the building and stayed too long. Terri's dead."

We drove away as they burst into tears. We would all have cried harder if we'd known that our friend, Rose Dischar, was also dead, still inside the Cabaret Room.

Paying little attention to where he was driving, I was surprised to notice we were on a **Newport** residential street. The policemen stopped in front of a house. "What's this?" I asked.

"My house," he said, opening his door. **"It's** on the way to the station, anyway." He walked around the car and opened my door. "Come on in. You've got some calls to make?"

When Betty answered the phone and heard my voice, she, along with her mother, who was visiting, and our children, all went wild. I can only imagine the relief they must have felt to know that I was alive and out of there. She said that everybody had been calling to see if I was OK, but she'd been telling them she wanted to keep the phone open in case I did call. "Where are you?"

"I'm on the way to the **Newport** Police station," I told her. "Meet me there as quick as you can get there."

The next morning at The Beverly Hills. (The Courier-Journal)

"On the way," she shouted into the phone as she hung up. I'm sure she was halfway to the station before the policeman and I could get to his car.

Traffic was unbelievably light. The police had the roads and Ohio River bridges closed to all but emergency vehicles. I was glad I was in a police car. Eventually, we arrived at the police station. The first sight I saw upon entering the building was the man I'd seen arrested for picking the pockets of the dead. Suffice it to say that the police were not happy with that young man. I stepped into another room to wait.

In a few minutes, I saw Betty and my two oldest sons on the sidewalk. I quickly thanked the policemen and dashed outside into the arms of my wife and children. We passed no words for the first few moments, just all clung tightly to each other. Before starting home, we took a moment to thank God that we were together and safe.

Richard, my oldest son, drove us home via the back roads. As the car reached the crest of the hills, we could see the glow of the fire at the Beverly Hills, a dull, red smudge against the distant blue-black spring sky. By now, I was numb, my brain and my body having absorbed all it could for one agonizing night. The full impact of the disaster had not hit me yet.

The search continues for bodies. (Dr. Fred Stine)

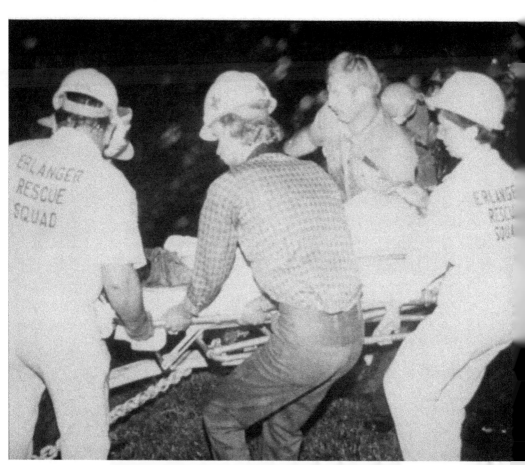

Chapter 13

At home that night, after I calmed a little and assured our two small children and the neighbors that I was OK, I could not pry my eyes from the television coverage of the fire. All the channels were filled, of course, with live and taped footage of the activities going on at the Beverly Hills.

As the night wore on, more of the drama of what had happened downstairs came to light through interviews with the firemen and a few of the surviving patrons. The officials in charge would not allow cameras at the actual site, because rescue efforts were still in progress, so there was a huge amount of speculation on the part of the newscasters. Among the few facts that they broadcast was a reminder that the Beverly Hills had no sprinkler or alarm systems, and that the employees had never been trained in fire prevention or fighting. They spent great amounts of time theorizing about how these factors may have contributed to the loss of life. Mixed in was conjecture concerning the cause of the fire and the point of origin.

The survivors were, naturally, quite confused. No one seemed to know how many people had been **killed** or injured, or even where the fire had started. This was to be only the tip of the iceberg for speculation.

Each of the survivors knew what he or she had experienced. Many told of how they'd been notified of the problem early, had taken the warning seriously, and escaped before the situation became dangerous. Some of the stories, however, were ghastly.

A man who thought he'd been one of the last to exit via the Garden Room said that he happened to be **looking** toward the building when the fire gained its full force. According to his account, flames shot from the exit twenty or thirty feet in a big "whoosh," reminding him of a military flame thrower in a war movie.

Another survivor told of someone bumping into him after he got out. He described turning to see a man and his wife, badly burned. His **por-**

120 Feared Dead, Scores Hurt In Beverly Hills Fire Disaster

By NEENA PS. LEGRINI
Enquirer Report-r

At least 120 persons were reported killed in a fire which ravaged and was still burning, apparently out of control, three hours after it began in the Beverly Hills Supper Club Saturday night.

By 11:30 p.m., a Ft. Thomas physician, Dr. Mark Schwegman, said he counted 120 dead. At the same time reporters were able to count the bodies of at least 100 victims. Authorities were covering the faces of the dead with sheets, clothing and any anything available.

A FIREMAN said about 200 people were trapped in the Cabaret Room of the Supper Club, and he feared most to be dead.

Ninety persons were confirmed dead at 1:35 a.m. by Lt. Ben Harney of the Kentucky State Police.

The Cabaret Room holds 800 people and was filled to capacity, according to a Beverly Hills spokesman. The total Saturday night crowd, including several parties in private rooms, was estimated at 3000.

They were there to hear singer John Davidson. Newsmen reported from the scene that Davidson was brought in to assist them.

SHORTLY AFTER midnight, an eerie light from two sources so brightened the grounds it appeared like daylight, creating what Enquirer Reporter Paul Harasim described as a "surreal scene." Flames continued to shoot 35 feet from the blazing north end of the nightclub, while nurses, doctors and rescue workers only 150 yards away moved from corpse to corpse, with the aid of spotlights brought in to assist them in their grim tasks.

Police were combing the bodies, many dressed in their best evening attire, for signs of life and looking in wallets for identification. A squad of six Catholic priests, on their hands and knees using flashlights, went from victim to victim administering the Last Rites.

At the same time, a crowd estimated at about 300 sat on a nearby hillside, gazing at rows and rows of the dead, in some cases their purses or other belongings put next to them by authorities anticipating that identification will become a major problem.

THE NIGHT club, on Alexandria Pike in Southgate, Ky., was described as an "inferno" and flames at times were reported at least 100 feet high from the intense blaze.

Bodies littered the hillside around the club. Others were reported jammed against a door leading outside.

PHYSICIANS ON the scene said many of those dead died of smoke inhalation. The morbid task of carrying out the bodies of the dead had to be halted shortly before 11:40 p.m. when fire engulfed the north portion of the supper club.

"It is the worst scene I have ever seen," said Wilder volunteer fireman Pat Tuemier, who pulled three

On Page B-1:
Photographs of blaze

bodies from the ruined supper club. "It is something you never want to see with your own eyes. People are charred all over in there."

Bellevue fireman Jack Krognan inside the north end of the Beverly about midnight, said: "Bodies are still strewn all over the inside. They'll find them in the morning but all they'll find will be bones."

AT 12:47 A.M., the walls of the Cabaret Room collapsed. A few minutes later the front walls of the night club also toppled.

Covington Fire Chief Jim Ruth said "there are a load of bodies in there. There are at least still fifty (bodies) stacked. They're stacked up in the hallways where they fell.

Red Cross disaster emergency team member Darrell Meader said "I have never seen anything like this, not even in Vietnam. There are still a lot of people in there. They were stacked up five feet deep in front of the bar where they all ran. They all panicked.

"We looked along the wall in front of the building and found a little girl trapped between some walls. We were able to drag her out but a lot of people suffocated," Meader said.

SOME PATRONS told a grisly tale, reminiscent of Boston's Cocoanut Grove tragedy, of panic and persons being trampled as they fled the club.

The fire broke out in the Zebra Room in the south end of the complex and quickly filled the club with smoke, Southgate Fire Chief Dick Reisenberg said. The Zebra Room had been cleared just moments before.

Deputy State Fire Marshal Tom Wald said the fire started under the floor in the Zebra room. Waitresses attempted to put it out with portable fire extinguishers but could not contain the blaze. Wald also said that a full team of fire and arson investigators would be at the scene early Sunday morning.

Wald estimated damages at "at least $2 million."

Two hours after the initial blaze began, fire had also broken out near the main entrance of the building and was being fought by serial fire towers.

BUSBOY WALTER Bailey instructed the 1200-capacity crowd gathered in the Cabaret Room to see entertainer John Davidson to leave. Bailey grabbed the microphone from comedians on stage and in a quiet voice instructed everyone to leave. Bailey said it took him a few minute to convince the crowd they actually was a fire. Many patrons apparently believed the announcement was part of the comedy routine.

"I told everybody not to go out front because that's where the fire was, and I pointed to two directions where I could go," Bailey said.

A patron said those in the room were calm until the front was opened and the flames were visible. "They panicked and ran for a single exit. At least one woman was trampled," said Henry Freeman, 136 Old State Raod, Cold Spring.

"THE DOORS suddenly opened and smoke was everywhere," said a patron in the club's Empire Room. "They just told us to run, stay calm, stay down below the smoke and get out as fast as you can.

"Suddenly the whole place was engulfed in flames. It was all black smoke. It all happened so fast. I heard a few small explosions, a few rumblings," said a woman who walked almost one mile to the nearest restaurant.

Eyewitnesses said the building's roof was engulfed in flames.

Police instructed Northern Kentucky's three major hospitals—St. Luke, Booth and the St. Elizabeth Medical Center—to be on standby to receive injured patrons from the fire scene and hospitals were implementing their emergency disaster plans to care for those injured.

THE FIRE broke out about 9 p.m. Ambulances were trying to make shuttle runs between the supper club and hospitals, but were slowed by heavy traffic on U.S. 27 (Alexandria Pike).

Fire officials at the scene put in requests for aid from Cincinnati fire

Victims Of Beverly Hills Inferno

trayal of their condition turned my stomach. "When I got to the outside a man bumped into the back of me. I turned around, and he was all burned. His hair and eyebrows were all gone. His hands were burned, and he was holding them at his sides, skin hanging from them like noodles. His wife seemed to be burned as bad as he. She was somewhat in shock and was starting to collapse. She had blisters all over her arms."

Only then did I realize that none of the dead I'd seen were badly burned. What evidence of burning I'd seen was minor. Clearly, those I'd prayed over had succumbed to the fumes. This realization gave me some idea of how toxic the smoke must have been. My friend, Mr. C., later told me that he'd talked to Paul Smith, another member of the orchestra, outside after they'd both evacuated the showroom, and everything seemed fine. The next day, Mr. C. was astounded to learn that his friend was dead. Apparently, Paul had inhaled enough of the deadly vapors that sometime after he was out, he'd simply dropped dead. I knew Paul Smith, slightly, and at the time Mr. C. told me this story, it occurred to me that the large man I'd help load into the second ambulance may have been Paul. Now, after nineteen years, I'm sure it was Paul. A great sadness attends that certainty.

Those who had endured the horror of the Cabaret Room and those who had helped rescue them had incredible tales. Through Ron Bridewell, a professional firefighter, I learned of the activity I'd ignored when I first went by the exit on the east side of the building. He told of his efforts to crawl inside after the trickle of people had stopped. He and fellow fireman Frank Santini had entered the service hallway on the south side of the Cabaret Room. They received no reply to their shouts, but did hear someone pounding on the wall. In smoke so thick that vision was impossible, they moved toward the sound. Upon reaching the doors into the service hall from the showroom, they encountered a stack of bodies jammed in the doorway. The man, who had indicated that he was a hardened professional, dissolved into tears as he told how he and his partner had just gripped a hand, or a foot, or whatever body part they could grasp and dragged a body down the hall to the landing outside. In some cases, he said through sobs, after grasping a body part, they had not been able to free the person from the tangle of bodies, and so had to just let that one go and grope around in the darkness for another. In response to a question, he said he had no idea of how many he'd managed to pull out in this fashion, or whether any one of them was alive or dead. The thought went through my mind that if those he'd pulled out were dead, and surely some of them were, then, at least, he'd saved them from being burned beyond recognition. I prayed that this would be of some consolation to the families.

Another of the images burned into my memory from that night is the picture of Kentucky's Governor, Julian Carroll, sitting in the garden area

Governor Julian M. Carroll's exhaustion is apparent as he is shown resting the following morning after having been there all night. He remembers, "I was entertaining the actor Lee Majors at the Governor's mansion in Frankfort when I was notified of the fire in progress shortly after it ensued. I immediately was transported at very high speed by a state trooper to the site where I remained until the next day attempting to help and provide comfort in any way that I could." (The Courier-Journal)

with his face reflecting his feelings. It's a portrait of anguish and frustration.

Every fire department in Campbell County had responded to the alarm. Additionally, ambulances or rescue units had been dispatched from **twenty-**four other departments. Kentucky's Boone and **Kenton** Counties, and Hamilton County, Ohio had provided all they could offer, and units had responded from as far away as Maysville, KY a distance of some 60 miles. Before the horrible night was over, a total of **32** ambulances had carried the injured away, and 522 firemen and rescue workers were on the scene.

One of the worst of the speculations was about a policeman at the south-east Cabaret Room exit. Several people reported that they'd witnessed this man attempting to close the door, while everyone knew that there were still people inside. Not all the facts became known at this time, of course, but according to the stories, a gust of flame shot out of the doorway, "like a strong wind." A few more people managed to burst out of the opening with flames at the top of the doorway before the door slammed shut in the wake of the out-rushing air. Some of those who had escaped via this exit were nearby, anxiously watching for husbands or wives who had not come out with them. These people began hysterically screaming for someone to open the door.

The policeman snatched up a piece of wood lying about and moved onto the landing. Many of those observing this activity swore that the policeman used the wood to bar the door, preventing its reopening. As the facts later came to light, what he actually did was wedge the point of the stick behind the edge of the door to pry it open. Successful in that effort, he and a young man opened the door and wired it to the railing to ensure that it would remain open.

At length, I became so enraged with the confusion and speculation that I decided to call the television station and tell them the facts that I knew. At least, I could tell them where the fire had started. A lady answered the phone, announcing the station's call letters.

"This is Wayne Dammert." I said. "I'm an employee of the Beverly Hills."

"What can I do for you?"

"I have some facts you might want to know."

"We're very busy right now," she informed me. "Give me your phone number, and we'll be in touch."

Initially, that response made me even more angry, but by the time the phone rang, about five minutes later, I'd decided that she had probably simply told me how it was. The call was from the news department of the television station. After I told the reporter a little of my story, he asked if he could come over and interview me. I agreed. He said he was on the way.

Waiting for the newscaster to arrive, I continued to watch the coverage for about 45 minutes. By midnight, all of the people who had escaped the fire were, like me, gone from the location. The Kentucky State Police had taken charge of the site, impounded all the vehicles in the parking lot, and arranged for transportation: home for the healthy survivors, to hospitals for the injured, and to a temporary morgue for the dead. As the final collapse of the building was imminent, the fire chief had ordered all the firefighters out of the building. At that point, the television reported that at least 70 people had suffered serious injuries, hundreds more were being treated for minor bums and smoke inhalation, and, worst of all, some 130 bodies had been recovered from the Cabaret Room. Speculation was that there might be several hundred more bodies still inside the building.

When the television newscaster and camera crew arrived, I was a bit nervous while they set up, but the newscaster was a professional, and we got through it. The next day, I got to watch myself on television telling of the origin of the fire in the Zebra Room and our escape from upstairs. I didn't know it yet, but I was to become an old hand at interviews before long.

By 2:00 AM, reports were that, aside from a small blaze here and there, the fire was out. Amid reports that the firefighters had done all they could do and were leaving the scene, and that the authorities were formulating a strategy to recover the fatalities from the Cabaret Room, I drug my exhausted body to bed.

Sleep did not come easily that night, or for that matter, for many nights thereafter. I tossed and turned, visions of not only my own plight, but all the others, my friends and the patrons and the Schillings, filling my mind Each time I closed my eyes, faces appeared. The peacefulness of those over whom I'd prayed, the sorrow of my co-workers, the smile of Terri Rose, the despair of the Schilling brothers, and anxiety of some of the survivors waiting for loved ones to exit the doors all paraded before me. The idea of dead bodies still lying in the Cabaret Room haunted me. The true horrors were not yet known: those who had endured them were not alive to tell.

Part Four

AFTERMATH

Chapter 14

S unday morning, the weather was as bleak as the news. A rain front had moved into the area overnight, and a steady drizzle fell from the gray, overcast sky. The ringing telephone awoke me early. "Hello," I said, my voice groggy. It'd been a long night.

"Wayne? Thank **God,**" my brother, Glenn, said.

"Yeah, I'm OK."

"I'm at Lake Cumberland, fishing with Don and Dad. We're camped way out in the boonies, but Dad has a transistor radio, so we got the news about the fire." Both of my brothers, Glenn and Don, had worked at the Beverly Hills at one time or another. "We were worried about you."

"I'm fine," I assured him. "It's a hell of a mess up there, though."

"Yeah. We've been listening to the news." I could hear the sadness in his voice.

Being awake anyway, I turned on the television. Coverage of the fire still filled the airwaves. According to the reports, the building was a total loss, with every part suffering major damage, including the Crystal Rooms upstairs. The basement was relatively intact, but there was structural damage even there. With great sorrow, I listened to the descriptions of my beautiful place of employment as a pile of charred rubble and ashes.

Reporters said that early this morning, rescue teams had removed what was left of the roof over the service bar at the northeast corner of the building, and knocked out part of the exterior wall to gain access to the Cabaret Room. Almost immediately, they found thirteen bodies, some of whom were behind the bar in the back corner of the service bar area. Apparently, these people had become disoriented in the dark, perhaps under the influence of the toxic gases and maybe alcohol, too, and wandered off the path to safety. Amid the smoke and ashes, the rescuers meticulously worked their way through the Cabaret Room, and then the remainder of the **build-**

ing. Before the day was over, a total of 26 additional bodies would be recovered, all from the showroom.

Betty's mother was scheduled to be on a plane for her return to New Jersey in mid-afternoon. In a cloudburst, I drove her to the airport. The mess this rain was making at the Beverly Hills and the impairment to the rescue efforts filled my thoughts.

After I'd dropped her off, a report on the radio informed me that a command post for vehicle retrieval had been established at the Southgate fire station. I decided to go there to see about my car.

Pulling into the parking lot, I could not believe the masses of people there. The lot, sidewalks and building were jammed with people who had come to claim either their own cars or those of friends or relatives who were known to be dead. The state police were in charge, and had established a procedure for claiming a car. After you waited in a long line to reach an officer, you had to describe the vehicle, present proof of ownership, and sign some forms. After the paper work was complete, a group of officers would go up to the site in a truck, retrieve the cars that had been authorized for return and bring them back to the fire station. At that point, the vehicle would be reunited with its owner. I had not brought proof of ownership, and it was a drawn out process, so I decided to just wait another day.

The trip was quite worthwhile, however, in that many of my friends who worked at the Beverly were there. We had a lot of smiles for each other, a lot of stories to swap, and much sorrow for those who were not in attendance, some of whom we'd never see again.

On television, I learned that the Southgate mayor had requested that the state police conduct an investigation into the fire. Governor Carroll had agreed, and before the day was over, he had appointed a complete investigation team, assigning them a straightforward mission: "Leave no stone unturned in your search for the truth about the fire."

Late Sunday evening, someone from NBC called to request an interview. I agreed to meet him on Monday at the Southgate fire station and gave him directions, thinking that I could retrieve my car at the same time. The National Broadcasting Company! Wow!

Leaving home with enough time to get my car before the newsman showed up, I arrived at the fire station early. Not nearly as many people were there this time, and I soon learned that the state police had changed the procedure. Armed with proof of ownership, I approached the officer and completed the required paperwork. He turned me over to an officer who drove me, along with several others, to the Beverly Hills.

The sight was sickening. As we came up the winding drive, I could see plumes of smoke still rising from the rubble, although, according to the

Front view of the building. Note the small portion of second floor that the only part remaining. (Jack Klumpe Collection, The Cincinnati Post)

news media, the fire was now officially out. "Out" meaning that the fire had consumed everything combustible and died due to lack of fuel. About all that was left of the building was the facade out front and some of the exterior walls. The roof was almost entirely gone as was most of the upstairs portion of the club. Noticing what was left of the Crystal Rooms, I thought now, for the first time since I'd climbed down the ladder from the roof, about the style show models. Evidently they were allowing television crews on the site now, trucks with satellite dishes were all over the place, as were photographers, reporters, policemen, firemen and the National Guard. From all the television trucks I saw, I took it that interest in the fire went far beyond the local area. Not only were all the area stations in evidence, but also all the major networks, and I even saw one Japanese television truck.

From the lack of crowd at the fire station, I'd expected most of the cars to be gone from the **parking** lot, but it was still pretty full. I'd guess there were still five or six hundred cars in the lot. One of the men in the police car with us was a member of the orchestra, who parked their cars in the small lot behind the Club. We drove around the building, taking the narrow drive behind the building to reach this lot. As we passed close to the building, we got an up-close look at the activity. Cranes and other heavy equipment were at work tearing apart the remains of the Cabaret Room. I suppose they were trying to ensure that all the bodies had been recovered. I sadly observed that the reports I'd seen on television were correct, the Beverly Hills was gone. In its place, a **smoking, stinking** heap of rubble marked the location of "the showplace of the nation."

After we'd dropped everyone else at his car, I was alone in the car with the policeman. At length, we found my car. I thanked the policeman and got in my car to drive away. Going down the hill, a great sense of sadness overcame me as I viewed the wreckage in the rear view mirror. The weather, the Beverly Hills and my spirits had all been fine when I drove this car up the hill a mere two days ago. Now, the weather was cold for this time of year, the Club was but a memory, and many people who were alive then were now dead.

I drove back to the Southgate fire station to meet the reporter. Just after I arrived, I saw the Southgate police chief **walking** across the **parking** lot. Remembering about the style show models in the upstairs dressing rooms, I shouted, "Hey, Chief!"

"What is it?' The dark circles under his eyes suggested he had not had much sleep lately.

"I was upstairs during the fire."

"Yeah?' His interest picked up a little.

"One of the parties up there was having a style show. They were using the upstairs dressing rooms. I tried to get over there before I got out, but it was impossible. I'm afraid some of them might not have gotten out. Have they searched up there?'

"I don't know," he said, a tired concern in his voice. "We'll find out. Where were these dressing rooms?'

"At the top of the stairway, on the east side."

"Thanks," he said with a sigh. "We'll check it out."

As the chief walked away, I saw a car sporting an NBC logo pull into the lot. I walked over and asked the man if he was **looking** for me.

"You Dammert?'

"Yeah," I replied.

"Then I'm **lookin'** for you." The newsman explained to me that he was in town for what he called **"special** interest stuff," that the network had plenty of people covering the fire itself. After we walked around for a while, he decided that the car retrieval system would make a good story. During the interview, I told him all I knew about how the state police were handling returning cars to their owners. Doing a story on the car retrieval seemed a little silly to me, but everybody's got their job.

When the interview was finished, I started for my car. I had my hand on the door handle when someone yelled, **"Hey!"**

I turned to see a state policeman running toward me. "You Dammert?' he asked as he approached me.

State fire investigator looking from the foyer into the Bar Room. (Jack Klumpe Collection, The Cincinnati Post)

Wreckage of the Garden Rooms soon after the fire. (Jack Klumpe Collection, The Cincinnati Post)

"Yes."

"Come with me," he ordered. "They want you up on the hill."

He ushered me to his car and we drove back to the club, my second trip of the day in a police car. As soon as we arrived, the policeman introduced me to a state arson investigator. This man, part of Governor Carroll's team, started questioning me. I didn't know much that interested him, so he soon turned me over to a federal investigator. I think this guy was from the National Fire Protection Association. Whatever he was, he asked me a bunch of questions about the origin and spread of the fire. He was very interested to learn that I'd been in the Zebra Room shortly before the fire was discovered. I told him that I'd noticed nothing unusual while I was there. It was then that I learned that they suspected that the fire had begun in that room, and had been smoldering, if not burning, in the concealed spaces for some time before it was discovered. While we were talking, a news reporter kept sliding closer, trying to hear what we were saying. When the policemen noticed, they gave the newsman a lecture that I feel sure impressed him with the inadvisability of eavesdropping on the federal government.

After many questions, the federal man asked me to walk around the building with him and point out the location of the various rooms. At the rear of the building, I pointed out the upstairs hallway where we'd been trapped. Only the rear wall where I'd crept along to the service stairway, the service elevator door, and the service stairway door were still there. Tables and chairs teetered precariously from the edges of what was left of the floor.

As we walked to the front of the building, I mentioned, "the Zebra Room is right through there," pointing through the brick facade.

"I'd like to see in there," he said.

"There's a window." I remembered. The old building had a window in the dealer's break room. Since the facade had been built, the window was hidden.

"What? Where's a window?' He seemed surprised.

"There's a small opening at the base of the false front," I said. "You can see the window through it."

"How do you know that?' I had his interest.

"I've worked here for a long time," I said. "I remember the window from before they built the facade."

"No, I mean the opening in the facade."

"I watched 'em build it."

"Show me," he ordered, moving toward the facade.

Approaching the wall, I pointed out the opening at the base of the brick. Before I could say anything else, he crawled through the opening into the narrow space between the facade and the front of the old building. Dropping to my knees, I scrambled through after him. Anyone who was never in the Zebra Room before the remodeling would not have known about the window, because it was concealed behind the false fireplace. All the covering material had burned or fallen away now. The window was now just a square hole in the front wall. He climbed through the opening with me right behind.

We dropped to the surface on top of a heap of rubble, most of which had fallen through from upstairs. Directly above the Zebra Room had been the bathrooms, so we were standing on sinks, toilets, roofing material and chunks of concrete. Even though it was a total wreck, one could get a good picture of what had been in the room at the fire's beginning. All the tables were still standing, including the table that had held the wedding cake on the day of the fire. All the paneling was burned away as were the double doors leading into the Hallway of Mirrors. In the rubble, we saw the fire extinguishers that the Schillings had used in the attempt to control the blaze. Naked steel skeletons of a row of chairs sat along where the wall had been.

Most of the debris was heaped in the center of the room. Evidently as the upstairs portion had collapsed, it fell into the center, missing the areas along the walls. The tray stands with dirty dishes on them were still standing along one wall. Most of the dishes were not even broken.

We poked around among the litter for a few minutes. Then I heard a shout from outside. "Hey! Hey you guys in there!"

I thought we were in trouble. The state police investigation was in full swing, and I thought they probably wouldn't care too much for us being in there.

"What?" my partner answered. I breathed easier when I remembered that he was a federal investigator.

"How the hell did you get in there?"

"Tell 'em," the investigator ordered.

"There's an opening at the base of the facade," I yelled. "Crawl through it and you'll see the window."

In short order, about ten members of the investigative team scrambled into the room. They immediately started picking through the debris. They knew what they were doing and set up a methodical search of the room, examining every bit of litter. The old saying, "sifting the ashes" came to my mind, as that is literally what they were doing. They worked so intently that I soon decided they didn't need me and exited via the window and crawled back through the facade.

Just as I came through the opening, on my hands and knees, another group of state authorities approached me. "You the guy that was upstairs?" one of them asked.

"Yes." Apparently, the word about me being on the site had gotten around.

They started questioning me. I told them the same story I'd recited several times already. After a while, one of them looked at his watch. "How 'bout some lunch?"

"I'm really not hungry," I answered, truthfully. The morning's activities had upset me.

They explained that the state investigative team had set up headquarters at the Fort Mitchell Holiday Inn, and that they wanted me to go over there with them. I went. In one of the rooms they'd rented, we ordered from room service. While they ate and I picked at my food, they asked me if I knew how to get in touch with any other employees who might give them additional information. Remembering talking to Pam Browning in the garden the night of the fire, I mentioned her.

"Pam was **working** in the Garden Room, I think," I told them. "I think she helped usher people out of there."

"Do you know how to reach her?"

"She lives in Cincinnati," I said. "She's probably in the phone book."

"Well," one of the men said, "you know her. Give her a call and see if we can go talk to her. We'd like to get her story." He handed me the phone book.

Her number was listed. She answered on the second ring. "**Pam**, there's some investigators here who want to talk to you."

"What do they want?" She sounded hesitant.

"**Just** to get your statement." I reassured. "I've already spent a while with them. They're nice."

"OK," she said, "bring 'em over."

The investigators were happy to hear this news. I gathered that this group's number one priority was to gather all the information they could from the employees. As we were **walking** out of the motel, I glanced through an open door to see Rick Schilling going over some blueprints with another group of investigators. I was impressed with how organized and professional these guys were. They were taking the Governor's charge to make a thorough investigation seriously.

To the delight of these men, Pam's three sisters, Marsha and Roberta **Vanover** and Cindy Schilly, were all congregated at Pam's house. I don't know if they were already there when I called, or if Pam had subsequently invited them. After they'd talked about their experiences for a while, the State's men wrote out statements for all five of us and we signed them. The men thanked the ladies and prepared to leave.

"What about the tip book?" one of the women asked as they were walking out.

"The what?"

"The tip book," she repeated.

He stopped and turned, a puzzled look on his face. "What's the tip book?"

"It's where the record of who worked what parties and the tips for everybody is kept," I explained. "We use it to determine how the tip money is to be distributed."

"Where was it kept?"

"In a cashier's cage in the **kitchen**," I said. "Near the time clock."

"Well," he replied, slowly, "I don't know anything about that."

"We have to have it," the lady insisted.

"What's the big deal?"

As I was a captain, such things were part of my responsibility. "It is a big deal. We usually distribute the money weekly, but it's been so busy lately that we haven't had time to worry about it for three weeks. So, there's a pretty good sum involved."

"I see," the investigator said, thoughtfully. After a moment, he added, "Well, we're going back up there anyway. I'll see if they'll let Wayne in the **kitchen** area." Then to me, "If so, you can see if there's anything left of the book."

When we arrived back at the Beverly Hills, I was surprised to see what the work crews had done while we were gone. The crane and other equipment had shifted their positions and efforts to the front of the building, and were busily **knocking** out anything that blocked access to the Zebra Room. I suppose they had found all there was to find in the Cabaret Room. An incredible number of television cameras and reporters were ganged around observing this activity.

The investigator I was with located a state police captain and explained that I wanted to look around in the **kitchen** area. "What for?" the captain asked me.

"There was a book in there that involves a lot of money," I replied.

"Whose money?"

"All the waiters and waitresses. A bunch of people's pay depend on it."

He fixed me with a hard stare while he considered the matter. At length, with a sigh, he said, "Well, all right. We'll see." He walked a short distance away and engaged the fire chief in conversation.

After a few animated gestures, the chief walked over to me. "Nobody is taking anything away from this site," he announced, matter-of-factly.

"I won't take it," I promised. "If I can find it, I'll turn it directly over to you."

He, too, glared at me for a long moment. "You say people's pay depend on this thing?"

"Yes, Sir."

After a slight hesitation, he said, "Well, all right. You can look." He looked to his left where a group of firemen were standing. "But, I'm going with you," he added. Motioning to the men, the chief started toward the back of the building. He, along with two firemen, accompanied me to the **kitchen** loading dock. A feeling of gloom rushed over me as we walked through the doorway from which I'd made my escape. I'd run what I thought to be the gamut of emotions since then, but this one was new. The instant I entered the area, the atmosphere seemed to close in on me in the kitchen area, and although I've never suffered from it, I felt just a bit claustrophobic.

Shuddering against these emotions, I surveyed the large room. Strangely enough, half the area was virtually untouched except for smoke and water damage, while the fire had totally consumed the other half. In the half that was **intact**, steaks still lay on the grills, and **din-**

Workers tear out the front partition and front wall of the Zebra Room two days after the fire. (W. Dammert)

ners sat on the counters, awaiting diners who would never show up.

In the vicinity of the time clock, everything was a shambles. A twisted, heat stained metal beam, already rusting, lay directly over where the time clock had been. The firemen and I searched, in vain, for the tip book. It, along with everything else in this area had been consumed by the fire. At that time, I thought that all was lost in terms of that money, but I underestimated the Schillings. Before the month of June ended, every employee of the Beverly Hills got whatever pay they had coming, and those of us who were due tips got that money, too.

The time it took to look around the kitchen and get out of there was much too long to suit me. Being in the Zebra Room earlier had not bothered me in the least, but the kitchen made my **skin** crawl. Perhaps the dinners sitting around made the difference, perhaps my having exited through there. I don't know, but I was happy to be back outside when I reached the service drive. Several minutes passed before I was breathing normally again.

By the time I walked back to the front of the building, I was astounded to see what the work crews had done while I was in the back. They'd used the equipment to scoop everything out of the Zebra Room, creating a pile of debris on the front driveway. As I watched in wonder, a crew of firemen were in the room, working with shovels and brooms, cleaning the area.

I was then, and I am now, confused about why this happened. By then, everybody knew that the fire had begun in the Zebra Room. To this time, the investigative teams had impressed me as professional and thorough. So, I would have thought that they would have gone through that stuff, where it was, with a fine-toothed comb. I know nothing about investigating a fire, but it seemed to me that the order in which the debris was layered would make a difference. But, as I watched, they cleaned the entire area, throwing everything helter-skelter on the pile. I realize that this is at odds with the official version of the investigation. All I know is what I saw.

On each of the next three days, the state investigators called me to the Beverly Hills. At various locations inside the structure, they questioned me thoroughly, and I did my best to inform them of what I knew.

On Wednesday (June 1), they questioned me in the comer of the main bar nearest the Zebra Room, where I observed some of the work crew brushing the burned-out electrical wiring. After about a half hour, they said that they were through with me for the moment, but that I shouldn't wander too far. Confused, and **thinking** perhaps they simply didn't want me to see what was going on, I took a seat on a rock across from the front entrance. By now, I was becoming a little concerned about the investigators calling me everyday — to my knowledge, I was the only employee, aside from the Schilling brothers, who'd been in the building since the fire.

In a short while, one of the investigators called for me to come back. We made a thorough tour of the building, even climbing part way up the remains of the spiral staircase. "We'd better get off this thing," he said. "It looks dangerous."

He was right, it was pretty shaky. Looking up to where the Crystal Rooms had been, I remembered about the upstairs dressing rooms. "Has anyone been up there?'' **asked,** turning to go down the stairs.

"Nope. Too dangerous."

"I'm not sure everyone got out of the upstairs." We were off the stairs.

"What?' He nearly shouted.

"They were having a style show up there," I said. "Some ladies were using those dressing rooms. I tried to check, but couldn't get there because of the fire."

"Show me," he demanded.

We couldn't get upstairs — there wasn't much left anyway — so we went down the hall to near the end of the Viennese Rooms. "Right up there," I said, pointing above us.

"Did you know that two people are still unaccounted **for?**" **His** voice was edged with concern.

"No," I replied. That had not been reported by the media.

We both turned to view the wreckage before us. I'm sure his **thinking**

Although taken nearly one year after the fire, debris from the Zebra Room (behind opening) still lay on the front drive. (Jack Klumpe Collection, The Cincinnati Post)

matched mine — anything in those dressing rooms would have fallen into the area where we were looking.

That afternoon, the radio informed me that two additional bodies had been found in the building. According to the radio account, they were two women who had been trapped in the upstairs dressing rooms. One of them was identified as Sharlene Matthews, the lady I'd worked with from the Choral union. As soon as I heard the name, I thought about moving those tables out, then back in. As the story unfolded, it was determined that she'd gone to the dressing room to see if anyone was there and been unable to get

Sharlene Matthews.

out. The reporters lauded **Ms. Matthews** for her heroic efforts. This story evoked mixed emotions in me. She had done exactly what I had tried to do, but I was driven back by the heat and smoke. On one hand, I wished that I had been able to get there because I might have helped Ms. **Matthews** and the other lady get out. On the other hand, had I managed to get to the dressing rooms, there might have been three bodies discovered in the wreckage — mine along with the two women.

Chapter 15

As the days rolled by, some events moved quickly while others made time drag. A very long evening was spent at a funeral home in Cincinnati where **Terri** Rose lay in a casket. She had been a cheerful, lovely young woman whose life had suddenly and tragically ended. Seeing her body was sad enough, but when her two young children, who I'd never met, hugged me (at their grandmother's urging), I nearly lost control of my emotions.

The next day, I drove ten miles to a small Catholic chapel to attend Rose Dischar's funeral. Rose was another fine young woman lost to the holocaust. Rose had five children, for whom responsibility of rearing now devolved on Rose's parents. The chapel was packed with Rose's friends, and the funeral was a sorrowful experience for all. I had the good fortune to talk with Rose's mother, Minnie Burtch, some fifteen years after the fire. She reported that Rose's children all grew up to be fine people.

At length, the final returns of the tragedy came in: 165 dead, many killed the night of the fire, some succumbing to injuries days and even weeks later. In terms of numbers killed, that made the Beverly Hills Supper Club fire the second worst in history. Only a fire at the Coconut Grove in Boston, November 28, 1942, which took nearly 500 lives, rates higher. Adding the hundreds of injured rates it as a major disaster, by any standard.

While funerals for my friends went slowly, other things moved much more quickly. On June 2, 1977, five days after the fire, Cincinnati attorney Stanley Chesley filed suit in U. S. District Court on behalf of one of the injured, seeking damages of $21,000,000. The Commonwealth of Kentucky, the City of Southgate and the 4-R Corporation (the Schillings' corporation) were named as defendants. This suit was merely the tip of the iceberg. Before the litigation was over, 90 suits would be filed, the aggregate damages sought amounting to more than $3,000,000,000.

This picture shows Viennese Room (left), Empire Room (bottom) Zebra Room (top center), and roof of second floor and spiral staircase (center). Note the circular hand railing of staircase. (Jack Klumpe Collection, The Cincinnati Post)

Meanwhile, some of the horror stories, primarily from the Cabaret Room, came to light. One such involved Caroyln Thornhill, eight months pregnant, who was shoved to the floor in the frenzy to exit the room. No one made any offer to help, so her husband, Larry, attempted to protect his wife and unborn child by shielding her body with his own. While flaming debris fell on them from the ceiling and the mob stampeded over them, Larry made every effort humanly possible to save his family. As fate dictated, one of the limbs in the tangle of bodies grasped by a firefighter belonged to Larry Thornhill. He was pulled from the inferno to live the remainder of his life scarred not only physically from the experience, but also by the memory of a wife and family lost to the fire.

The morning following the fire, Southgate mayor, Ken Paul, accompanied state officials into the Beverly Hills and came out with a story that he won't forget. Paul's heart was heavy as he trudged past the various emergency vehicles into the smoking rubble. Among the horrifying sights he witnessed that morning, he reported that the spectral display of five bodies, seated upright at a table in the Cabaret Room, patiently waiting for the show to begin, would remain forever in his memory.

Another spine-tingling story was provided by Donnie Hammond, a Cabaret Room cocktail waiter. When the fire invaded the Cabaret Room, Donnie found himself groping through the darkness toward the service bar in the northwest corner. He stumbled over something or somebody in the doorway leading from the Cabaret Room. As others tripped and fell on top of him, he soon found himself near the bottom of a pile of screaming, struggling humanity, his head in the service bar, the remainder of his body pinned to the Cabaret Room floor. He related that as he fought the rising panic, he attempted to rationally evaluate the situation. The air was fresher near the floor — he could breathe — and the bodies above protected him from the flames and heat. He knew the way to an exit, but was unable to move due to the weight piled on him. Through the smoke and fumes and screams, he heard a voice calling from the outside door, some 20 feet away. "Come this way! The door is over here."

"I'm stuck!" he screamed.

"We can't get to you," came the plaintive reply. "The smoke's too thick!"

In the tangled mass of bodies, some unconscious, some writhing silently, some screaming hysterically, he struggled to free himself, but it was impossible. He could not move toward the exit. "I talked to myself while lying there. I thought it was all over, but I kept saying, 'Get hold of yourself and take it easy.' When you've got a crowd of screaming people around you, that's hard to do. It seemed like a long time I laid there and I tried not to breathe. I held my breath so that I wouldn't use much air."

Some of the more intrepid rescuers got close enough that Donnie could actually see them trying to reach the stack of bodies. The heat and smoke were too much for many of them. While he waited, more of the bodies around him grew quiet, overcome by the fumes and heat, creating more terror for Donnie. Eventually, some rescuers braved the harrowing conditions, reached the pile, and started, slowly, to untangle the bodies. "The voices called out for help from a pile of people two-and-a-half to three feet high. I couldn't see a thing. I felt around and grabbed the person who held out his hands, pulled him to the outside and returned for another," related one of the brave rescuers.

After what seemed an eternity, the rescuers managed to work the pile down enough so that when the next one grabbed his hands, he managed to pull Donnie free. Exhausted, burned and suffering from smoke inhalation, he lay on the grass in the garden giving thanks to God and the brave men who rescued him from that nightmare.

On June 10, Kentucky State Fire Marshal Warren Southworth issued a press release which provided some insight into what the fire investigating team was finding:

> "Based on the investigation to date, including both interview evidence and evaluation and examination of physical evidence, the investigative team has concluded that the fire originated in a concealed space within the Zebra Room.
>
> "The most probable cause of ignition within this area was electrical in nature and would have been fed by combustibles located there. Specifically, the presence of concealed, combustible ceiling tile and wood materials used for supports provided a fuel supply for continued spread of the fire through the original and other concealed spaces. On-site analysis of the construction of the concealed spaces within the Zebra Room indicates that the fire burned for a considerable time prior to discovery. Interviews with occupants of the Zebra Room and adjacent areas support this conclusion.
>
> "The above mentioned ignition sequence led to an intense heat build-up within the concealed space which ultimately resulted in the accumulation of smoke and hot gases within the Zebra Room itself. It was at this point when the fire was discovered, and attempts were made to extinguish it. Some time thereafter, various actions were initiated to notify occupants of the building and the fire department.
>
> "During the time attempts were being made to extinguish the fire within the Zebra Room, flashover occurred.

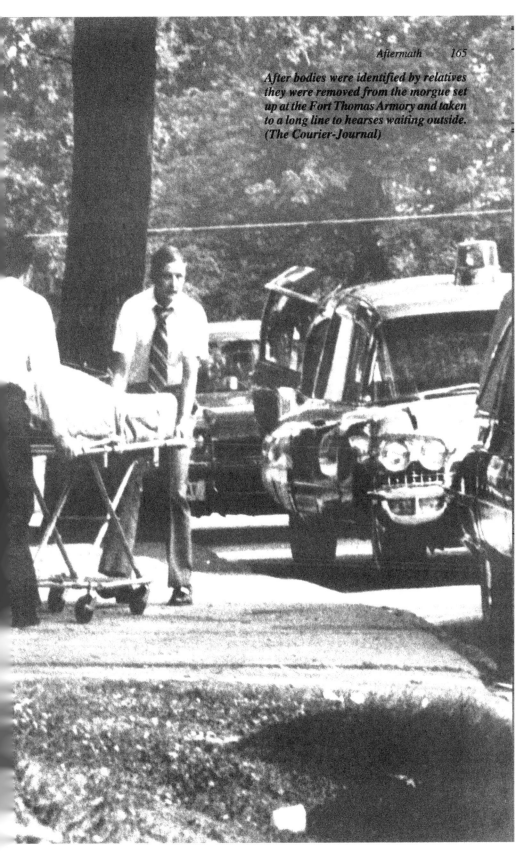

After bodies were identified by relatives they were removed from the morgue set up at the Fort Thomas Armory and taken to a long line to hearses waiting outside. (The Courier-Journal)

In other words, simultaneous ignition of all combustible materials within the room occurred.

"Following the occurrence of flashover, the fire continued to build until it broke out of the Zebra Room through double doors located at the north end of the room. The fire then spread rapidly throughout the structure."

A federal investigator built what he considered "a most probable scenario for the action of the fire" on the fire marshal's premise.

"When flashover occurred in the Zebra Room, the room resembled a furnace... This furnace-like fire had only one immediate flue or vent available to it and this was the pair of doors at the north end of the room... The venting of smoke through this doorway resulted in the passage of smoke, flames and heat through the upper part of the doorway at relatively high velocities, with an in-rush of cold, fresh air at lower velocities near the floor. As the smoke, flames and hot gases left the Zebra Room they were propelled across the ceiling of the small corridor directly outside the Zebra Room until they hit the far wall, some 20 feet distant. Here, the flames and hot gases split, with part of the flames and hot gases turning down and part turning sideways in both directions. The thin, plywood paneling, on the far wall of the small corridor, would have ignited readily under the impact of this flame and hot gas exposure."

These reports touched off a whole new round of speculation, part of which was that there was a great delay in notifying patrons of the fire. This speculation was based, in part, on the "fact" that smoke was discovered in the Zebra Room as early as 8:30 **PM**. This is simply not true. I, personally, was in the Zebra Room for about three or four minutes, beginning at 8:35 **PM**. As it happened, I was worried about my party upstairs being late, so I verified the time with Shirley Baker. Therefore, I'm certain about it. Neither I, nor any of the several others present, noticed anything unusual at that time. I was standing within a few feet of the concealed space that the investigators identified as the source of the fire, and I am absolutely sure that had there been any smoke in the room, or had the temperature been elevated, I would have noticed it. When I left, there were still several of the wedding party in the room, as well as a couple of employees. When the guests departed, the room was cleaned and the dishes stacked on trays. I don't know how long all that took, but I am certain that the smoke in the Zebra Room was not discovered before 8:55 **PM,** at the earliest.

Speculation also swirled around failure to promptly notify the fire department, and I have something to say about that, also. Upstairs, I learned of the fire at exactly **9:00** PM. Having no opportunity to check the time, I do not know how long we were trapped upstairs. It seemed an eternity, but my best guess is that it was no more than 10 minutes. By the time I made my escape through the kitchen and walked around to the front of the building, at approximately 9:15 PM, a fire truck was sitting under the awning. Given that Southgate had a volunteer fire department, the firemen had to be notified after the alarm was sounded, rush to the fire station and then they had to gather their equipment. From the Southgate fire house to the Beverly is a four or five minute trip. The fact that they accomplished all of that and were already on the scene by the time I escaped bears testimony to timely notification.

Amid the speculations and survivor's experiences, a fascinating, morbid glimpse of the activities at the temporary morgue established at the Fort Thomas armory was provided by Campbell County coroner Fred Stine.

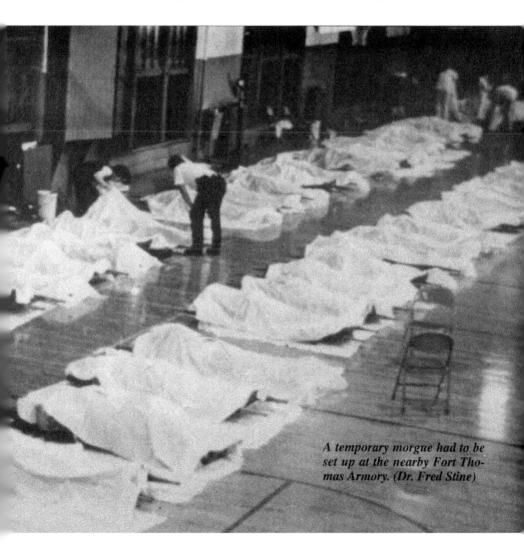

A temporary morgue had to be set up at the nearby Fort Thomas Armory. (Dr. Fred Stine)

"I was at a holiday cook-out when I received the call, 'Report to the Beverly Hills Supper Club.' Leaving immediately, I responded to the order. I hadn't heard about the fire in progress at the club, but realized that someone had to have died at the site if the coroner was being called in.

"Approaching the club, I was struck by the deep red glow emanating from the top of the hill, the light of it dominating even the myriad profusion of red and blue flashing lights.

Dr. Stine at a daily press conference. (Dr. Fred Stine)

Walking swiftly along the path beside the building, I kept tripping over obstacles in the dark. To my horror, I realized that these 'obstacles' were the bodies of people who had successfully egressed from the club only to fall dead in their tracks from the effects of inhaled toxic smoke. I now realized that we had a tremendous disaster on our hands, and mentally reviewed the carefully detailed disaster plan recently set up in the county by Saint Luke Hospital.

"As I entered the garden area, I witnessed many more dead bodies and immediately put into action a system to transport the victims to a temporary morgue in the nearby Fort Thomas armory. I then proceeded to the armory myself to begin the gigantic task which would totally dominate the next two weeks of my life — identifying all the bodies and returning those identified to their loved ones for proper burial. My task was made all the more challenging because one of my assistants was in Florida, visiting his sister, and my other assistant informed me that he would have to leave around noon on Sunday to attend a relative's funeral.

"Throughout the first night, some 130 bodies were delivered to the morgue on stretchers covered with bright, white sheets. The delivery was accomplished in an orderly fashion according to the county's plan. I ordered the bodies brought into the building's gymnasium via a back basement door to avoid possible traffic accidents on the busy North Fort Thomas Avenue which runs past the front of the armory.

"*Doctors, dentists, morticians, clergy of all faiths, nurses, a pathologist and high school students were among the many who volunteered to assist us in our task, As the bodies arrived, one group cleaned the victim's faces then sent them to another section to be placed in rows according to gender. Large, new tarpaulins protected the highly polished basketball floor. At this point, each victim's clothes were removed and placed in a bag. The body was then completely cleaned and covered again with a white sheet. When this procedure was complete, the body was ready for identification.*

"*Reporters and photographers from across the country had gathered around the site of the morgue. Because I thought constant questioning of the workers would hinder our efforts, I arranged to keep the reporters informed on events and procedures by holding three press conferences a day.*

"*Sunday morning, we received news at the armory that additional bodies were being discovered in the smoldering ruins of the Beverly Hills. The assistant still on duty said that he would go to the site and stay as long as possible. My other assistant, in Florida, had been informed of the disaster and immediately flew back to Cincinnati.*

"*During Sunday and Monday, over 30 more bodies, most badly burned, were delivered to the armory, this time in black, plastic body bags. Identification of these victims would prove to be a **difficult,** time consuming task. As a result of an urgent telephone call to the F. B. I. in Washington, D. C., five experts were sent to assist us in this duty. A specially cordoned section of the gym enabled these specialists to work in privacy.*

"*Jewelry, purses, clothes and other items were delivered to the armory with the bodies. A nurse volunteered to take charge of these personal effects. 'You've got the job,' I eagerly responded, 'but why do you want it?'*

"*'I was in the Air Force,' she replied. 'One of my duties was to go to the site of plane crashes and perform this same task. I know exactly what to do.'*

"*Amazingly, in just one day's time, this woman and a few other volunteers had all possessions tagged, boxed or bagged, and ready to be claimed by the next of kin.*

"*When a body was properly identified, volunteer high school boys carried the corpse out to a waiting hearse. Each night, the remains that were not yet identified were*

Firefighters load bodies into trucks to be taken to the temporary morgue at the Fort Thomas Armory. (The Courier-Journal)

stored in refrigerated trucks parked outside the building and then returned to the gym floor the following morning. The task of embalming the bodies had been accomplished by several local morticians and students from a Cincinnati based mortician's school. During the week-and-a-half ordeal at the armory, we used such a large quantity of embalming fluid that no more was available in the entire area. More embalming fluid was donated from other cities and flown, free of charge, to the Greater Cincinnati International Airport courtesy of TWA.

"The clergy was an integral part of the overall plan. A person arriving at the armory to identify a loved one would first be accompanied to a private room to meet with a priest, minister or rabbi. The grieving relative would then be informed of exactly what to expect and was not permitted to view the remains until their composure indicated readiness. In some cases, this procedure was quite lengthy, but no incidents of fainting or panic occurred during the entire body identification process.

"Looking down the long lines of bodies, one could distinguish the burned victims from the clean ones by the color of sheet covering them; black coverings shielded the burned remains, while the less disfigured were covered in white. The unburned bodies were being identified and claimed relatively easily. The temperature in the Cabaret Room had soared to some 2000 degrees Fahrenheit. Therefore, although they had died as a result of inhalation of toxic fumes, the remains of those victims who had not been removed before the intense combustion were so badly burned and mutilated that identification was extremely difficult.

"One of the first burned corpses to be identified was a woman whose family had noticed her purse lying by her side. They claimed her remains before the F. B. I. specialists and a dentist had checked her out, took her away, held a funeral, and buried her. This proved to be a mistake. A week later, the body of a young woman, just returned to this country from a stint in the Peace Corps, could still not be located. Positive that her body was not among the remaining unidentified few, another dental check was run on the already recovered victims. This resulted in a solution to the mystery — this body was confused with the one who had been identified by her purse. That body had to be

exhumed, and proved to be the Peace Corps worker. A determination was made that she had evidently tripped over the purse and died on the spot. Rescue workers, assuming the purse belonged to her, had placed it beside the body.

"Another woman was so badly burned that only a small portion of her palate remained. Not knowing this corpse was their mother, her family kept returning, day after day, hoping to find her. When they told me that their mother never wanted to be without her dentures so she owned two sets, I asked them to bring in the second set. With the dentures, the experts were able to match up the palate and thereby establish her identity.

"The last horribly burned person to be identified was a woman whose leg had been protected from the fire by a table which had fallen on her. By the process of elimination, we could assume who she was, but these situations require proof positive. As well as protecting her leg, the table had preserved her shoe. I directed the F. B. I. agent to check out the shoe. As we had an excellent idea of who she was, the agent carried the shoe to her home in Lexington, Kentucky, opened the closet in her bedroom and searched along the neat row of shoe boxes. The serial number on one of the empty boxes matched that on the shoe, making the identification positive.

"After three days, it was presumed that all but two bodies had been recovered. Confusion among the survivors made a definite decision **difficult,** *however. In some cases, entire families had been wiped out, or an entire group* **of people** *had perished. Hence, in these cases, there was no one to notify us of how many bodies should be at the make-shift morgue. Nevertheless, our best information was that two bodies were still missing. On the fourth day after the fire, two final bodies, both women, were found and pulled from the wreckage. These were not to be the final casualties, however. Deaths of injured fire victims taken to hospitals would continue to occur for some time."*

Reading that account made me realize that the tragedy of the Beverly Hills fire was not limited to those who lost their lives, nor even to those of us who managed to escape. Grief for many people, some of whom didn't even know about the fire yet, would last for many years to come.

Opposite page: Volunteers load bodies into a refrigerated truck for overnight storage at the temporary morgue at Fort Thomas. (Jack Klumpe Collection, The Cincinnati Post)

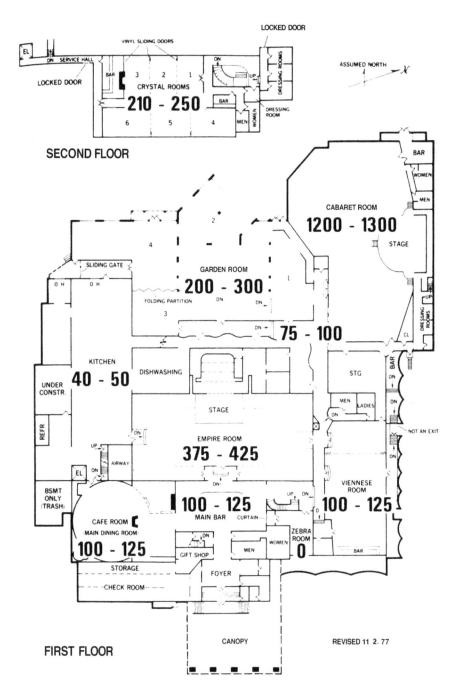

ESTIMATED ACTUAL OCCUPANCY AT TIME OF THE FIRE
(National Fire Protection Agency)

Chapter 16

Following the state fire marshal's press release, the State Police released the Beverly Hills site to the owners, and the investigating team moved their headquarters to Frankfort, Kentucky's capitol city. They'd interviewed more than 600 witnesses, including not only surviving employees and patrons, but also architects, contractors and various state and city officials. Once established in Frankfort, they developed a questionnaire designed to gather information from those who were not available for interview. The questionnaire was sent to 917 persons, and amazingly, a total of 1,117 responses were received, as recipients duplicated it for use of friends or family members who were present but did not receive a form from the State. The state police computer was used to tabulate these responses, adding to the volume of data available to the team.

As the summer sun heated the earth, the heat was also turned on the state teams to answer all the questions raised about the fire. The public wanted to know, officially, where the fire had started, how it had spread so rapidly, what factors and people contributed, and, most importantly, how a disaster of this proportions possibly could have happened.

Through August and the first half of September, the team worked long hours to digest the information they'd collected. On September 19, 1977, the "Investigative Report to the Governor - Beverly Hills Supper Club Fire," detailing the investigator's findings, was released. In the document, the investigators disclosed their methods of search, their conclusions, provided an analysis of applicable laws and made recommendations. Acquiring a copy, I read the voluminous document with great interest.

The report brought the Beverly's safety violations to full light.

"At the time of opening, (February 1971) there was considerable publicity about the failure of the club to comply with state safety codes. We have found records indicating concern for the existence of at least ten major Stan-

dards of Safety violations at, or just prior to, the opening of the club. We have been unable to find any official records indicating that these were corrected. However, in a 1971 news article, the State Fire Marshal and the Southgate Fire Chief were quoted as having been assured that the corrections had been made. The facts indicate that certain of these violations were never corrected."

It also exposed the fact that much of the construction and remodeling on the building had been accomplished without the permission, and in some cases, the knowledge, of the state or city.

"In December 1975, the Zebra Room was paneled, and a suspended ceiling with recessed lighting fixtures was installed. No permit was issued for this work, nor was an electrical inspection made...

"Investigation of the fire scene revealed new construction on the south side of the existing kitchen for which no record of a building permit could be found. Also, evidence was found of an addition to the Chapel for which no record of a building permit could be found."

Following a lengthy discussion of the structure of the building, the investigators addressed the allowable occupancy load for the club and the requirements for exits based on that load. Using the published safety standards giving required square footage per person, they determined the total allowable capacity of the Beverly Hills to be 1,511 persons, putting the capacity of the Cabaret Room at approximately 525. By the same standards, it was determined that the club, in general, and the Cabaret Room, in particular, were woefully lacking in exits. In contrast to the calculated allowable occupancy, the report stated that while the entire building was overcrowded,

"After analysis, the Investigating team has concluded that excess occupant load was a direct contributing factor to the loss of life or injury only in the Cabaret Room.

"Various procedures have been used to estimate actual occupancy of the Cabaret Room at the time of the fire. The final estimate of 1,360 persons is based on a seating diagram developed by a hostess who has worked in the Cabaret Room for several years. Supporting evidence for this estimate is based on interviews and responses to questionnaires which total 848 people who said they were present in the Cabaret Room at the time of the fire. When added to the more than 150 occupants of the Cabaret Room who perished, the Investigating Team has direct knowledge of at least 1,000 people who were present."

The section on over-crowding, as do most sections of the report, concludes with,

> "*This factor... is in the opinion of the Investigating Team a direct contributing factor to the loss of life and injury.*"

Tucked away in the section regarding sufficiency of exits was a paragraph of particular interest to me.

> "*With regard to the Crystal Rooms, the failure to enclose the circular or spiral stairway, which provided primary access to that area, and the resulting **immediate passage** of smoke to the area of the Crystal Rooms after the fire was discovered in the Zebra Room, forced occupants of this area to use secondary exits. One of these exits was a doorway to the roof over other sections of the club, which was locked and which the occupants could not force open. Had they been able to force open the door, they would have been unable to leave the roof without jumping because of the absence of any other means of escape. Ultimately, occupants of the Crystal Rooms had to turn back from the two most obvious means of egress. They were led by an employee through a service stairway which connected with the kitchen area on the first floor of the club... Statements indicate that the two deaths which occurred in the area of the Zebra Room were the result of confusion and possibly panic on the part of the two deceased individuals during their attempts to find an exit.*"

I assume that they meant "Crystal Rooms" rather than "Zebra Room" in that last sentence, and that they were referring to the two women from the dressing rooms.

In conclusion,

> "*...it is the opinion of the Investigating Team that the Beverly Hills facility was constructed with insufficient exit units and that this insufficiency was a direct contributing factor to the loss of life and injury.*"

An analysis of the spread of the fire from the Zebra Room to the Cabaret Room,

> "*...indicates that hot gases and smoke spread rapidly down the corridor, traversing the entire 150 foot length in five minutes or less. This analysis further indicates that the actual spread of fire down the corridor was somewhat slower.*" The team concluded that as

> "*the initial blast of hot gases was probably responsible for the majority of deaths... it is the opinion of the*

The spiral staircase before the fire. (National Fire Protection Agency)

The spiral staircase after the fire. (National Fire Protection Agency)

*Investigating Team that as many as twenty minutes may
have elapsed from the time heavy smoke was originally
discovered in the Zebra Room until the busboy notified
occupants of the Cabaret Room to evacuate."*

Concerning training of employees, the Team concluded,

*"...training in emergency evacuation procedures was
practically nil,"* and that this factor, too *"...was a direct
contributing factor to the loss of life and injury."*

The report reiterated and supported the earlier press release by Fire
Marshal Southworth with respect to the place of origin of the fire and its
cause, stating,

*"Since the release of that report, no evidence had been
discovered contrary to the initial conclusion."* The only
addition is, *"Due to almost complete consumption of combustible materials in the area of origin, it has not been
possible to develop a more specific conclusion as to origin, source or cause..."*

The simple conclusion on these matters is,

*"In summary, the Investigating Team remains of the
opinion that the fire was electrical in nature and that the
fire originated in the concealed spaces of the Zebra Room."*

The investigators concluded that the lack of an alarm system, as well
as the absence of a sprinkler system,

"...contributed directly to the loss of life and injury."

Moving into compliance with applicable law, the report noted that,

*"Violations of the National Electrical Code (NEC)
abounded at Beverly Hills,"* indicating that many would
have been discovered only by an expert, but cited more
than a dozen violations which were, *"obvious to even a
layman."*

With regard to the National Building Code, (NBC) the Team determined violations in the absence of a sprinkler system, the unenclosed spiral stairs, modification of the structure without building permits, and lack
of inspections. Concerning the electrical wiring, the report described the
work as "

"...an electrician's nightmare," and noted that,
*"...since the fire was electrical in origin, compliance in
this regard would have avoided tragedy."*

Lack of employees training, locked doors in the facility and **over-crowd-**
ing were cited as violations of National Fire Codes (NFC).

Analysis of these violations produced scathing indictments of many
individuals. I found the following discussion particularly interesting.

"There were other special circumstances that should

*have alerted officials to the fire hazards extant at Beverly Hills. There was, of course, the history of prior fires at Beverly Hills. But in addition, the following striking chain of events. After the fire at Beverly Hills in June of 1970, Southgate officials were justifiably concerned about fire hazards. This prompted the Mayor of Southgate to write the fire marshal's office on November 23, 1970, stating that the extensive remodeling at Beverly Hills, 'has caused myself, and other members of the Board of Council, to wonder if all the plans and specifications are being submitted to your office for approval, and if so, have they all been finally approved. <u>Our concern is **about fire** hazards.</u>'*

"*The fire marshal's office responded to the mayor's letter on December 2,1970, indicating that that office had not yet received plans for renovation at Beverly Hills and that no approval had been given. On December 7, 1970 Deputy Fire Marshal Boyd, after checking the plans submitted, found ten areas of concern which he put in a memorandum to Fire Marshal Culvert.*··

Under questioning, the deputy stated that his having been directed to review the plans and write a memo on what he found wrong, "*wasn't normal.*··

The report goes on,

"*Apparently, the day after Boyd's memo to Culvert, an inspection was made and an inspection form signed by a State Inspector, Edward Eviston, indicating 'Date Inspected — December 8, 1970.' On the form, the following handwritten statement appears in a space entitled 'deficiencies noted':*

'*I have discussed the ten items listed in your memo of December 7, 1970 with Mr. Schilling and he assures me that all will be complied [with] in the completion of his building. He will let us know prior to completion so that we can make a final inspection.*'

"*...No final inspection was made, although a partial inspection was reported ... The submitted form indicated that there were deficiencies in the portion of the club inspected...*··

The report then notes that the public was informed of these events via the newspapers, and that the resulting furor, which precipitated the 1971 grand jury investigation,

"*was more than sufficient to alert state and local inspectors that there might be some life safety problems at*

Beverly Hills. Even the myopic inspector who somehow could fail to perceive that the spiral stairs were not enclosed with this type of advance notice should have at least directed his attention to that area of the club.

*"...It is clear that prior to the Beverly Hills tragedy of May 28, 1977, the State Fire Marshal's **Office** and Southgate officials were aware that the issue of danger to life and violation of Standards of Safety at Beverly Hills had been raised... If the stairway and main corridor had been enclosed... the spread of the smoke and fire from the Zebra Room down the main corridor to the Cabaret Room would be impossible, and perhaps no loss of life would have occurred."*

In addressing how this comedy of errors and omissions occurred, the Team laconically noted,

"Certainly part of the answer lies in the phenomenon that for most of us, fire is not personalized and is instead perceived as a very unlikely occurrence that happens to others."

I'm reserving my evaluation of the report for the end of this chapter, but I can't resist commenting that's a hell of a capricious attitude for the State to profess!

Later, the report becomes specific about the officials' negligence.

"The picture that emerges is that the State Fire Marshal knew of fire hazard problems at Beverly Hills based on inquiries from Southgate, notifications of deficiencies by deputy fire marshals, a complaint by a Kentucky senator and newspaper publicity... Inspections were not complete or thorough, as admitted by at least three deputy fire marshals. We are compelled to conclude that during the period of time from December 1970 until May 28, 1977, the Fire Marshal's Office did not implement a proper inspection program which would have revealed the code violations."

Dick Schilling was not exempt from the Team's indictments.

"Surely the most culpable acts which created and contributed to maintenance of fire hazards were intentional violations of known safety standards."

The electrician who installed the wiring in the Zebra Room admitted that he was aware that failure to place wiring in metal conduit was a violation of the NEC. He told the investigators that,

*"Mr. Schilling provided all the materials used in the Zebra Room... The wiring was a number twelve, **non-me-***

tallic wire, was not run through conduit as specified in the code... and [Mr. Schilling] advised [me] that he had permission to use these type supplies and wiring in the building. ··

Then, warming to the subject of Mr. Schilling, the report states that,

"*A major factor in keeping Beverly Hills in operation without compliance was the owner and operator's surreptitious behavior and failure to live up to commitments made. First, as to surreptitious activities, frequently construction was going on without a permit and was discovered by accident when almost completed. Deputy Fire Marshal Bramlage came upon the Garden Room addition construction by accident. He confronted Mr. Schilling and told him that he had to submit plans to the State Fire Marshal's Office...*

"*Second, another significant factor was the matter of unkept promises and misrepresentations. We have already noted that [the] electrician reported that Mr. Schilling indicated that he had permission to violate the NEC and use non-metallic cable. It also appears that Mr. Schilling told [Inspector] Eviston that he would correct all deficiencies noted, including the unenclosed stairway.*"

Turning to the Southgate officials, the Team noted that,

"*Both the Southgate building inspector and inspector for the local fire department hold other full time jobs. In a real sense their willingness to take on the difficult and arduous task of inspecting local facilities is a manifestation of dedication to public service. Unfortunately, local inspectors do not generally possess any great expertise in understanding of the electrical, building and fire codes. Therefore, it is specially important that the state fulfill its duty to aid local officials in enforcing fire safety laws and ordinances of the state.*

"*Nonetheless, the primary responsibility for inspecting to assure that safety requirements are complied with is placed on the city.*"

The Team reported that the local Southgate inspectors reported a list of nine violations to Mr. Schilling following an inspection in October 1971, and then,

"*We note that unfortunately this inspection did not reveal a host of violations of the NEC, NBC, and LSC* [Life Safety Code] *that we know were extant.*"

This oversight caused the Investigators to,

*"wonder whether the local **officials** were ever given*
any training in the application and scope of the relevant
codes."

In response to their wondering, they discovered that not only were the local officials not trained, the copy of the National Building Code supplied to the Southgate building inspector was obsolete!

With a modicum of kindness, the Team concluded,

*"It appears that the Southgate **officials** did inspect Beverly*
Hills but obviously were unable to perceive the existing haz-
ardous conditions that violated the Standards of Safety and
created a high risk to life and property."

The report concludes with a discussion of how the victims of the tragedy might recover some compensation, noting that even if they took everything the Schillings' had, a very small portion of the damages would be satisfied. The possibilities they noted were workers compensation, suing state employees (e.g. the fire marshal), insurance companies, utility companies, the City of Southgate and the Commonwealth of Kentucky. The Investigative Team advised the Governor that none of these possibilities, except perhaps suing the utility company, was likely to produce any good result. With respect to the utility company, they noted,

"that the NBC makes it unlawful to supply power to a
facility unless a certificate of inspection has been issued."

Tucked away in the middle of the discussion is the fascinating possibility that the victims might recover some money through criminal prosecution.

After reading the report through several times and attempting to digest its content, I came to a few conclusions of my own. The parts of which I had personal knowledge were accurate, and the sections which involved me were just as I had given the state's investigators the information. That, plus other knowledge that I had through my involvement with the club for so many years was correctly reported, and so I tend to think that, overall, the report is accurate and thorough. I am disappointed in the simple conclusion that the fire was *"electrical in nature."* It has always been my understanding that the actual cause of the fire was that aluminum wiring was spliced to copper wiring in the Zebra Room. I'm told that this is a violation of electrical codes because the two materials are incompatible, and that, over time, such a junction will corrode and overheat. I think that with all the resources at their disposal, the state should be able to come up with a better explanation than "electrical in nature."

As I've already noted, I think they are completely wrong about *"twenty minutes delay"* in notifying the occupants of the Cabaret Room.

The part about "confusion or panic" on the part of the two ladies who died upstairs made me feel a little better, but still does not lessen my regret at not being able to reach the dressing rooms.

They were right on about the locked doors. I understand why the Schillings wanted to keep various exits locked — expensive items did tend to disappear — and perhaps if they'd been open, lives would have been saved. I know for sure that on May 28, 1977, I wished that the door from the upstairs hallway out to the roof had been unlocked! There were other such doors in the facility, generally in locations not accessed by the guests, and the State is probably correct in their conclusions about them. I don't think that's any great issue, however. Exiting the Cabaret Room was the only trouble area, and there were no locked doors there.

As concerns the lack of training, the State is correct, we never received any training of any kind on fire prevention or fighting, or emergency evacuation of the building. Again, perhaps these items would have made a difference. Worth noting in passing, my brothers, sons and I have many man-years of experience in nightclubs and restaurants. No one of us, at any location, have ever received any of this kind of training.

About the Schillings, I liked them and enjoyed working for them. Yes, they certainly bear some responsibility for the tragedy, but I hold them no more answerable than any of the others who might have prevented it. Governors, United States congressmen and senators, fire marshals of surrounding states, state, county and city judges and inspectors, police chiefs, fire chiefs, electricians, builders, contractors and elected officials of every description at every level were patrons in the Beverly Hills every night. Any one of them, at any time, could have noted the violations which were "obvious to even a layman," and taken some action. Nobody did.

This photo was taken months after the fire when clean-up finally begun. (Jack Klumpe Collection, The Cincinnati Post)

Governor's report. (John Snell)

Chapter 17

When Kentucky's Governor Julian Carroll read the Investigative Report, he was outraged by what he considered evidence of favoritism shown by the State to the Beverly Hills. Taking time only to consult with his staff, he suspended the state fire marshal, the chief deputy and the inspector who had performed the inspections of the Beverly Hills. Governor Carroll also scheduled a press conference for Sunday, September 18.

After praising the work of the Investigative Team, Governor Carroll gave vent to his emotions. "I am appalled; I am shocked; I am disturbed at the clear indications that it (the report) shows of disregard of human life... "

In specific language, Governor Carroll addressed the disregard for life on the part of the fire marshal's office and the Schillings. He went particularly hard on Mr. Schilling, citing construction activities in violation of the law because of no building permit and using non-code materials, employing an unregistered architect and then modifying the drawings himself, lack of reasonable care in developing an evacuation plan, and over-crowding. In response to a question about criminal charges, Governor Carroll gave his opinion without hesitation : "Indictments will likely be returned by a grand jury and prosecution will be pursued."

As a result of the report and the press conference, the Beverly Hills returned to the headlines. The newspapers translated Governor Carroll's words, in large print, to, "CARROLL RIPS CLUB OWNERS, INSPECTORS," "BUILT TO BURN," and "EVERYONE KNEW CLUB WAS A FIRETRAP." The Governor's remarks generated almost as much publicity as the fire itself had.

In response, the Schillings scheduled a press conference of their own a few days later. If Mr. Schilling feared criminal charges against him, an attorney in his employ evidently thought Governor Carroll had done them a favor. "We feel that irreparable damage had been done in that a fair trial is now impossible," said the lawyer, then adding, "His (Carroll) remarks were not only unwarranted, but were also defamatory, scurrilous, irresponsible and unprofessional." The attorney finished by stating that Governor Carroll, who was a lawyer himself, had appointed himself "special prosecutor for Campbell County, judge and jury."

This kind of furor was to rage through the remainder of 1977. The newspapers seemed to think that Governor Carroll had prejudiced the case to the extent that no criminal action was possible, but I still expected something at any time. Near the end of February 1978, some action occurred — a special grand jury was impaneled to investigate the fire. As I understood it from what I read, their objective was to determine if crimes had been committed in conjunction with the fire, and to return indictments if they so found. All the grand jury members were residents of Campbell County and would , no doubt, have been exposed to all the publicity, so I wondered about the so-called prejudice.

After about a month, spent, I suppose, wading through all the written evidence and testimony already collected, the grand jury called for testimony from the Kentucky State Police Commissioner, who had headed the Governor's Investigative Team. He'd been interviewed many times since the fire, and so his views were fairly well known. He'd been quoted as saying that the local officials had done as well as possible given the circumstances under which they worked, but those at the state level were a different story. The state officials were better trained and in a more powerful position to prevent the disaster. He'd also indicated that he thought that Mr. Schilling had not acted with ill intent, but had operated recklessly and disregarded safety requirements for the sake of profit. One supposes this is what he conveyed to the grand jury.

Through a spring that saw the first anniversary of the fire and a long, hot summer, the grand jury labored in secret, hearing about 100 witnesses and analyzing thousands of pages of evidence. On August 2, 1978, they entered a court room to deliver their 28 page conclusions to the judge and the public saying that they were,

> "...able to hear testimony from many witnesses that had never been contacted by the State Police and had access to materials and evidence that was found after the initial investigation was concluded... The jury did not accept at face value any reports submitted to it, but reached its conclusions independently after considering all of the evidence."

The courtroom was packed with reporters who had come to get the names of those against whom indictment would be returned. They were to be surprised. The jury found that the Cabaret Room had contained only 900 to 1,000 people on the night of the fire — 360 to 460 less than the 1,360 the State had reported — and hence was not overcrowded.

The biggest surprise concerned the reasons the Jury found for the loss of life.

> "*It seems there was a sudden surge of the noxious smoke, hot gases and fire that burst into the Cabaret Room from the main corridor... The result of this occurrence was to create panic among those who had not yet exited the room from the exits which were still available. Testimony also indicated that some patrons of the Cabaret Room, even though notified to evacuate, failed to react and remained seated until the conditions of the room itself indicated the need to exit. By this time in some instances it was too late.*"

Making little or no mention of the State's findings, the grand jury blamed the patrons for their own deaths! In my opinion, while the State's attitude was capricious; this attitude on the part of the Grand Jury was absurd.

The reporters threw away their prepared list of candidates for indictment when the report concluded,

> "*Although the Grand Jury feels that there were instances shown where there was negligence involved, it was of the opinion that this negligence was not criminal in nature. The Grand Jury did not find any evidence that would tend to raise the possibility of indictment for criminal negligence **and/or** conspiratorial conduct indicating such negligence.*"

Once again, controversy raged in the press. "DON'T THINK JUSTICE WAS DONE," and "JURY REPORT SHOCKS FIRE SURVIVORS," screamed the headlines. The articles rehashed the state's report and contrasted it with the grand jury's findings, and indicated that the public was overwhelmingly in disagreement with the grand jury.

While the general citizenry may have been upset over the grand jury's findings, Kentucky's first citizen, Julian Carroll, blew a fuse. Evidently, the Governor had planned that criminal indictments, hopefully leading to convictions, in combination with the suspensions he'd already enacted, would help cleanse the State's record. Within hours of learning of the grand jury's decision, he was seeking advice from the Attorney General. Governor Carroll was told, as he surely already knew, that to tamper with secret grand jury proceedings would be not merely illegal, but unconstitutional. As for the options that he did have, he could submit the State's evidence to another grand jury, or appoint a special investigator to look into the case.

The phone wires in Frankfort must have been hot as the Governor, the Attorney General, the State Police Commissioner and the Fire Marshal consulted with each other and their staffs. In a few days, the **recommenda-**

This photo was taken near the Cabaret Room entrance looking down the long hallway towards the Zebra Room to the front of the club. This is the hall where the fire came roaring down in towards the camera. (Jack Klumpe Collection/The Cincinnati Post)

tions came in. The state officials raised questions about the thoroughness of the Campbell County Grand Jury's investigation, noting that they had heard testimony from only some 100 witnesses while the state investigating team had interviewed more than 600. They also strongly questioned the Jury's conclusion that the facility was not overcrowded, and, in the end, suggested that the Governor take action.

Governor Carroll promptly acted on that recommendation. In an August 9, 1978 letter to the Attorney General, he said,

> *"...I hereby request that your **office** review the actions of the Campbell County Grand Jury in regard to **its** findings concerning the Beverly Hills fire to determine whether the Grand Jury thoroughly investigated all relevant matters and reached a proper determination as to its legal conclusions. I base this request upon apparent inconsistencies between the findings of the Grand Jury and those made by the special investigative team for this Commonwealth...*
>
> *"I feel it is my duty to make this request to ensure a fair, just, and accurate adjudication of the Beverly Hills tragedy, and to maintain the public trust in governmental institutions. The conflicting conclusions concerning the fire make it absolutely essential, in my opinion, that you undertake a review of all evidence and determine **if further** action should be taken."*

The Attorney General responding by pointing out that the Commonwealth of Kentucky was named in several of the pending civil actions filed on behalf of the victims, and that, in his opinion, for his office to address any criminal proceedings would, at least, give the appearance of a conflict of interest.

Down to his last option, Governor Carroll appointed an independent investigator. Mindful of the Attorney General's advice, he wanted someone not connected with state government. He chose a law professor from Northern Kentucky University. He challenged the professor to examine not only the State's evidence about the fire, but also anything the Campbell County Grand Jury had unearthed. The Governor made it clear that he'd accept the investigator's recommendations.

Having access to all the State's evidence, and the transcribed testimony presented to the Campbell County Grand Jury, the professor launched the third investigation into the circumstances surrounding the fire at the Beverly Hills. All fall and into the winter he poured over the mountain of written material, and personally interviewed many witnesses attempting to examine every pertinent fact. In the end, he covered the same ground as the other investigations and had to face the

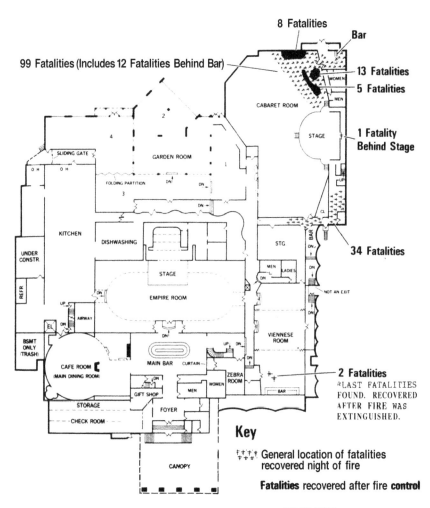

8 Fatalities

Bar

99 Fatalities (Includes 12 Fatalities Behind Bar)

13 Fatalities

5 Fatalities

1 Fatality
Behind Stage

34 Fatalities

2 Fatalities

*LAST FATALITIES
FOUND. RECOVERED
AFTER FIRE WAS
EXTINGUISHED.

Key

✝✝✝✝ General location of fatalities
recovered night of fire

Fatalities recovered after fire **control**

REVISED 11/7/77

FATALITIES

same questions. Finally, in February 1979, he reached his conclusions and reported to the Governor.

The first of his conclusions fell halfway between the State's conclusions and the Grand Jury's decisions. He found that there were not as many people in the Cabaret Room as the State had said, but, accepting the State's estimate of the room's allowable capacity, he found that the room *was* overcrowded, in contrast to the Grand Jury's finding. The exits from the Cabaret Room, he found, were insufficient, both in number and width, and the time between discovery of the fire and notification to the occupants of the Cabaret Room was not the twenty minutes the State had suggested, but more in the range of eight to ten minutes.

As to blaming the patrons for their own deaths, he reported,

> *"Whether or not the failure of some to heed the **warn-**
> **ing** about the fire might have contributed to the loss of life
> in the fire is impossible to determine. Until heavy smoke
> entered the Cabaret Room... evacuation proceeded
> smoothly and without panic. Had everyone proceeded
> immediately after the fire announcement to move simulta-
> neously toward the exits, it is possible that the evacuation
> would have been even less successful than it was."*

He's right. Who is to say that if everyone in the room had immediately heeded Walter Bailey's warning and stampeded for the exits that the loss of life might not have been worse?

This report went a little easier on the various officials. While clearly indicating that the state and county inspectors failed miserably in their responsibilities, the professor also gave some consideration to the conditions under which they served. Noting that the Southgate positions were unfunded (i.e. the men served without monetary compensation,) and that the state's offices were woefully understaffed, he determined that given the lack of training and poor coordination among them was, while regrettable and ultimately tragic, understandable.

> *"The critical issue... is not whether the conduct devi-
> ated grossly from the manner in which a reasonable per-
> son might have acted under ideal circumstances. Instead,
> it is whether their conduct deviated grossly from the man-
> ner in which a reasonable person might have acted under
> the same circumstances."*

In summary of the culpability of the officials, he found that while they were clearly guilty of various malfeasances, there was no ill intent on anyone's part, and no conspiracy among them. Hence, there was no criminal liability sufficient to seek indictments for homicide.

Dick Schilling's behavior, he found, was another matter. While determining that Mr. Schilling had not acted with malice, the report noted that

Mr. Schilling had used an unlicensed architect to produce plans for remodeling the structure, modified those plans himself, and implemented them without permission from the state or county in the form of a building permit, and opened the areas so constructed without a certificate of occupancy. All of these activities were in violation of the law. Therefore, the professor thought, Mr. Schilling was more responsible than any of the others, and he suggested that indictment and conviction of Mr. Richard Schilling were within the realm of possibility.

So, after plowing through the evidence and reaching his conclusions, the investigator now had to make recommendations to the Governor as to whether the Commonwealth of Kentucky should take further action. One possibility was to recommend that a second grand jury be impaneled. His thoughts on that were that such a jury would be composed by the same kinds of citizens from the same area as the first, and that they would examine basically the same evidence. Hence, the professor did not see much point in that option. Another option was for the State to pursue criminal prosecution. His recommendation, reached with some agony, I am sure:

*1. The evidence... that could be produced against individuals other than the principal owner of the Club is clearly **insufficient** to **warrant further** proceedings.*

2. The evidence that could be produced against the principal owner is stronger than that which could be produced against any other individual. In absolute as opposed to relative terms, however, it falls short of making out a good case of criminal liability against him.

3. The probability of a grand jury returning indictments against anyone connected with the fire on the basis of presently available evidence is very small... The probability of... convicting someone of the basis of such an indictment (should one be returned) is even smaller. I would say that the latter possibility is remote at best.

4. The sum of these three factors... leads me to my most certain belief in this case. That belief is that nothing is to be gained from additional efforts to pursue criminal prosecution in connection with the fire.

5. Thus, it is my recommendation that you not proceed to have a second grand jury impaneled to consider the case.

Governor Carroll kept his word and accepted the recommendation. No prosecution would ever take place, and the Commonwealth's criminal involvement with the fire at the Beverly Hills was over.

View looking up the driveway. Chapel is visible to the far right. Cabaret Room was behind the telephone pole. Partial demolition had begun by the time this photo was taken. (Jack Klumpe Collection, The Cincinnati Post)

Chapter 18

A ll may have simmered down on the criminal side, but the civil litigation was boiling. The end of the State's criminal involvement came
nearly two years after the fire. Long before then, some 90 civil actions
seeking aggregate damages of approximately $3,000,000,000 were pend-
ing. While the City Of Southgate and the Commonwealth of Kentucky
figured prominently in most of those suits, The **4-R** Corporation, consist-
ing of Dick Schilling and his three sons was the primary defendant.

Cincinnati attorney Stanley Chesley was heavily involved in these actions, and he was concerned about the ability of the 4-R Corporation to
meet whatever judgments might be lodged against it. And rightly so. The
Schillings had total assets of less than a tenth of the total sought, counting
the 1.3 million in insurance and all personal assets, including homes, cars,
and the land on which the Beverly Hills sat.

The cases fell under the jurisdiction of the Eastern District of Kentucky and Campbell Circuit Court Judge John **Diskin**. Federal Judge Carl
Rubin of Ohio's Southern district, realizing that Kentucky's court was already overloaded while his own docket was current, volunteered to take
the cases, and it was so agreed. On behalf of the various victims, one of
their first actions was to certify the Beverly Hills case as a class action
suit, thereby merging all the suits into one. Judge **Rubin** explained that this
action would ensure that not all available award money would go to the
first cases heard.

The consolidation also placed Chesley in overall charge of the suit.
Many attorneys shied away from the action, feeling that there was simply
not enough money to go around to all the victims and still make it worth
their while. **Chesley's** associate, Thomas Spraul, summed up the position
of some: "Some of the attorneys involved at the outset became discouraged over the limited assets available for damages, only about three million dollars. **A** lot of lawyers weren't willing to gamble their time plus

expenses. We had to go on the hook to personally guarantee payment to the experts."

Another associate, Louis Gilligan, had previously been primarily involved in corporate law. When victims contacted his office following the fire, he had his doubts about representing them. "Quite frankly, we weren't sure whether we wanted to get involved because it was obviously going to be very complex and time consuming."

Chesley, on the other hand, sought ways to up the ante, diligently seeking out other defendants who might have been a contributing factor to the disaster. Among these possibilities was the Union Light, Heat and Power Company (ULHPC), supplier of electrical power to the Club. As the State's report had noted, supplying power to an uninspected facility was a violation of the National Electrical Code. Attorney Chesley contended that the ULHPC had failed to inspect the Beverly Hills' electrical system following several of the remodelings.

On more or less the same basis, Chesley implicated Iso-Fair, an association of some 1000 insurance firms, contending that Iso-Fair had issued policies to and collected premiums from the 4-R Corporation without inspecting the premises.

Additionally, over 40 manufacturers of aluminum electrical wiring were involved via the allegation that such wiring was capable of overheating to the extent of ignition of any nearby combustible material. Chesley also contended that polyvinyl chloride (PVC) emits toxic hydrogen chloride gas when it bums. Therefore, manufacturers of products containing PVC were added to the growing list of defendants.

As the action moved along, the number of **plaintiffs/victims** rose to 286 and the count of defendants swelled to over 1000. Chesley accomplished his purpose, the money involved rose in proportion to the number of defendants, ultimately amounting to approximately $30,000,000.

Given the lengthy list of defendants, Judge **Rubin** and Judge **Diskin** assigned them into categories: the 4-R Corporation, the aluminum wiring industry, manufacturers of PVC products, manufacturers of various other products, the Union Light, Heat and Power Company, **Iso-Fair** and governmental agencies. The latter category encompassed the City of Southgate, the Commonwealth of Kentucky and the relevant employees. Once these assignations were accomplished, preparations were made to go to trial.

As the elements fell into place, Chesley learned that the Commonwealth of Kentucky planned to bulldoze the remains of the Beverly Hills over the hillside. Upon appeal for a restraining order on that issue, he was informed by a U. S. district judge that the court was powerless until a law suit concerning the fire was filed. Robert Schuman had already approached Chesley about representing him concerning the death of Mr. **Schuman's** wife. Chesley had been reluctant to file so soon after the fire, but, given the judge's ruling, he felt that it was time for action. The day after he filed a suit on behalf of Mr. Schuman, he received the court's permission to search through the charred remains of the Beverly Hills.

Mr. Chesley was subjected to some criticism for filing litigation while the community was still in mourning over the event, but he'd preserved the evidence. After the cases were settled, he commented, "As we look back now, a great deal of history would have been changed if we had not elected to do what we did and go in there with qualified experts. The public just didn't understand what we were dealing **with**."

Just before the legal action began, an associate of Mr. Chesley contacted me to inquire if I'd be interested in accompanying them to the site. I declined the offer on the assumption that they were going to prosecute the Schillings. I did not care to be a party in any such proceedings.

Before the action involving the 4-R corporation came to trial, however, the Schillings settled out of court for approximately $3,000,000. Thus ended their involvement with Beverly Hills.

Things went so far as jury selection for the trial against the ULHPC, but they also settled before the trial, adding $5,700,000 to the pot.

Iso-Fair went to court. After a lengthy trial, in October 1979, the court awarded a judgment of approximately $3,000,000 to the plaintiffs.

The case against the aluminum wiring industry also went to court in December 1979, and was to last fourteen months. Before the verdict was reached, several of the companies involved settled, the settlements amounting to about $4,5000,000. At the end of the lengthy proceedings, the jury decided in favor of the defendants.

In another long trial, a jury ruled against the PVC industry. Before a monetary award was announced, however, the companies settled for some $1,800,000.

As for the other product manufacturers, the suit was settled for $4,000,000. In a separate action, one of the companies involved in this category, the Cincinnati based firm which had installed the Cabaret Room air conditioning system, continued the fight and received a judgment in their favor.

Just as the state investigative team had predicted in their report to Governor Carroll, the courts evoked sovereign immunity on behalf of the City of Southgate and the Commonwealth of Kentucky. The same constitutional provision, barring legal action against governmental agencies without their own permission, covered the various employees. Hence, actions in this category never came to anything. Stan Chesley was particularly interested in this action and pursued it all the way through the legal system, but, to no avail.

As the money awarded through the judgments and settlements came in, it was invested in an escrow fund until disbursement could be made. The total amount to be distributed included the interest paid on the deposits as the proceedings were in progress.

When, at long last, all the suits ended, the courts then had to face the issue of how to allocate this money. In addition to the 268 plaintiffs, some 100 attorneys had been involved, and they had to be compensated for their services. These lawyers consisted of the team headed by Chesley and the many counsel retained by the individual victims or families, in the case of the deceased. Without great caution, legal fees would consume a major portion of the money. An equitable distribution of the available funds — a daunting task — now became Judge **Rubin's** main priority.

To assist with this problem, Judge **Rubin** appointed Cincinnati attorney Lawrence Kane, Jr. to serve as trustee of the invested funds. Kane's chore was to consume the next 18 months of his life. Under the court's direction, a forty page questionnaire designed to determine the respondent's economic profile was developed. A questionnaire was mailed to each claimant to the fund money. A computer was used to help analyze the responses, resulting in a lifetime economic dollar value for each of the dead or injured.

All the returns were in by July 1981. Kane and his staff then met to hammer out a plan for distribution of the money. In three day marathon meetings, their first determination was that all victims' medical expenses should be paid in full. As it happens, this amount was the smallest of the three economic areas they had to address. Next on the dollar scale was payments to victims or families for pain and suffering, which was over four times the medical figure. The largest piece of the pie was allocated to compensate victims for economic loss.

On September 16, 1981, Kane disclosed his plan to all the attorneys involved. It is difficult to imagine more than 80 lawyers agreeing to anything, but the payment plan was approved with only a few modifications suggested by the attorneys.

Kane, under Judge **Rubin's** direction was resolute in his conviction that legal fees should not consume too much of the funds. In such civil actions, the normal attorney's fee is thirty per cent of the amount awarded, but the gentlemen felt that the attorneys should not be the only ones to benefit from the money collected. One suspects that there was probably some haggling over the matter, but in the end, the attorneys were awarded $5 million of the $30 million total. The major portion of that money went to four attorneys: Stanley Chesley, Thomas Spraul, Louis Gilligan and William **Hillman.**

I had testified in Judge **Diskin's** court in the product manufacturers trial, spending an entire day on the witness stand answering a multitude of questions, mostly concerning the chairs in the Zebra Room and the conditions in there following the fire. As it happens, these four gentlemen were

Fred Cianciola (Mr. C) and me standing behind what had been the Frontenac Room, above the garage. Above that had been the Crystal Rooms. Note the two doors in top left of photo. The door on the left is the elevator with the door still firmly in place. The door on the right is the door where I escaped from down into the kitchen. This photo clearly shows there was nothing remaining from the rear area of the upstairs Crystal Rooms. (W. Dammert)

involved in that trial. After the Schilling's were out of the picture, the attorneys had reiterated their request for my help. On that basis, I had worked with them in preparation, so I knew a little about their labor. I firmly believe that these men earned every nickel of the money they received. Not only did they employ large staffs and work long and hard on the legal issues involved, but they personally delved into the evidence, too. I happen to know that Stanley Chesley spent several weeks of his time meticulously picking through the Club's wreckage. At any rate, if not for these gentlemen's efforts, the fund would not have been nearly as large as it was. Even after the legal fees were deducted, the victims received much more than they would have had these men not involved the various companies as defendants.

Thomas Spraul found a great deal of satisfaction in his work with the Beverly Hills cases. "The single most interesting thing was the concept of being able to obtain some type of satisfaction for people when the circumstances had looked rather bleak."

Louis Gilligan addressed the amount of work and hardship involved, mentioning the long hours they put in, and the fact that he had to turn his corporate work over to his associates. "The case had a lot of effect on a lot of people's lives. Some of the defense guys even got divorced." But still, he felt a great sense of accomplishment. "It was like climbing Mount Everest. I'm not sure I'd do it again, but I'm glad I was a part of it. It was an opportunity to take part in the biggest and one of the most complex cases in legal history."

As for Stanley Chesley, he became the American expert on such cases. Since that time, he's represented victims of the Las Vegas MGM Grand fire, and had a hand in the recent multi-million dollar settlements over silicone breast implants. After the Beverly Hills fire dominated five years of his life, Chesley remarked that he must have been partially insane to get involved, but clearly remembers why. "All you had to do was visit the site and meet the clients. You could recognize the hurt, the anger, the distrust that these people had. I got swept up by it, no question."

Judge Carl **Rubin,** who waged a personal battle with cancer while the attorneys battled before him, feels that the Beverly Hills litigation proved that our legal system, antiquated as it is, still works. "Everyone got their day in court. I think the system functioned, which, in the final analysis, is the test for success. If the court system can handle a case of that complexity, then we have the right to say we can function late into the twentieth century." Concerning the overall experience, Judge **Rubin** said, "I had aggravation. I had anxiety. I had all sorts of things, but, I'd do it again."

Right: Walter Bailey going over some of the many letters he received after the fire. (W. Bailey)

Chapter 19

At the time of this writing, the fire at the Beverly Hills occurred almost exactly 19 years ago. My collection of newspaper clippings is yellowing, the legal action is merely judicial history, the dead are long buried and the survivors, including me, healed our wounds as best we could and life went on. Memories, however, remain fresh.

I remember the smiling faces of my friends who died in the fire. When the grim reaper's final toll was counted, nine of my friends were gone. Their faces, their lives, their children and their aspirations, frozen in my mind as they were in 1977, sometimes still haunt me.

Other memories are less haunting. I remember Walter Bailey, the 18 year-old busboy, well as he worked on my team many times. He was a quiet young man who performed his assigned tasks well. When I consider all the employees who were on hand that night, Walter would come in low on the list of potential heroes, but hero he was, and I continue to feel pride for the service he performed so well on that tragic night.

When I reflect on all the lives tragically snuffed out on that long ago May evening, part of me is glad I did not personally know them, but yet, another part of me wished I knew something about their lives. In the intervening years, the latter emotion has occasionally won out. I'd like to share some of what I've learned about those who perished in the fire.

Norbert and Helen Castelli, came to the Beverly Hills from nearby Grant County, Kentucky. Helen's eighty-four year old mother, Otillia Vollman, joined them as did her sister, Ruth, and her husband Walter **Backus,** from Cincinnati. None of them were to survive the evening. The five **Backus** children, who had remained at home, lost their entire family on that night.

Josephine Carson, of Covington, attended the Club that evening with a party of eight to celebrate her retirement from St. Elizabeth Hospital, where she was a dietitian. Additionally, her husband, Howard, was on the verge of retiring from the Heekin Can Company. Included in the party were the Carsons' friends, Noralee and Elmer Ellison, Amelia and William Authur, Clarence Gripshover and Dorothy Nie. With the exception of Dorothy Nie, who suffered bums on her hands, this entire group, too, was to die. Initially, Mrs. Authur was listed as missing, but the reason turned out to be that the Carson children had difficulty in identifying her body at the morgue.

Mr. Gripshover's son, Eddie, was a 17-year-old dishwasher working in the kitchen that night. Knowing that his father was in the showroom, Eddie rushed in that direction as soon as he heard about the fire. Despite his desperate efforts, he was not able to get there to help his father. Although Mr. Gripshover survived the night of the fire, he was critically injured and died, after suffering great agony, several weeks later.

Eighteen year-old Tammy Kincer and her 19 year-old fiance, James Crane, were found by rescuers, the bodies lying side by side. They had met on a blind date in March 1977, and had been engaged for three weeks. Now, they were deprived of the bright future they had expected. Tammy, who was an honor student at Lebanon (Ohio) High School, was to have graduated May 29. She had landed an exciting summer job at King's Island Amusement Park, north of Cincinnati. James, from Waynesville, Ohio, had just begun a new job as a design engineer for a container company in Centerville, Ohio.

Mary Louise and Raymond Bohrer, of Bridgetown, Ohio, were treating their family to a belated 31 year anniversary party at Beverly Hills. Participating in the celebration was their son, Thomas, and his wife, Barbara Ann, the Bohrer's daughter, Mary Susan, and her husband Edwin Vogel. Completing the group were the younger Bohrer girls, Judith and Jane. Jane was just past her sixteenth birthday. Judith had been on assignment with the Peace Corps, and part of the reason for the delay in the anniversary part was to await her return to this country. Judith Bohrer is the young woman mentioned in the coroner's gruesome tale of mistaken identity. Edwin Vogel was the sole survivor of this group, escaping with an injured ankle and suffering from smoke inhalation, to rear his and Mary Susan's five children. The deaths of Barbara and Thomas Bohrer left a three month-old infant an orphan.

Fredica Fryman had traveled to the Beverly from Cynthiana, Kentucky for her fortieth birthday party in the Garden Room. She, along with her husband, Williard, their children, 17 year-old Tracey, and fourteen year-old Scott, were treating friends Herb and Martha Morford and their daughters, Mindy and Joetta, Joetta's boyfriend, James Estill, and Mrs. Thaxtor (Sally) Sims to dinner and John Davidson's show. Service was a little slow in the crowded Garden Room, so they arrived late, about 9:00, in the showroom. They had no more than gotten settled when Walter Bailey made his announcement. Directed back out into the hall through the door which they'd just entered, Mr. Morford asked Mrs. Sims about the remainder of the group. "They're right behind the children," she replied.

"Shut up and get moving!" an anxious voice behind them shouted, so they hurried out into the garden. Once outside, they turned to see dense smoke pouring from the door from which they had just exited. Fredica, Willard, Tracey and Scott **Fryman** and sixteen year-old Mindy Morford did not emerge from the building.

Thirty-seven relatives, friends and fellow teachers threw a surprise retirement party for Ona Mae **Mayfield** in recognition of her 43-year career at Wayne Elementary School in Hamilton Ohio's **Edgewood** School system. Mrs. **Mayfield** had been quite happily surprised by the party and especially delighted that her son was able to attend. **Clarkie Mayfield** was a former football player at the University of Kentucky, and in 1977 was the head football coach at Jacksonville State University in Alabama.

After dinner, the **Mayfield** party proceeded into the Cabaret Room eagerly anticipating John Davidson's show. Originally, they were to have seats in the lower section, near the stage, but a mix-up placed them in the rear of the room, in an extremely crowded area. Somewhat disgruntled, the group had some discussion about making a scene, but in view of the jovial occasion, they decided to just make the best of the situation. Of the large party, only twenty-four were to survive the evening. Witnesses stated that football hero **Clarkie Mayfield** was near the exit door when the smoke blasted into the room. Near the final moment, he literally heaved his wife and young son through the exit to safety. **Clarkie** himself never exited the building. His body was found in the rest room area, leading to speculation that, in the smoke and confusion, he made a wrong turn and ended up trapped in that area.

The guest of honor, Ona Mae Mayfield, survived the event. Six of her fellow teachers did not. Tiny Wayne Elementary School lost one-third of its faculty that evening.

For several months, the Thornhill family had been attempting to arrange eight people's schedules to allow them all an evening together at the Beverly Hills. At last, they managed to settle on May 28. When Barbara Thornhill called to confirm the reservations, she was informed that their names did not appear on the sheet. After the trouble they'd had arranging a time, she would not be put off. After insisting that they be scheduled, she managed to get her group booked for the show. The Thornhill party was seated in what was to proved to be one of the worst possible areas, where even Larry Thornhill's heroic actions could not save his wife, Carolyn, and their unborn child.

One member of the Thornhill family, Donna, experienced a sudden outbreak of poison ivy on her face and neck on the afternoon of May 28, so she and her husband were unable to attend the party that evening.

In addition to Larry, Barbara Thornhill and Ron Lape managed to escape the holocaust. Mr. Lape permanently lost his power of speech to a badly

Taken at the Beverly Hills Memorial Fund meeting in Fall of 1977. L to R: Wayne Dammert, Kay Dee (club's publicity director) and Bill Lane (club's orchestra leader). (W. Dammert)

burned larynx. When Barbara turned in the doorway to assist her husband, Robert, she swallowed a mass of smoke and hot gases. In the hospital, unable to speak or breathe without assistance, she suffered unspeakable agony. After enduring four major, unsuccessful operations, Barbara succumbed to her injuries. Nine months after the fire, Barbara Thornhill became the one-hundred-sixty-fifth and final victim of the Beverly Hills disaster.

The Roadrunners Club of Ashland, Kentucky, a community about 150 miles up the river from Cincinnati, loaded chartered busses with 84 members on May 28, 1977. The Roadrunners regularly traveled as a group to various locations to enjoy entertainment and companionship. John Davidson's Saturday night show was to be one of their biggest outings of the year.

Club President William Mordica, and his wife, Janas, arrived in Northern Kentucky on Friday to spend the evening with her father who lived near the Beverly Hills, in Fort Thomas. The remainder of the club left Ashland at 3:00 PM on Saturday afternoon for their scheduled dinner at 6:00 PM.

The Mordicas arrived at the Club early and spent a few minutes conversing with Rick Schilling. After dinner, the entire group was ushered to their tables in a prime location of the Cabaret Room, right down front near the stage.

When Walter Bailey grabbed the microphone from one of the comedians and announced that there was a fire in the building, some of the Roadrunners took it as a joke. Mordica, however, felt that one never jokes about such things. He urged his wife and the other club members into the hall via the exit the busboy had indicated. When he arrived in the garden area and counted heads, some of the club members were missing.

William Mordica covered his face with a handkerchief, reentered the building and fought the smoke and crowds half-way back to the showroom. He managed to locate none of the missing party before the smoke, fumes and intense heat forced him to flee for his life.

Returning to the garden, he asked Janas to watch for the missing while he hurried to another exit to try again to locate the stragglers. He was one of the heroes who braved the torturous conditions inside the building assisting firemen pulling bodies from the tangle at the showroom doors. Mordica reports great sadness when he recognized Roadrunner Buzz Fowler as one of the dead he pulled from the inferno. Dazed and grief-stricken, the surviving members worked their way down the hill and began the grisly chore of identifying the missing. That accomplished, they had to face calling **Ashland** to break the tragic news to friends and family.

Although he survived the evening, William Mordica fell ill to the effects of inhaled smoke the next day and spent several days recovering in St. Luke's Hospital before he was able to return home. The toll of dead among the Roadrunners was 18 members lost.

There are, of course, many other stories. Mary **A.** and Richard **Gorman** of Lexington, Mrs. Alberta **Pieper** of Louisville, Larry Phelps of **Lakeside** Park, Kentucky, Fred Cooksey and Marian **Adkins** of **Ashland,** Kentucky, 72 year-old Sara **McClain** of Miamisburg, Ohio, 71 year-old Minnie Knight of Germantown, Ohio, and 70 year-old Dottie **Issacs** of Dayton, Ohio all perished in the fire. And the list goes on. These few stories suffice, however, to define the true proportions of disaster the fire at the Beverly Hills visited upon so many people.

Some things changed as a result of the Beverly Hills fire. The Commonwealth of Kentucky undertook some reform of state agencies, creating a new department to regulate the construction and use of public buildings. The Department of Housing, Building and Construction was assigned reduced responsibility, more money, and a staff of lawyers to help them enforce their decisions. A registered architect headed the new department, beginning the job charged with protecting the public and assured that he was immune from any political influence on his efforts to carry out the charge.

The State also allocated additional funds to fire protection and inspection agencies, and adopted a new building code. Purchasing a new computer system for the purpose, Kentucky implemented a tracking system to ensure regular, methodical inspection of public buildings, including schools, health care facilities and, of course, nightclubs.

These things changed, and certain is that owners and operators of the establishments paid heed to the State's inspectors, for a time, anyway. Given that, could such a disaster strike again? Despite the State's efforts, the major contributing factor in the disaster — the fallibility of human nature — did not, and will not, change.

Part Five

OTHER VOICES

Chapter 20

S o there now, that's the Wayne Dammert story. Mine, however, was just one of many lives touched by the drama played out on top of that Southgate hill. Here are the stories of some other survivors. As you read these, you may note that they do not agree in all details concerning the events of May 28, 1977. No editorial attempt has been made to make the accounts consistent with the facts as reported elsewhere or with one another; indeed, these incredible accounts are recorded here just as reported by those who experienced them. The inconsistency of multiple human observations of the same events is part of what made the investigators task so difficult. Here, we gain some insight into the problems they faced in compiling the facts.

Pete **Sabino**
Cincinnati Fireman

I was at the Beverly Hills as a patron on May 28, 1977. My wife, Delores, and I were celebrating the engagement of our son. We planned on enjoying dinner and then attending the late floor show.

We arrived at the Club at approximately 8:45 PM. After ordering drinks at the bar, we were ushered down a wide hallway, lined with mirrors, turned left and entered another corridor to the dining area. I made a **joking** remark to my son, also named Pete, about the trouble we'd have deciding which way to turn for an escape route if there was a fire.

Suddenly, a waitress and a busboy rushed by us, bumping Delores. Within a minute, a woman at a podium nearby announced the existence of a "small problem" and directed us through a short hall which led into the garden at the rear of the building. We exited immediately. Glancing in, I observed two comedians performing on stage as we were **walking** by the Cabaret Room.

As soon as we were in the garden, I heard the shout "Fire!" After I identified myself as a firefighter, a busboy accompanied me back into the building via the door where I'd just exited. Smoke had already darkened the corridor. From the crackling noises, I knew that a major combustion was in progress. Bending low in the empty hall, I raised my hand into blistering heat. In the darkness, I held the busboy by his belt as we moved on down the hall until the heat at head level reached a too uncomfortable temperature. We turned back. In the course of our retreat, we again passed the showroom doors. I heard screaming from within, and I knew that a major fire was happening. I also knew that without a mask, there was nothing I could do except get myself and the busboy out of there.

Outside in the garden once again, I checked on the safety of my family then returned to assist people who were stumbling out the door. They poured out, coughing and choking, gasping that many more were trapped inside. I peered inside to discover that while the smoke was thick and oily at eye level, the air up to about three feet from the floor was relatively clear. No more people were coming out, so I crawled through the opening to the double doors that opened into the showroom. My blood turned to ice water at the sight that met my eyes. The double wide **entryway** was stacked all the way to the top of the door frame with bodies. I was looking at a wall composed of human heads!

At the level of the pile where I was on my hands and knees, I saw a conscious man, his hand extended toward me. I grabbed it and attempted to pull him from the tangle. With so much weight piled on him, I could not extract him from the tangle of bodies. I was amazed at how calm he remained, even as I released my grip. Apparently, he was resigned to his fate. I reached up into the inky blackness to the top of the stack. I managed to pull two people free and drug them down the hall to the outside.

Although I'd inhaled some smoke, I was able to get some fresh air near the floor, too. So, I recruited some men to help and ventured back inside again. We made several trips pulling whoever we could get a grip on from the pile and dragging them outside. On my final trip, I grabbed a woman who appeared to be tightly wedged and pulled as hard as my waning strength would allow. She screamed, and I immediately regretted the pain I had caused her. By now, the smoke was all the way to the floor and my lungs had reached their limit. I released the lady and turned to exit, knowing that I would not be able to come back to get her.

Outside in the fresh air, I collapsed in exhaustion. Amazingly, my watch told me that a mere ten minutes had passed since my family and I first exited the building! There were no firefighters evident at this time, but patrons and employees were venturing in to drag people out.

I got up and walked around the kitchen side of the building, attempting to regain some strength and breath. When I reached the front of the building, two pumper engines were sitting under the canopy. I introduced myself to the captain and explained that a pumper was desperately needed around back. "Take one," he immediately said. "Do whatever you can back there." I jumped on the running board and ordered the startled driver to take us around the service drive to the rear. We managed to lay down a line and did battle the flames, but it quickly became evident that the pumper's small hose was next to useless against a fire of this magnitude.

Pete and I joined others in turning over the victims lying about. Their noses were black. He and I were able to save at least one, possibly more, by applying C. P. R.

After a while, my family left for home, but I remained on the scene. Father James Breghetto, Cincinnati fire Department Chaplain, and Assistant Chaplain **Collini** spent the remainder of the evening cleaning up the bodies and making them ready for identification.

My actions of that evening have been deemed "heroic," and I've received many awards, including the Ben Franklin Award (the firefighters "Medal of Honor") and an award from the Ohio House of Representatives.

When I think back on the tragic event, I feel far from heroic. I still do not believe that I, a professional firefighter, walked right past a room where a major fire was festering, and did not smell it, hear it nor feel any heat. My heart also fills with sadness that I had to leave that last woman. I wish to God that I could have done more on that disastrous evening. There's small consolation in knowing that I worked to the maximum of my stamina and ability.

Willie Snow
Head Dishwasher

By 1977, I had worked for Mr. Schilling for twenty years, first at a concession that he ran at the **Newport** Steel Mill, then at his first restaurant, Schilling's, then at the Lookout House. I was employed at the Beverly Hills from the minute it opened. I knew the Schilling sons Rick, Ron and Scott from the time of their births, and watched them grow up. He and his wife, **Terri,** always took good care of me, and I was a guest at their home many times. In return, I always gave him my best effort.

During the interval between Mr. Schilling's selling the Lookout House and the opening of the Beverly Hills, I remained at the Lookout House. This time was a little over a year, including that lost to the fire during remodeling.

On May 28, 1977, I reported for work at **2:00** in the afternoon, fully expecting to stay until about 3:00 AM. Yes, that's long hours and the work was grueling, but I enjoyed it and also the friendships I had with my co-workers. Because the time clock was located in my area, most of the **em-**

ployees would visit a little while as they clocked in. Working at the Beverly was like being part of a huge, caring family.

Early in the evening, a busboy rushed into the **kitchen.** "Willie," he exclaimed, "the customers in the Zebra Room are complaining about how hot it is in there." In a short while, waitress Roberta **Vanover** (we called her **"Hubba"**) made the same report. In response, Ronnie Schilling and I went downstairs to check the laundry room, thinking perhaps a lighted cigarette had been deposited along with the soiled linens. Everything appeared to be normal in there. Less than 30 minutes later, we got a report of actual smoke being sighted in the Zebra Room.

Ronnie and I dashed back to the basement into the area behind the linen room which put us directly under the Zebra Room. Through a small opening in the ceiling, we saw flames, inside a wall of the Zebra Room. There was no fire in the basement, and as a matter of fact, it never did get down there.

Ronnie hurried back to the first floor to direct traffic out of the building. Neither of us realized that we had a major fire at that time. Being dressed in kitchen work clothes, I did not want to go into the dining rooms, but did go up the service stairway to warn the bartender working at the bar in the back of Crystal Rooms 1, 2 and 3. I told him there was a fire, to remain calm, but to get everybody out of there. His major concern seemed to be his stock of whiskey. He argued for a minute before I commanded, "To hell with the booze, man. Get these people out of here now!"

I was in the service hallway upstairs directing the patrons to the service stairs to escape through the **kitchen** and into the garden. A woman near me was concerned about soiling her dress. "My God, woman," her husband snapped. "You can always buy a new dress, but I can't buy a new you!" At that moment, the electric lights failed but we were eventually able to move down the stairs.

Outside, voices were screaming, "Cabaret Room. Cabaret Room." I rushed to the rear showroom exit and joined two other employees, Curtis, a cook, and Tyrone, a kitchen worker at the door. No firemen were on the scene yet, so the three of us began pulling bodies out of the smoke-filled entry way. No one came out under their own power after I arrived, although I'm sure some did before I got there.

Scottie Schilling arrived and joined in our efforts. Somehow, we developed a system whereby we'd pull someone from the building and others would carry them away to safety while we returned for another. The time became blurred, and I have no idea of how long we toiled there or how many people we pulled out. When I saw Tyrone emerge from the smoke carrying Terri Rose's dead body, my throat tightened and tears streamed down my cheeks. Earlier that evening, Terri had, as usual, taken

Roberta (Hubba) Vanover and her three sisters were
all waitresses at the Beverly Hills. L to R: Pam Browning, Cindy c h e e M a c Vanover, Roberta and their
mother, Audrey Schelle (front). (Marcia Vanover)

a minute from her busy schedule to say hello. This was an actual nightmare, but I still couldn't believe it was happening.

After we evacuated all the bodies we could see, I dropped to my knees. From that position, I could see a short distance along the floor. Higher, the smoke was an impenetrable pitch black. I could see no more bodies. Placing a napkin over my mouth and nose, I crawled into the room, my face an inch from the floor. The heat was nearly unbearable, but I managed to go about thirty feet, inch by inch. I was still unable to see anyone and my groping fingers detected nothing, so I eased my way back to the exit. When I arrived at the door, waitress Jean Bethel noticed that I was exhausted and notified Dr. Stine, who was attending the injured nearby. "No more for you," he said after one look. "Don't go back in there again."

I did not argue. I staggered out into the garden to get some fresh air and ended up sitting next to busboy Walter Bailey. I was to later learn that it was Walter who sounded the alarm in the Cabaret Room, a heroic action. I have not seen Walter since that night.

Horror and the body count rose around me as I rested near the chapel. Doctors worked frantically with anyone who showed any signs of life. After a short rest, I returned to the Cabaret Room exit. By now, no visibility at all was possible, only thick, black smoke was to be seen in there. I walked around by the kitchen and looked into the window openings. The heat had blasted the glass outward, but, strangely, the kitchen was relatively free of smoke. I felt I had done all I could do to help anyone, so I left that area, went around front and walked down the hill.

The next morning, I went to the Southgate fire station to retrieve my car. The large crowd gathered there told me that many other people had the same idea. Southgate Mayor, Ken Paul, pulled me aside and said I wouldn't have to wait in line. "I saw what you did last night, Willie," he said. "You were just great. I'll get a state policeman to drive you up to get your car right now as a gesture of gratitude." While I waited, I saw Tyrone and George, a cook. I invited them to go up with me.

For many nights following the fire, I could not sleep. Mental images of the victims haunted me. About a week after the fire, Rose Dischar's mother called me. She asked me to come over to her home. When I visited with her in Alexandria, she thanked me for my rescue efforts even though I couldn't save her daughter. While I was there, I met Rose's five children who were now their grandmother's responsibility.

Even through all these years, that tragic night seems only yesterday. I shall never forget the destruction and horror of the fire at the Beverly Hills.

Dove Craig
Cabaret Room Waitress

I am unable to clearly recall the name or face of anyone I served that night, and I do not want to. Over all these years, whenever I meet anyone who tells me that they lost friends or relatives in the showroom that night, I immediately ask that they not tell me in what area they were seated. I could not deal with knowing that any of those I served had not made it.

On May 28, my first indication that all was not normal came when I observed the Cabaret Room manager, Pauline Smith, walk wordlessly past me, her face grim. Pauline marched silently past the patrons at the bar — normally, she would have greeted them — opened the fire doors, then tuned and retraced her steps into the showroom. Although her face was set, there was no panic in her actions, and no apparent concern.

I assumed that a customer had fallen and injured himself or perhaps someone had become ill and that Pauline had opened the doors to allow emergency medical personnel easy access. Under that assumption, I stepped outside to see if an ambulance was coming up the drive. Seeing nothing unusual out there, I walked back into the building. Immediately upon re-entering, I experienced a gut-level feeling that something was dangerously wrong. Something within me — I couldn't say what — urged me to get out of the building.

Giving in to that urge, I again walked to the fire door and outside. Still, nothing seemed amiss. But, when I turned to go back in, orange flames were licking around the top of the doorway from which I'd exited only a moment before. I rushed back to the door to help in any way I could.

I, along with the comedians, Teeter and McDonald, and others, remained at that post and assisted people as they staggered out of the building. Eventually, John Davidson joined us and helped in our rescue efforts although he was quite concerned about the safety of his manager, who was walking on crutches at the time. As I'd seen him leave, I assured John that his manager had exited the building and gone down the hill to the Oasis to call his family in California.

We circled the building in search of John's conductor, Douglas Herro. We didn't know it, of course, but Doug was still inside and was to die in the fire. Reaching a Cabaret Room exit, we stood in helpless agony and listened as people still trapped inside screamed in terror.

John Davidson and the two comedians walked with me down the hill to call my husband, Rudy, who was a **Newport** policeman. In the darkness, I stepped in a hole and sprained my knee. I was in such a state of shock, however, that I did not feel the pain until the next day. Dazed, I don't remember much about being at the bottom of the hill, but I do remember rudely fighting off a reporter who was trying to get to John Davidson. I'm usually an easy-going person, and such behavior is unusual for me. Rudy was on duty and I could not reach him, so I went back up the hill.

Wandering into the garden, I saw Rudy working there, just like a movie script would have had it happen. In fact, my husband is the man who arrested the man who was looting the dead. He did not know if I was alive or trapped inside, but when he saw me in the garden, alive and well amid the dead and dying, he ran over and swept me into his arms. We embraced for a moment, happy to be alive, before he returned to his duties.

I remained on the scene until 6:00 AM when the last truck departed for the morgue. When I did get to bed, I was unable to sleep, and did not sleep for four nights. Even today, I still sometimes experience nightmares.

For quite a while after the fire, I was angry with Pauline Smith for walking right by without giving any indication of the danger. At the time, I felt that this was a lack of caring and respect for those of us she walked past. Now, however, I realize that Pauline was probably focused on her mission and was giving her top priority to those in a packed showroom rather than the few of us in the bar area.

The service held for Steve Taylor, my bartender, was the only funeral I was able to attend. I did suffer enormous loss over the deaths of my friends and co-workers Terri Rose, Rose Dischar and Stuart Coakley.

I also retain great admiration for Walter Bailey for his heroic action, and for John Davidson, who never attempted to capitalize on the tragedy.

Father John Riesenberg
Priest

My former sister-in-law, Shirley, and I share a common birth date, May 28. As a joint celebration, we had planned to go, along with my brother, Richard, and our mother to the Beverly Hills for dinner and John **Davidson's** first show. Fate stepped in, however, and dictated that I'd officiate at a wedding that evening, so we agreed to attend the 11:00 PM show.

While we sat at home, nibbling birthday cake and watching All *in* the *Family* on TV, Richard, who served as fire chief of the Southgate Volunteer Fire Department, was summoned to respond to a fire at the Beverly Hills. As Richard prepared to go to the fire station, I joked, "Put that fire out fast and get back here so we can go to the show." My last joke of the evening, as he walked out the door, was, "And don't get any smoke on your clothes."

In a short while, I received a call from Richard **asking** me to bring **drinking** water to the site. His manner of speaking made it clear that there was to be no birthday party this evening.

Upon arrival, I was informed that there was an urgent need for a priest in the garden at the rear of the building. Father Jack **Kroger,** who had also just arrived, and I walked around the building and surveyed the ghastly sight. We spent the remainder of the night administering last rites to the dead, consoling stricken survivors and helping people locate or identify their loved ones.

Cari Kettman
Victims' Child

At the time of the Beverly Hills Supper Club fire, I was two-and-a-half years-old living with my parents, Robert and Susan Kettman, and my two sisters, Christi and Pam, in Mt. **Carmel,** Ohio. I did not understand at the time, but when our parents did not return from their night out, I soon realized that my sisters and I had been left parentless. Being so young when the tragedy occurred, I remember nothing of my parents or the fire.

Soon, we three girls were sent to live with my father's sister, her husband and their three children in New Richmond, Ohio. I remember little about the first year, but my first distinct memory is from about a year after the fire. I recall clearly watching as my two sisters packed their belongings and were moved out. I simply could not understand why I wasn't going with them.

Christi and Pam were sent to live with some friends of our parents in Mt. Lookout, about 20 miles away. At that point, I'd lost not only my parents, but my sisters as well. Twelve years were to pass before I got to know my sisters.

Ironically, at the time, my mother's brother in Colorado wanted to take all three of us in, but he wasn't deemed to be qualified. Colorado was too far away, and my other aunts were not married or were too young. So, I stayed in New Richmond.

After the separation, we were able to visit occasionally, and some-

The Kettmans. Clockwise Robert (Bob), Christine (Christie), Susan (Sue), Carin (Cari), and Pamela (Pam).(Cari Kettman)

times I even spent the night with my sisters. The occasions became less and less frequent until I only saw them at Christmas, and rarely, on one of our birthdays. My sisters' guardians made the effort to keep us in touch, but my aunt and uncle would not cooperate, so we slowly drifted apart. I did not have an easy life, young and frightened in an atmosphere where communication was non-existent.

Each year, on the anniversary of the fire, my aunt and I would go to church and light a candle, but she never told me anything. In fact, nothing whatsoever was ever discussed concerning the fire, and what few comments I heard about my parents were negative. I wished someone would have told me more, or at least told me anything. I assumed that I would not be allowed to ask, either. I felt that the fire had also caused my aunt and uncle a lot of pain, so I never asked. Sometimes, I'd see something about the Beverly Hills on television or in the newspaper; that was how I learned the little I knew.

When I was eight, my father's mother died, providing my first experience with death. That brought many questions to my mind, but I was still afraid to ask. The night my grandmother was buried, I had a nightmare, dreaming that there were three coffins under my bed. I was so scared that, for the first time, I ran to my aunt and uncle's bedroom and got in bed with them.

That turned out to be the first night of some seven years of sexual molestation. I never went to their bedroom again, but he soon found his way into my room. From that time on, I was totally unable to sleep, and I really don't know how I survived.

Despite these hardships, I kept my school grades up, did what was asked of me, and was a good girl. My "therapy" was a nightly battle with my pillow. I'd bury my head in the pillow, scream at my uncle for his behavior, at my aunt for her mistreatment, and at my parents for leaving me. This was my emotional release.

Nothing about my environment suited me. I did not like red meat or onions, and they were both on the table every evening. I especially disliked sloppy joe's, a frequent dish. One evening I came to the dinner table smelling sloppy joe's, but was delighted to see a Kentucky Fried Chicken box at my place. I thought they were finally going to be nice to me. My mouth watered and my spirits soared. I opened the box only to discover an extra large helping of sloppy joe's. My aunt, uncle and cousins laughed uproariously. I cried, and was sent to my room. This kind of thing happened often, and my punishment was to sit alone in my room behind a pink chair, a spot with which I became very familiar. I got no dinner that night, not even sloppy joe's.

When I reached middle school, I found a new family in the 4H Club. I had friends, most of whom were older, they communicated with me, and for the first time in my life, I had some fun. Even though I knew that drinking was wrong, we did it — a lot. My friends watched over me to ensure that I didn't go too far. I still feel that it was wrong, but I needed something, and I suppose alcohol helped.

By my ninth grade year, I had become a little rebellious. Until that time, I had used my uncle's name, but now I started printing "Kettman" on my school papers. I loved using my father's name for the first time in my life.

Through the years, I had discussed the abuse only with my older cousin, Jody. She listened, cried with me, and said that she'd tell her mother-Jody did tell, and her mom said that she'd look out for me, but, to my knowledge, she never did.

Abuse, like murder, will come out. My aunt and uncle had some problems, and in sessions with a marriage counselor, my abuse was revealed. The law required the counselor to inform the authorities. In court, my two sisters and I fought against the rest of the family. My sisters spoke out for me, and my uncle, after admitting to the abuse, was sentenced to a year in jail. This case was kept out of the media, and my aunt and uncle were quietly divorced. I received an apologetic letter from my uncle while he was in jail.

The court hearing gave me my chance to speak out. I was a little older then and not so frightened. I told them that I wanted to live with my sisters. Within a month, I was reunited with them in a house in Hyde Park which my sisters had purchased with money they had received from the Beverly Hills litigation and our parents' estate. My life-long dream was a reality! My sisters and their friends told me everything they knew about the fire and our parents. Our friends' parents' said that our parents had been loving and caring people.

I learned that Christi and Pam had not had an easy time of it, either. But we were together and happy now. Despite the doubts of our family about their ability to do so, my sisters provided more guidance than I'd ever had before. Among other things, they kept my financial situation intact. This allowed me to attend Summit Country Day High School and Xavier University, where I am now working on a communications degree.

The idea of a memorial for the victims of the fire excites me. I am deeply involved in the project, and we hope to have something up on that Southgate hill soon. Not long ago, I drove to the site of the Beverly Hills. I didn't know what I'd find, but I was compelled to go. Walking up the driveway, now overgrown with weeds, my thoughts turned to my parents. What were they thinking and feeling as they made the last drive of their lives up this hill? I didn't know much about what had been there, but walking around the site brought me a little closer to reality and gave me a kind of an emotional release.

In the weeds, I noticed a statue which had fallen from its pedestal during the fire. I am thinking that it would be nice to include it in the memorial. I'm going to work on that.

Bill Rowekamp
Wilder, Kentucky Fire Captain

We played a softball game which ended at 7:00 PM against the Southgate fire department on May, 28, 1977. Two hours later, we were all one team locked in a life and death struggle against a common opponent.

Following the softball game, I attended a neighborhood cookout in an area that overlooked the rear of the Beverly Hills Supper Club. When the call announcing the fire came, I immediately glanced in that direction. Only a slight amount of smoke was discernible at that time.

Fellow firefighters Bill Siebert, Jerry Stiltenpohl, Bernie Watkins and I all arrived at the fire house at the same time. Station pumper #1401 was pulling out, its pre-designated assignment to go to the lake just below the Beverly's parking lot. The pumper could pump 800 gallons per minute up the hill, the water to be distributed as needed. This was not to be. Although a clear path to the lake should have been a priority, the way was clogged with many parked cars, and the pumper could not get to the water. Pumper #1402 was enroute.

Riding in the department's rescue van, we pulled a 1,500 watt electrical generator to the scene. Arriving at approximately 9:20 P.M., I grabbed two oxygen bottles and headed for the front Cabaret Room fire exit. Evidently, some people had managed to escape from that door, but several had been overcome by smoke just as they reached the threshold of safety. As these people lost consciousness and collapsed, the door, which could be opened only from the inside, slammed shut, trapping the remaining patrons. When the entry was finally reopened, rescue workers where horrified to find dead bodies stacked inside as high as the top of the door in mute testimony to their frenzied escape efforts.

Corpses were also scattered on the ground in this area, as though they'd dropped as they walked. I vividly recall attempting to resuscitate one victim, a beautiful red-headed woman, about 40 years-old, dressed in a lovely green and white patterned dress. Her color was normal and she appeared to be sleeping. A passing doctor watched a moment, then said, "Forget about working on her, she's gone." He was right, she was beyond help. I spent the remainder of the nightmarish evening pulling bodies from the ruins.

Ron Bridewell
Newport Assistant Fire Chief

Five years after the fire, I was forced into early retirement by the critical condition of my lungs, aggravated, I believe, by my actions at the Beverly Hills fire.

During my time on the witness stand in the litigation concerning the fire, I vividly recalled first entering the Club's foyer and venturing into the bar area, flames all around me and my companion, Dayton, Kentucky fireman O'Day. We used the hose to extinguish some "spot fires" burning on the floor and ceiling of the bar, acutely aware of the roaring blaze on the right of the Zebra Room, the ominous glow back in the Empire Room, and the crackling sound being produced by the flames in the main dining-room. After a short while, the smoke and intense heat forced us to retreat from this area.

I then proceeded to the east side of the building with Captain Yutze in response to reports that people were trapped in the Cabaret Room. Despite not having any equipment, we entered the building and turned right. After going about five feet, we encountered a hallway going to the left. Crawling, we moved into the hall, groping about in the murky darkness for victims. I can still hear the crackling sounds of flames devouring the building while we were in there.

Checking a diagram of the Club later, I realized that the path we had taken led directly to the stage area. Still crawling on my belly, I came upon several bodies in the hallway and some others in a couple of small rooms off to the side. Firefighter Frank Santini and some others joined us at that time, and we set about the task of dragging these bodies out of the hall and down some steps. Once there, other rescue workers removed them from the building.

Continuing my search, I happened upon a room where I noticed what appeared to be a closet door, partly open. To my horror, when I opened the door fully, I saw numerous dead bodies stacked upon one another. I later learned that these were members of the orchestra who had traded their lives for an attempt to save their musical instruments.

Finally, when reddish-yellow flames broke out in the ceiling and doorway by the exit, I made a final rescue mission and then returned to the front of the club. By this time, I was experiencing great difficult in breathing.

Although "eating smoke" is one of the hazards of being a firefighter, and it was not a new experience to me, I had never suffered such serious effects from it. After I returned to the fire station, I was barely able to call for oxygen before I passed out. The firemen rushed me to St. Luke's Hospital, where I was to remain, in serious condition, for several days.

I suffer from emphysema, which is unpleasant, and I think all the smoke I inhaled that night was a factor. Still, if it was 1977, I'd go in again. But knowing what I now know, I wouldn't go in without a mask. There's no doubt in my mind that acting as I did on that evening took some years off my life.

Mindy Stricklen
Nurse

In 1977, I was on the nursing staff at Saint Luke Hospital and President of Kentucky District 3 Nurse's Association.

Because I was such a big fan of John **Davidson's,** I had planned to attend both shows at the Beverly Hills that fateful evening. At the last minute, my brother, Vince, convinced me to accept a blind date that he had arranged. As we drove up to the Brass Key Lounge, south on U. S. 27, in Alexandria, we noticed an unusual number of emergency vehicles heading north. I wondered where they were going.

It was usual for me to inform the hospital of where I could be reached when I was off duty. Toward that end, I went for the phone in the ladies lounge as soon as I entered the Brass Key. A man rushed in and shouted, "There's been a terrible explosion at the Beverly Hills! They need you at the hospital right away. We've got to get you out of here."

Enroute to the hospital, our car was met by a Highland Heights police cruiser which escorted us to the emergency entrance. As we sped through Fort Thomas, I could see ominous black smoke hanging in the sky above the Beverly. I also observed many people, looking dazed and bewildered, with soot smudging their faces and formal clothing, emerging from cars and wandering aimlessly. I later learned that volunteers were transporting survivors away from the fire scene, dropping them off along the highway, and returning for more. Residents of the area took these people into their homes, doing whatever possible to aid and comfort them.

Dashing past a group of clergymen in the emergency room, I made my way into the operating and recovery area. Having received training as an E. M. T. in the Navy, Vince was of great help that night.

Remaining in the operating and recovery area until **2:00 AM,** I worked with ten badly burned victims. Later, on the way through the lobby, I saw a stunned John Davidson standing in a daze, his jeans and black leather jacket covered with dirt and soot. Approaching him, I saw that he had bums on his hands and face. With shaking hands and a trembling voice, he told me that he'd been unable to locate his music director, Douglas Herro. He also told me that he'd been helping people out of the building when he discovered, to his horror, that he was pulling dead bodies from the inferno. I checked the computer listings of patients at all area hospitals, but could find no listing for Mr. Herro. I advised Mr. Davidson to go to the Fort Thomas Armory where a temporary morgue had been established. There, his worst fears were realized when he found Douglas Herro lying under one of the white sheets.

Unable to reach my family in Brooksville, Kentucky, I finally called Father Lou Blinker, a friend who lived in nearby Augusta and asked him to keep trying to contact my family. Father Blinker was glad to hear from me. He said that he'd heard reports of a girl named Mindy being **killed** in the fire and feared it was me. That victim was actually sixteen-year-old Mindy Morford from Dover, Kentucky.

My emotions got away from me while I was talking to the priest. At length, he settled me down, and I headed for my next duty at the temporary morgue. When I arrived at **4:00** AM, I volunteered for the section nobody wanted — **working** with the badly burned bodies. Because of the newly implemented county disaster plan, procedures were running smoothly despite the magnitude of the tragedy. It was no easy task, but I was eventually able to identify ten of the bodies, one from a ring she was wearing. On another body, all that was left was a shoe. By checking the serial number from the shoe, we were able to identify her when a matching serial number was found on a shoe box in her home.

My first patient from the fire was Karen Barker, a young woman from Alexandria, who was attending a farewell party for her husband, Dan, who had been transferred to New Jersey. Karen told me that their friends Donald and Patricia Bezold, did not get out. Dan, we learned, had been sent to a Cincinnati hospital. Despite being severely burned, Karen's main concern was about her husband and baby.

Karen was badly burned about her neck and shoulders. Although she had difficulty in speaking, she explained that it was unusual for her to wear a low-cut dress such as she had that evening. Despite the serious bums on her body, her face was untouched.

For the next few days, Karen, in great agony from her injuries and unable to speak due to heat and smoke damage to her larynx, sent **mes-**

sages to her husband and eagerly awaited a return communication. Then, ten days after the fire, Dan died and Karen had to find the courage to battle her grief as well as her injuries.

Months were to pass before I could eat or sleep with any regularity. The sights, odors and raw emotions of the entire ordeal are branded forever in my mind. In 1987, on Memorial day week-end, my brother, Vince Stricklen, who played a big part in the Beverly Hills tragedy, was **killed** in a tractor accident in Augusta.

Michael **Mullen**
Busboy

I was in the kitchen near the main service bar when Ron Schilling burst through the doors from the Empire Room in a high state of excitement. "Mike, get a fire extinguisher. Fast!" he exclaimed. Because of the danger of grease fires, the cooks always kept extinguishers handy. I grabbed one and dashed into the Empire Room.

The Empire Room was mostly vacant, the patrons having already exited, but a few were in a line going through the door into the bar and out the front entrance. Light smoke was curling above their heads, but I could see heavy smoke in the bar. Suddenly, I felt a little silly when I realized that I hadn't even bothered to find out where the fire was.

As I paused, Ron came up behind me, grabbed the fire extinguisher from my hand and dashed through the smoke in the direction of the Zebra Room. In that direction, the heavy smoke indicated a major fire, and I remember **thinking** that the tiny extinguisher wasn't going to do much good. When Ron disappeared into the smoke, I checked the room to make sure everyone was out. The lights were burning brightly, but heavy smoke was rolling in by now. Everyone was gone.

I ran back into the **kitchen thinking** about how crowded the Club was tonight. I wanted to warn as many as possible. My first thought was of those upstairs. As I approached the bottom of the service stairway, it was jammed with people coming down. Obviously, they'd already been alerted.

My mind now turned to the Viennese Rooms, where I'd been **working**. Moving in that direction, I passed a young dishwasher who was screaming hysterically. I feared he'd panic the customers, so I took time to try to calm him. When he settled down, I told him to leave with the others. The last I saw of him, he was in the line moving outside.

I raced through the service hallway which connected with the main hall. When I reached the double doors leading into the main hall, I jerked them open. Instantly, thick, black, oily smoke crawled through the top of the doorway, two feet down from the ceiling. Stooping low, I peered up the hall toward the Zebra Room, expecting to see it engulfed in flames. Although the air was clear near the floor, I saw nobody and nothing in the hall. I guess I froze for a few moments, because the next thing I knew, a wall of flame was roaring down the hall toward me. Smoke rolled from the top of it as it barreled closer to me, consuming the carpet and the ceiling tile as it came. I doubt that three minutes had passed since Ron Schilling grabbed the extinguisher from me.

Reaching the Viennese Rooms was out of the question. I prayed that everyone had gotten out of there. Mesmerized, I watched the wall of fire for a moment, then decided to get the hell out of there. The next thing I knew, I was outside in the garden, stunned and dazed. I have no recollection at all of how I got out of the building.

At the rear exit of the showroom, men were pulling people from the interior. I helped rescue a woman who was having great difficulty breathing. When we got her out, I noticed that the intense heat had molded the fabric of her dress to her body. When her husband tried to pull the fabric away, she screamed in agony as her skin came away with the material.

There were many displays of heroism in the rescue attempts, Willie Snow's efforts among them. Before any firemen arrived, Willie had already made several trips into the building pulling people back out with him. The ground was littered with bodies, none of them burned. I suppose they'd expired from the smoke and toxic gases.

When I'd seen all I could take, the thought occurred that I should let my parents know that I was OK. I walked over the hill and caught a ride with a guy on a motorcycle. At his home, I called my parents who. were overjoyed to hear from me.

Over the next few weeks, I spent a lot of time with the State's investigators telling them about my extraordinary eye witness view of the fire roaring down the hallway.

Judy Holiday
Waitress

I was working on the second floor when I smelled just the slightest hint of smoke. Even thought the scent was faint, I knew that there was a problem somewhere in the Club. "Do you smell smoke?' I asked another waitress.

"Yes, I do." I could hear the concern in her voice.

We stood together in the hallway, warily looking around. In just a few seconds, heavy smoke came pouring into the hall. I couldn't believe it came so quickly.

Wayne **Dammert,** the captain in charge up there, ran into the rooms on one side of the hall. I took the other side. I told the people in there that there was a fire and directed them out the back, into the service hallway.

Judy Holiday

Already, we were having trouble breathing. I was scared.

After the last person exited the room, I took one more look around and then dashed into the service hall, expecting an easy descent down the service stairs, through the kitchen and outside. To my horror, dense, black smoke surrounded the people jamming the narrow hall. Nobody was moving! My emotions broke down as I burst into tears.

As I stared in disbelief, Wayne came into the hall. Seeing the motionless crowd, his face turned white — he was as scared as I was. He gathered himself, however, and directed some men to try to knock out a door leading out onto the roof. My spirits sank even lower when they failed to break it open. Wayne disappeared down the hall just as Robert, a waiter, came up to stand behind me. Terror gripped me when the lights went out. Robert talked to me and helped keep me calm.

We struggled to breathe and fought the panic rising in us. Robert had just placed a towel over my face when, miraculously, the people started moving. I was so weak, Robert nearly carried me down the stairs. He had not worked at the Club for long, and was not sure of the way out. He made several false turns, pulling me along, before we finally found the loading dock out back. I do not remember anyone else being around, so I think Robert and I must have been the last of the upstairs group to get out.

Robert held on to me as we walked to the top of the hill behind the Club. I was happy to see several other waitresses standing there. We hugged with joy. Robert said he was going to check on his car and went back down. I've never seen him again. The other ladies and I stood there for a long time watching the flames devour our beautiful club.

When someone noticed that we were standing directly under some power lines, we ran away, screaming. Eventually, we worked our way to the bottom of the hill where the others turned toward **Newport.** I ended up walking alone, in a state of shock, right down the middle of U. S. 27. I don't know why I wasn't hit by a car. Fortunately, a policeman stopped, put me in his car, and took me to Highland Country Club, where rescue workers had established an aid station.

They gave me a cold drink, examined me for injuries, calmed me and suggested that I call home, an idea which had not even occurred to me. My husband, Michael, was not at home. His mother, visiting from Hazard, Kentucky, answered the phone. To say that my family was relieved would be an understatement. In the background, I could hear my youngest son, Kevin, shouting, "My mommy is alive. My mommy is alive."

My older son, Michael, Jr., had heard about the fire on his car radio. He rushed to the Beverly Hills, only to be turned away by the police. "You can't go up there," he was told. Fear for me welled up in him as the policeman added, "There's dead and injured all over the place."

Terrified, Michael rushed to Saint Luke Hospital where he spent hours checking each ambulance to see if his mother was among the victims. He did not know how close I came to being in one of those emergency vehicles.

He finally learned that I was OK and started home, arriving at the same time as I was dropped off. Even though I was coated from head to toe with soot, we hugged each other tightly and gave thanks that I'd been spared.

Although the weather was unseasonably cold following the fire, I would not allow the furnace to be turned on. I was still in shock, still scared, and I could not bear the odor of the furnace. Sleep was impossible. When my husband offered to take me out to dinner, I discovered that I could not tolerate even the idea of being in a crowd.

Michael decided that a little vacation would do me good, so we drove to Gatlinburg, in the Tennessee hills. I could not force myself into the hotel elevator. With a great amount of persuasion, Michael managed to get me into one of the tram cars going up the mountain. When the car began to fill with other tourists, panic gripped me and I had to rush out.

Many years have passed since then. Almost every day, thoughts of the fire, the horror, my friends who died and the Schillings are in my mind. The Schillings were demanding employers, but fair with their employees, always concerned about the customers, and did a good job of running the Beverly Hills. I feel badly for the victims, of course, but I feel badly for the Schillings, too.

Buddy Bethel
Busboy

My mother, Jean, was a waitress at the Beverly Hills when she decided that I, at age fourteen, should begin work as a busboy. My first night on the job, Rick Schilling discovered my age and fired me. Before I got out of the building, I was also fired by Ron and Scott Schilling for the same reason. As Mom had worked for Mr. Schilling for many years, she had a good relationship with him. She talked him into letting me stay.

On the day of the disaster, — I was sixteen by then — I arrived for

Jean Bethel (left) in her Beverly Hills waitress uniform with members of her family. Her son, Doren (Buddy) Bethel, (center) and Tammie Bethel Golf (far right), also a waitress at the club. Both were working the night of the fire. (B. Bethel)

work about noon, prepared to work a double shift on what figured to be a very busy evening. The afternoon parties went off OK, and those of us working then prepared for the evening crowd. We'd finished setting-up when the evening crew began to arrive. Included in the group were Mom, my aunt, Fran Oaks and cousins Shirley Baker and Bridgette Walls. My sister, **Tammy**, also worked at the Beverly, but she was off on that fateful evening.

I was **assigned** to the Viennese Rooms where a group of doctors and their wives were having a dinner party in one section, while a Bar Mitzvah party occupied the other end of the room. I was talking with **Scottie** Schilling when the head hostess, Dottie Eberle, walked up to tell him that the wedding party guests in the Zebra Room were complaining about it being hot in there. That news surprised me — I'd been in the Zebra Room just a few minutes earlier, and everything was normal.

Perhaps ten minutes later, I was in the kitchen when B. J. Bailor, another busboy, rushed in shouting, "There's a fire in the Zebra Room." He and I rushed back in that direction, passing through the main hallway, by the Cabaret Room and the Garden Rooms. Many people seemed to have already been alerted; the hallway was pretty crowded with people making their way through the light smoke to the exits.

After we ensured that everyone was out of the Viennese Rooms, we headed for the Zebra Room, which was just around the corner. Black smoke was rolling from the top of the double doors, which were jammed shut by a tray stand wedged in the door knobs. The smoke was wafting up the spiral staircase. I saw some expended fire extinguishers lying on the floor and realized that someone had attempted to put the fire out. Failing in that, they'd evidently jammed the doors in an attempt to contain the blaze until the fire department arrived. I grabbed the stand, burning my hand. At that time, I realized that a major fire was in progress inside the Zebra Room.

Suddenly, the fire burst through the doors, singeing us. "There's nothing we can do," I said to B. J., "let's get the hell out of here." He did not argue, and we started down the hall toward the rear exits. We'd only gone a few steps when I heard a shrill scream behind me. In the mirrors on the wall, I saw the reflection of a woman hit the bottom of the spiral stairs, she having fallen, or maybe jumped, from the second floor landing. I hesitated a moment, **thinking** I should go to her aid. By this time, however, the fire was raging down the hall. B. J. had picked up a fire extinguisher somewhere and was standing beside me with it in his hand. We looked into each other's eyes only a second before panic hit us both. He threw the extinguisher aside and we ran like hell out of there. I guess someone helped the woman as no bodies were found in that area.

B. J. and I became separated in our dash to safety. I ended up, alone, in the Empire Room. The lights were on, and there was no fire, although the drapes were smoldering and appeared ready to burst into flame. Moving through there into the **kitchen,** I saw people from upstairs coming down the service stairs. I took time to advise them to keep low and head for the back of the room. At that time, I realized that my mother and Aunt Fran were working upstairs. I got about halfway up the stairs before the rush of people from the opposite direction forced me back. The thick, black smoke roaring through the stairwell made visibility impossible, anyway.

As soon as I exited into the garden, the screams of people trapped in the Cabaret Room assaulted my ears. Those noises are my worst memory of the fire — I shall never forget the ghastly, unbelievable sounds of that human agony.

Searching for Mom and Fran in the garden, I bumped into fellow busboy, Mark Johnson, who agreed to help me look for them. As we talked, something caught our attention inside the Garden Room. It gave the appearance of a streak of fire flashing across the room. Mark and I looked at each other in terror as we realized that we were witnessing a person, engulfed in flames, running across the room in panic. Without communication, Mark and I dashed inside, wrapped the lady in a tablecloth and drug her outside. She screamed in agony as we rolled her on the ground, patting the tablecloth to extinguish the flames. We thought we had all the fire out when a policeman passed by and took her away for treatment.

At that time, Pam (Browning) and Hubba (Roberta **Vanover)** walked by and told me that Mom and Fran were out and safe. A wave of relief flooded over me, and I realized that I was exhausted. I walked around the building, noticing flames shooting out through the roof. As I reached the Cabaret Room exit, I witnessed the rescuers pulling bodies from the building, a sight which brought the full impact of what was happening crashing down on me. I'd thought that everyone got out. How could there be so many dead bodies lying around?

Scottie Schilling was one of those pulling bodies out. When he turned and saw me, I burst into tears. "Buddy," he said, "you can't help here. Go around the bodies and put their rings and valuables in their pockets. The police already picked up a guy looting the bodies. I don't want any more of that going on."

I didn't relish the idea. I turned, but before I'd moved, a policeman who'd over heard what **Scottie** said told me to go on down the hill. "You look pretty shaken up," he said, "and I think you'd be better off leaving." The policeman escorted Mark and me to the front of the building.

My mother was standing out front. As we hugged each other, the emotional and physical drain hit me. I was suddenly desperate to get away from the site — Mark and I had done all that could be expected of **sixteen-year old boys.**

Mom stayed where she was, as Mark and I started down the driveway, both of us sobbing in reaction to what we'd endured and witnessed. We met Wayne Dammert on the way and told him of the critical situation in the Cabaret Room. We eventually made our way to Latonia, where Mark and I spent the night at the home of Dave Brock, another busboy.

In 1979, I enlisted in the Marine Corps, still experiencing nightmares of the Beverly Hills tragedy. One night on the aircraft carrier Saipan, I jumped out of my bunk, screaming, just as the duty officer walked by. My buddies explained to him that it was not unusual for me to do that. Two years of intensive counseling were required to relieve the problem.

Although he's not, Mark Johnson, my best friend, should be listed among the casualties of the Beverly Hills fire. I am sad to report that Mark fatally shot himself in December of 1991.

-Nola Ballinger
Waitress

A s I reported for work at **5:00 PM**, my usual time, I knew that because popular John Davidson was appearing in the Cabaret Room, a busy evening was assured. The beautiful Frontenac dining room was my assignment for the evening. This exclusive room, located to the left of the bar, offered only a la carte dining to our patrons.

In my charge were five tables, each seating four customers. Early, the tables were turned at least twice, so I estimate that I served some forty customers who then moved on to the Cabaret Room before the first show was to begin.

At **9:00 PM**, business was slow in the dining room, although we knew that it again would soon be packed as the time for the second show, which was sold out, approached. Only a man and his wife were at my tables.

After taking their order, I was in the kitchen getting their salads when

Scottie Schilling ran in. "Drop those salads, Nola!" he shouted. "Get the hell out. Fast!" I had no idea what was wrong. He then yelled to all in the **kitchen,** "There's a fire! There's a fire!"

Instantly, I started back to the Frontenac Room to warn my customers and anyone else who might be in there. **Scottie** had not said where the fire was, and the club was so large that it might not even be a threat to us. In the service hallway, there was no smoke or flame, but I saw waitresses Ann Egan and Shirley Robinson directing people out the exits. When everyone was out, Ann, Shirley and I made our way outside through the **kitchen.**

We walked up the hill a short distance and turned to watch. No one of the three of us had seen any fire or even any smoke, so we thought we'd soon return to work. In a few minutes, we decided to walk around the building to see what was going on. We walked down a narrow, gravel drive passing by a large oil tank which sat just outside a basement entrance. Rick and Ron Schilling were at this location, frantically giving their best efforts to accomplish something around the tank. I never learned what they were trying to do, but the intensity on their faces remains vividly in my memory.

At the top of the drive, near the front corner of the building, we witnessed victims being loaded into ambulances, our first indication that the fire was serious. I thought that they must be alive or they would not be being placed in ambulances. We were still unaware of what was going on in the Cabaret Room.

We attempted to walk down the hill but were held up for some time by the police. While we waited, I noticed all the fire trucks and emergency vehicles sitting around. When we were allowed to go on, water from all the hoses ran down the drive in a small river.

Ann, Shirley and I entered the Oasis Club at the bottom of the hill to call home. This proved impossible due to the large number of people doing the same thing. Somehow — I know not how — we ended up at Bev Warndorf's house in **Newport** and made our calls from there.

From the television at Bev's house, we learned the magnitude of the disaster, which hit me forcefully. I realized how lucky I had been to have happened to be in an area which wasn't threatened and allowed an easy, quick exit. I hadn't even witnessed any of the horrors that so many others did.

Over the years since the fire, I've wondered about the customers that I served that evening. They were all excited about their special evening. Everyone of them had said something like, "Hurry and give us our check so we won't be late for the show," when they finished eating. I wonder if some of them were rushing to their doom.

Only after it was gone did I realize how much I loved working at the Beverly Hills. The atmosphere, the friendships and the working conditions there were better than any place I ever worked, before or since. After the disaster, I experienced an emptiness, a void in my life. I'd worked for the Schillings at the Lookout House before the Beverly, and everyone in that family always treated me with the utmost respect. They were demanding employers, but they didn't expect anything that they wouldn't and didn't do themselves. The Beverly Hills was not the success story that it was just because it was so elegant. The popularity of the Club was a tribute to the Schilling's hard work and dedication to make every evening a special occasion for each customer.

Cindy Schleicher Teal
Waitress

Late in 1975, I, at sixteen years of age, began work as a waitress at the fabulous Beverly Hills Supper Club. My aunts, Karen Watts and Phyllis Delaney, plus several of my school friends worked there, so it was a family atmosphere. We tried hard to please the customers, and they, in turn, were always pleasant and courteous to us.

On May 28, 1977, I arrived at 4:00 PM, excited because it was to be my first chance at working a banquet alone. A wedding party of about 50 people to be held in Garden Room 4, the newest in the Club, was all mine. This room was in the comer of the huge Garden Rooms, right next to the kitchen. Later, I realized that it happened to be the safest place in the building that fearful night.

All went well through the afternoon, and the guests started arriving, on schedule, at 6:30 PM. The three piece band and the portable bar were in place. The wedding was performed in a lovely section of the garden at 7:30 PM.

By 9:00 PM, the salads and fruit cups were in place on the tables. It was my party, but the busboys carried all the food and equipment into the room through the partition which separated us from the rest of the Garden Rooms. We were just getting ready to serve dinner when someone knocked on the partition door. I opened it to be informed that there was a fire in the building. I saw no smoke or flames, but I did observe a great amount of commotion going on in the Garden Room. Assuming the situation to be serious, I immediately led the wedding guests through a sliding glass door into the garden outside.

When everyone was out, I ran back into the kitchen, only to find it empty. Therefore, I assumed that the fire must be in the front of the building. Since that was were Aunt Karen was working, I worried about her. Where was the fire? How serious was it? Where was Karen?

I ran back into the garden area. Many well dressed customers were wandering there in great confusion. Now, through the glass wall, I could see smoke floating around inside the Garden Room. I decided to search for

Aunt Karen. Passing around the building, I witnessed horrifying sights and sounds as rescuers carried and dragged victims from the flaming structure. As I watched them gently deposit bodies on the grass, tears streamed down my cheeks. I screamed Karen's name, merely adding my voice to the profusion of plaintive cries for missing loved ones. Then I saw Karen. She was safe! In the midst of the chaos, we clung tightly to each other, crying.

Cindy Schleicher Teal.

Like a nightmare, bodies were being placed all around us. Then we thought of calling home. We were prevented from going around to the front, so Karen, another waitress, Cindy Shilly and I hiked over the hill in back leading through the highway construction area.

At the crest of the hill, I turned to look back. I wish I hadn't. Consuming fire now completely engulfed the Beverly Hills. A plume of black smoke, illuminated by flickering flames, rose vertically into the dark spring sky. The screams which had torn my heart earlier were silenced now. Silenced forever. I could see survivors and rescuers milling around in shock. The grassy areas of the garden were littered with bodies, people who only a short while before had been enjoying a special evening.

The scene was too much for a 17 year-old girl to bear. I ran down the steep hill, stumbling several times before I finally reached the bottom. Even though the nightmarish scene was out of sight, it was not out of mind. It still is not.

Phyllis Delaney
Waitress

When my husband's company transferred him to Pittsburgh, I hated to leave my job at the Beverly Hills. I'd worked there since 1972, and I loved it. My sister, Karen, my niece, Cindy and many of my childhood friends worked at the Beverly. With Wayne Dammert, Pam Browning and her sisters, and their friends, it was a real family affair. On my frequent returns to Northern Kentucky, I never passed up an opportunity to work there.

It's difficult to describe the horror that struck me on May 28, 1977 when the Pittsburgh television program I was watching was interrupted by a news flash announcing that the Beverly Hills Supper Club was on fire. According to the news, many people had been killed and injured and the fire was raging out of control. My heart was pounding as I telephoned my mother in Cincinnati to inquire about our family members, who I assumed were working that night. Mom didn't know anymore than I did. As the news reports grew more and more ominous, I kept calling. The answer was always the same, "No news."

Relief finally came about 11:00 PM. Cindy had called from the Oasis, a little club nestled at the foot of the long drive leading up to the Beverly. Karen and Cindy were safe, and as far as they knew, so were all our friends.

As deeply as I was joyful for their safety, I was also filled with despair for the tragic victims of the fire and for the beautiful club that I loved so much. My sorrow deepened a few days later when I learned of the deaths of my friends and co-workers, **Terri** Rose and Rose Dischar.

When the state investigators finished with the property and turned it back over to the Schillings, I loaned them my two German shepherd dogs to guard the place. On several occasions, I went up to the ruins and just walked around, sometimes sifting a handful of ashes through my fingers as I attempted to comprehend the reality of what had occurred here. That was truly an eerie experience. Viewing the pitiful remains, I realized that the Beverly Hills was gone. **There'll** never be another.

Claude **Farwick**
Cashier

A full time position with the L & N railroad was my day job, but like many, old and young, in the Northern Kentucky area, I worked part time at the Beverly Hills. I worked there partly for the money, but also partly because I enjoyed it.

On the evening of the fire, I was to work in a small bar room attached to the Crystal Rooms upstairs. The bar and two restrooms were located at the top of the spiral staircase, directly above the Zebra Room. My assignment was to check the drinks and cashier the money for the Afghan Hound Dog Owners Club party. Some 90 people, from all over the nation, were attending this get-together.

My wife, Angie, also worked at the Beverly. We usually rode together, but, as her assignment for this evening was as a cashier in the showroom, she'd be working very late. So, we drove separately.

The patrons were lining up for a buffet dinner while we were just closing the bar about 9:00 PM when someone yelled, "There's a fire in the building." By the time I got to the top of the stairs, smoke was boiling up the staircase, so I realized we could not go down that way. I told everyone around to come with me and ran down the hall toward the service hallway in the back. A waitress was standing at the doors directing people through. When I reached her, black smoke had filled both of the party rooms, convincing me that a major fire was in progress. I had no idea where the fire was.

To my complete horror, the hallway was jammed solid with people, not moving. I was one of the last ones in there, so I was at the end of the line and was extremely scared for all of us. Smoke in the hallway grew thicker as the lights failed, then flickered back on. I later learned that as the fire was in the Zebra Room, the stairway acted as a chimney, bringing the smoke up to us. At the time, I thought perhaps the explanation for our being trapped was that the fire had erupted in the **kitchen**. If that had been the case, we would not have gotten out.

The lights failed again, this time permanently. Terror filled the hall. We instructed everyone to place a hand on the person in front of them and to try to keep calm. In the heat, dark and suffocating smoke which made breathing difficult, keeping calm was a tall order. I'd had some previous experience as a volunteer firefighter, so I'd grabbed a **napkin** before the lights went out. Holding it over my mouth and nose allowed a little help in breathing.

Through some stroke of luck, the line started moving. We moved down the narrow stairs and into the **kitchen** without mishap. Somehow, Wayne Dammert had reached the stairs. As he rushed down, the others followed him to safety. Once in the kitchen, which, thank God, was not on fire, exiting to outside was an easy thing. With so many people in there; however, I decided to make a left turn and exit through the main dining room. I found it was full of thick, oily smoke. After I stumbled over a table in the dark, I quickly turned back and exited through the kitchen.

In the garden, I was surprised to see bodies lying on the grass. I'd assumed that the fire only affected the area where I'd been. If we'd gotten out OK, how could these people be dead? The Beverly Hills was such a large facility that I couldn't comprehend that the fire had spread so quickly all throughout the building.

Suddenly, I thought of Angie. My mind had been so occupied with my own plight that I hadn't given her a thought. I had to find her! I said a quick prayer for her to be out of the inferno.

On the east side of the building, high above U. S. 27, I went by the Cabaret Room exit. I searched frantically, but couldn't find Angie. God, where is she? Running toward the front of the Club, I saw her standing on the grass! I ran to her, and we embraced as never before. Neither of us said a word, we just held each other tightly.

Angie, our children and I were a close knit family even before the fire. Since that night, we've become even closer, our love and appreciation for each other made stronger by the terrible tragedy.

Angie Farwick
Showroom Cashier

In addition to being a full time wife and mother and selling Avon cosmetics, I also worked part time at the Beverly Hills. The Beverly gave me a little extra income, an occasional night out, and the opportunity to meet the many celebrities who appeared at the Club. It was fun! My husband, Claude, had the same duties as I, checking drinks and taking money at service bars.

On the fateful night of May 28, I arrived at 7:30 PM and went to work at the south service bar, to the right of the stage, in the Cabaret Room. This was the location where I usually sat, right next to an exit into the service hallway that led backstage. I liked it as it was an ideal location for meeting the stars as they came into the room. Many times, they'd stop by to get a drink or just to chat.

On this particular evening, I was working with Larry Baumback, who was in charge, and two bartenders. The room was packed for the Memorial Day week-end, and the waitresses were kept busy running to us for drinks and delivering them to the customers.

The showroom hostess, Pauline Smith, came by to check on us a few times. She was quite concerned about getting everyone seated before the show began. Although the waitresses and bartenders were very busy, I had time to chat with Pauline because most customers just ran a tab to pay for their drinks at the end of the evening.

About 9:00 PM, Pauline ran into the bar area. "There's a fire in the building," she announced. Before leaving, she added, "Take your time, but get out." I picked up my purse and went out the door. Larry stayed to collect the money boxes. I made it outside with no problem. Although there was a crowd of us, exiting was orderly. I remember thinking it was a little like a fire drill. Soon after I exited, Larry came down the steps, money boxes in hand. Thick, black smoke followed him out the doorway. That was the moment the fire became a reality for me.

I walked to the front corner of the Club, near the front entrance and looked back toward the door through which I'd exited. People were still streaming through the door. I knew from Cabaret Room experience that these people had not been in the "pit" area as their dress was normal. That area contained the best seats in the house, and patrons seated there were always the most elegantly dressed. As it turned out, most of those in the pit perished because it was farthest from an exit.

I happened to overhear some firemen talking about the low water pressure and a pump problem. Things did not look good.

Just then, I thought of my husband. Claude was working upstairs, an area with which I was unfamiliar, so I had no idea of how he might have exited, if, in fact, he had. Where could he be? He had previously been a volunteer fireman, so I felt sure that if there was a way out, he'd find it. Something told me that **he'd** have an easier time finding me if I stayed where I was. I stood still, waiting and praying. At last, he came running along the same path I'd taken. He, like Larry, had brought his money boxes with him. After a grateful embrace, we walked to the bottom of the hill to contact our family.

After a long wait at the Oasis, we finally got to the telephone. As we left the restaurant, I glanced up the hill just in time to see a blast of flame spew out from the rear of the Club, right over the showroom where **I'd** been working a short time before. Words cannot express how happy I was to be out of there.

I thank God that I was sitting right by the door and that it was un-locked. Otherwise, I would not be alive to tell my experiences. Since that night, I have always been aware, wherever I go, of the exits to a room and fire safety. Not a day has passed in all the years since the fire that I fail to remember the Beverly Hills victims and their families. God bless every one of them.

Leslie Henry
Rose Dischar's Daughter

M y mother was a very beautiful woman. By 1977, she had five chil-dren: I, at 18, was oldest, Rick was 16, John was 11, Nicole was 7, and Joshua was two-and-a half. Mom was divorced, so Rick, John and Nicole lived on a farm in Campbell County with Mom's parents, Minnie and Puis Butsch, while Josh and I lived with Mom in an apartment in Highland Heights. Our apartment was located on U. S. 27, about two miles from the Beverly Hills. This was a good arrangement for all. The boys liked working and living on the farm and the schooling was better. I, as oldest, and Josh, as youngest, were closer to Mom, so we enjoyed being with her.

On the day of the fire, I was ready to leave the apartment about 3:00 PM. Mom was not due at work for a few hours yet, and prided herself on having a good suntan, so naturally, she was out by the pool. I went out to tell her good-bye.

I went to a party in **Newport** for a while and then with some friends to a marina near Wilder, Kentucky. One of my friends had a sort of dune buggy. We were trying it out over the hills and paths around the marina. About the time it started getting dark, we noticed some smoke in the sky in the direction of the Beverly Hills, which was some two miles away. Then we heard sirens, many of them, some loud and near, some farther away. A passing girl who had a portable radio informed us that the Beverly Hills Supper Club was on fire.

My first thought was of my mom. I thought, and even said aloud, "My God, I hope she's not trapped in there." We left the marina for a friend's house so I could call my grandparents. Grandma knew about the fire from television, but she knew nothing else. My friends were assuring me that Mom would get out if anybody did because she'd worked there for quite a while and knew the layout well. I tried hard to believe it.

One of my friends agreed to drive me to the Club. The police road-blocks prevented us from getting very close. Despite the radio reports about people being trapped inside the building, I was not scared because I figured she'd get out. I was concerned, though.

We returned to my friend's apartment. In a little while, someone suggested that I should go home so I'd be there when Mom called. We had to take back roads because of the road blocks, but we finally made it. Some of my friends said they'd stay with me until Mom got home.

About midnight, the phone rang. That was the first of many calls that night, mostly from Mom's co-workers inquiring if she'd gotten out all right. They were upset when I told them that I had not heard from her. I particularly remember that Willie Snow and **Lise** Bohannon called several times.

Around 4:00 AM Lise called again. I told her that I'd still heard nothing, despite the fact that I'd called all the area hospitals, and was becoming desperate. She hesitantly suggested that I call the morgue. After Lise hung up, I lifted the receiver to call the morgue, but couldn't do it. I called Grandma instead. She'd heard nothing, either and was as concerned as I. Where was my mom? There were reports on television about injured people wandering along the highways and in residential areas in a daze. I prayed that she was one of them.

Finally, the sun came up on Sunday morning. I remember nothing else about that day. I guess I was just too tired and too worried. Grandma asked me to come out to the farm, but I had to stay where I was until I found out something. I got no sleep that night, either.

By Monday morning, my hopes were almost all gone. Grandma and my aunt Charlotte, who'd come in from Chicago, came by and told me we'd better go to the morgue in Fort Thomas. It so happened that a friend of Mom's was a nurse working at the temporary morgue. She knew Mom was listed as missing and had already checked all the bodies. She tried to comfort us by ensuring us that Mom was not there.

Not finding her there did little to raise my spirits. I cannot describe the feelings I had as we slowly drove back to the apartment. What had happened to my beautiful mother?

On Tuesday, the state police had me identify Mom's car so they could try to match fingerprints from it with the unidentified bodies. They, along with us, were also trying to get her dental records. This was difficult because Mom was so fussy about her teeth that she had been through several dentists trying to find one whose work suited her. We couldn't remember all their names. The police spent all day Wednesday trying to locate her records.

Finally, they were down to only five unidentified bodies at the morgue. I happened to mention to one of the doctors that I thought she was on her monthly period, and that proved to be the key. Her body was finally identified by a tampon, as strange as that may sound.

One of those days, I'm not sure which, Jerry Lubbers, a bar boy and friend, drove me to one of the Schilling's houses where I was able to retrieve my mother's purse. It was not burned, and the contents were perfectly intact.

Thursday, I think it was, Grandma got the dreaded call. The morgue had double checked and had identified my mother's body, or so they said. From what I'd heard about the intensity of the fire, I doubted there was much of her left to identify. A few days later, I watched four pallbearers carry a casket to the grave. How could I ever be sure that that casket contained my mother's body?

After the funeral, I gave up the apartment and moved to the farm to help with the children. Before the fire, Josh's father wanted nothing to do with him, but now we were embroiled in a paternity suit. His father won out, so now we had to face a custody battle. We all needed each other and we were especially close to Josh, because he was the youngest. The long custody suit took a year, but we won with Grandma being appointed Josh's guardian.

I tried to get welfare and social security for the children, but failed in both cases. They denied welfare because I was working and owned a car. How was I supposed to get to work without a car?

Being good Kentucky farm people, my grandparents took excellent care of the children. I am very proud of the job they did. I would have tried to keep us all together under any circumstances, but without them, it would have been difficult. After a long fight, we finally did get about $125 per month in food stamps. They kept demanding so much from us that Grandma finally told them to just keep the food stamps.

I'm happy to report that today, all five of Rose **Dischar's** children have grown up to be fine people. All except Josh are happily married and all are living productive lives.

Nicole and I, along with many others, are working on having a memorial to those who died on the site of the Beverly Hills. We've contacted many other families who lost someone in the fire and we feel a common closeness. Through employees and survivors, we've managed to learn quite a bit about that tragic night. I feel it's important to know as much as we can.

My siblings and I loved our mother very much. We miss her. Not a day has gone by since I saw her last that I don't think about her. Occasionally, I go to the site, park at the bottom of the hill and walk up the long, winding driveway. As I stand on the ground where the Beverly Hills once sat, sometimes I feel as if Mother is standing there with me.

Lise Bohannon
Cabaret Room Waitress

B ecause the Memorial Day Saturday looked to be very busy, I went to work a little early on that May evening. After I'd served wine for a party in the Empire Room, cocktails for a wedding reception in the garden and for a style show party in one of the upstairs rooms, it was time for my regular shift to begin.

Despite all the extra work, I was in fine spirits. I'd participated in the joyous remarriage of my father earlier in the afternoon. My father and I were very close, and we were all very happy. He and his new wife, Janet, had made other plans for the evening, but at the last minute, they decided that they'd like to attend John **Davidson's** show at the Beverly Hills. I asked Pauline Smith if she could get them in. Her answer was a somewhat frustrated, "We're tremendously busy, but tell them to come see me. I'll try to get them in somehow."

The weather was gorgeous and everyone was having a lovely evening. About 8:30 PM, I reported to my station in the Cabaret Room. I was to work the "pit" area to the right of the stage, serving some **60** to **80** people. While my area was filling quickly, my father and his bride showed up. Pauline squeezed them in at an excellent table in my area, which they shared with another couple who were friends of the Schillings.

I was so busy getting people settled and taking care of the first round of drinks that I took little notice of anything else going on in the showroom. On one trip to the service bar, which was on the right side of the room, I did notice several empty tables. By the time I got the drinks and started back, the show had begun and these seats were still vacant. This struck me as unusual because they normally did not begin the show until everyone was seated and calmed down. Even stranger, there were still people standing in the doorway and seated in chairs on the ramps leading up to the stage.

With so many patrons in the room, I has having to work hard. On what turned out to be my last trip to the bar, I was the only one in the area. It was not unusual for the bartenders and cashiers to be gone for a few minutes, so I simply got on with why I was there. As I placed glasses on the tray, I noticed people streaming through the service exit. They weren't rushing, but did seem concerned. I heard someone say, "I don't know. They just said we should get out of here." Being so busy, I took little notice and kept on with what I was doing. As I turned with the tray, the volume of people coming through the bar had increased, so I then knew something was wrong.

The crowd of people was orderly, no panic was evident. I wasn't sure what was going on, but I decided to get out, too. Calmly, I picked up my purse from the pile belonging to the waitresses and joined the line of people going out the door. Just after I reached the platform outside, I felt a huge blast of air from behind me as thick, black smoke encircled our heads.

With that, the orderly behavior of the crowd disappeared. People screamed and the line behind me started to push. My thought was to get to the bottom of the steps and away from the building. This I managed without great difficulty.

On the grass a few yards from the building, I thought of my father. He should have come out this exit, too. Aloud, I shrieked, "My God. Where is my father?" As I started to rush back to the stairs leading down from the platform, my fellow employees tried to hold me, but I broke loose and ran. I fought the mob to get back into the building. I'd gained the landing when a huge, jagged arm of orange flame shot through the doorway. The heat singed all of us on the platform. By this time, three of the other waitresses had followed me up the stairs and were trying to hold me back. "No!" they shouted. "You cannot go back in there."

In my panic, I was determined to get inside. I fought them with a strength born of hysteria. Finally, one of my friends hauled off and punched me in the nose with a blow that knocked me off the landing. When I stopped rolling down the hillside, I'd come to my senses.

I walked back up the hill, rubbing my sore nose, to a point from which I could see the exit doorway. John Davidson was standing in the crowd near me, his eyes, like all of us, fixed on the exit. Only a trickle of people were coming out. We could hear people inside screaming, we could see a few of them packed together in there, and we could even smell the fear. They were tangled like a ball of twine full of knots. I saw a young girl, with long blonde hair wearing a beautiful prom dress lying near the door. The rescuers were trying to pull her out, but apparently her legs were stuck. She screamed in agony and fear as they attempted to drag her from the snarl of bodies.

Then, an unbelievable event occurred. A man in uniform dashed to the opening and closed the door! My God, what about those people still in there? I screamed at the top of my lungs, "NO! You've got to open that door." The door sealed shut. I couldn't understand why he'd closed the door with people still inside.

Larry and Terri Rose at Sharon Woods, OH.
(Shawn Earnest, their son)

My mind reeled from so much horror. Suddenly, two explosions erupted from inside in rapid succession. Thinking the building was going to blow up, everyone scrambled away. I was still thinking of my father, praying that he had gotten out.

Standing with five or six waitresses on the grass, I still wanted to go back to check on my father. I walked back up. The area around the exit was now deserted except for a few firemen. Because the door was still closed, I moved around to the front of the building, where the front door was open. I went inside, but didn't get far before the smoke and heat drove me back.

Out front, I saw one of my bartenders giving mouth to mouth resuscitation to a victim. The two bodies lurched in unison as the victim's lungs expelled a gust of air. The bartender lifted himself, vomited, and went right back to his work. Witnessing such heroism comforted me a bit.

Moving to the rear of the building, I could hear people screaming in pain and calling the names of their loved ones. I added my voice to the bedlam, calling for my father. I checked every one of the many bodies lying around. I asked everybody I saw about my friends and co-workers. Nobody knew much of anything, but I was happy to learn that some of my friends had gotten out.

All the while, I was yelling, "Dad, Dad," as loud as possible. Finally, I heard a voice calling, "Lise." Running toward the sound, I saw my father and Janet standing on the grass. Through hugs and tears, he explained that some unknown hero had led them out through the Garden Room.

Dad and Janet soon left, but I stayed to look for my friends. My heart sank when I saw Terri Rose's dead body lying on a tablecloth. I, along with many others, searched unsuccessfully for Rose Dischar and Steve Taylor, my new boyfriend. About 2:00 AM, exhausted, I gave up and left. I ended up at the Holiday Inn in Covington with a group of employees who had gathered, to make calls and comfort each other.

When all the reports were in, I had lost three dear friends. Terri Rose, Rose Dischar and Steve Taylor, all perished in the fire. Terri, Steve and Rose will live forever in my heart. I loved them all and still miss them.

Also forever etched in my memory are the faces I saw inside that Cabaret Room exit and the smiling faces of my customers. Some got out and some didn't. The same unforgetfulness holds for the bodies and dazed people that I saw wandering in the garden calling for loved ones.

Now, nineteen years after the fire, with those memories still in my mind, I'm working with the group to build a memorial on the site of the Beverly Hills. The best thing about this activity is that I've been re-united with some old friends and been fortunate enough to meet the families of some of the victims. We've all become very close and help-ing the families is a source of comfort to me.

George W. Zadek
Patron

My girlfriend, Judy Beck, had been asking me for some time to take her to the Beverly Hills. She especially wanted to see John Davidson's show. I talked my older brother, Bob and his wife, Victoria, and my sister Harriet and her husband, Dick Schewene, into going with us on May 28.

We arrived at the Club early and had a drink at the bar before being ushered into the Frontenac Room for dinner.

After we ate, we took a walk down a long hallway to the Cabaret Room. The hostess seated us in a back corner of the room, a location that did not suit us at all. Judy was not happy, saying, "We're not going to spend all this money to end up with bad seats." As a former Schilling employee, she knew what to do. She walked over to the hostess desk. The next thing I knew, we were being moved to a more central location. We were re-seated, still in the back, but on the upper level, near the entrance. We had an excel-lent view of the stage from this new location.

Lovely dance music was provided by the orchestra while the room filled with people. Shortly after the show started, a busboy came on stage, took the microphone from one of the performers and announced a fire in the building. "Don't panic," he said, "but, get out." He pointed out the exits. Everyone in our group, except Bob and I, got up to leave. He and I often attended the Cincinnati Bengal's football games, and we always re-mained seated to wait for the crowd to thin out before we got up. I suppose we were doing the same here.

In a few minutes, we did head toward the exit on the left of the stage.

The line was moving slowly and orderly, there was no panic at all. Somehow a table was knocked over into our path. Bob, who was a volunteer fireman in Cleves, Ohio, righted the table, climbed up on it and started yelling at people not to shove and not to panic.

As I stood on the floor beside Bob, another table was knocked into the aisle. Bob told me to get it out of the way. I bent over, attempting to pick up the table, and was shoved to the floor. Instantly, it seemed, people were trampling over me. I managed to get up just in time to see a sheet of flame roar into the room through the door.

A huge volume of smoke accompanied the flame into the room, making it very dark and difficult to breathe. I grabbed a wet towel from a champagne pail and placed it over my face. At this time, the room was almost totally dark. I decided it was time to get out. The mass of people trying to cram through the narrow doorway created a bottleneck. In trying to squeeze through, I became stuck in the opening. Fighting panic, I struggled through the doorway, but fell and ended up at the bottom of a pile of people. I had no idea of where I was or how to get out.

Somehow, I managed to crawl out of the mass of bodies. Looking around, I saw a blue light which I took to be the night sky. I crawled toward it and was soon in the garden. Dick, my brother-in-law, found me quickly. He said that no one had come out the door for some time before me. He helped me to the back of the garden where the rest of our group was waiting. After I'd had a few gulps of fresh air, Victoria asked, "Where's Bob?"

In my heart, I knew he was still inside. For lack of something more encouraging, I told her that he'd gone back to help some people get out.

Hoping to find Bob, I went back to the exit and started helping the rescuers pull people out. A reporter, armed with a television camera equipped with a bright light, was trying to get pictures. When someone asked him for the light to help located victims, he replied that he needed it for his camera. With little hesitation, the guy knocked the reporter to the ground and took the light. I don't think the reporter got any pictures.

I have no idea how many bodies I pulled out or whether they were alive or dead. In an emergency situation like that, you don't think, you just do what you have to. I tried to revive a couple of people, but to no avail. There was so much horror, one couldn't tell what to do or where to start.

Finally, some firemen showed up with a hose which proved to be too short to do any good. A bunch of us grabbed the hose and had a tug of war with whatever was holding it up. Somehow, the hose became long enough to allow them to spray water into the door. Sometime in there, the firemen let us breathe through their masks. The oxygen felt good.

We started to go inside in pairs because it was too much for one person to pull somebody out. We could see nothing in there. We'd just grab an

252   *Inside The Beverly Hills Supper Club Fire*

arm, or a leg, or a hand, or a head, whatever our hands fell on, and tug with all our might. If the person came free, we'd drag them outside; if not, we'd feel around for another.

I had not given my group a thought. I later learned that Judy had stayed waiting for me, but everyone else, thinking that I'd gone back in and perished, had left the scene. Judy and I left about 4:00 AM. I remember dropping her off, but I haven't the slightest idea of how I reached my home in Monfort Heights, Ohio.

The next morning, I was in the shower when the phone rang. Water dripped from my body to the floor as I was informed that my brother's body had been located. I was asked to go to the make-shift morgue in Fort Thomas to identify him. When I arrived, they counseled me for a short time and then led me to a body covered by a white sheet.

The sheet slowly rolled back to reveal Bob's purplish face. A little blood was in his nose, ears and mouth. His color and the blood made me think that he'd held his breath as long as possible, and probably burst some blood vessels in the process. I loved my brother, and seeing him there like that was a very traumatic event. I asked the attendant if I could see the rest of him. When he pulled the sheet from Bob's body, it was some comfort to see that he was not burned.

My brother, Robert Zadek, was given a fireman's funeral in Cleves, Ohio. I, along with his many friends, said a mournful farewell to a genuine hero.

Fred and Edna Donsback
Patrons

When my cousin, Kathleen **Booher,** learned that she and her husband, Joe, would be in town for the Memorial Day week-end, she asked me to make reservations to see John Davidson, one of her favorites, at the Beverly Hills. I made the reservations for Saturday, and, since we didn't want to be rushed, I chose the second show.

We arrived at the Club about 8:30 PM. Kathleen and I stopped off in the ladies room near the front entrance while our husbands browsed the gift shop. At this time, the front area of the club was pretty empty as the first show was about ready to begin back in the Cabaret Room.

Kathleen and I both noticed how hot it was in the ladies room. In fact, when I touched the water faucet, it burned my hand. Our eyes were watering and burning by the time we got out of there. I was to later learn that this room shared a wall with the Zebra Room, and that the fire was probably burning inside the wall while we were in the ladies lounge.

We'd just rejoined our husbands and started for the dining room when a hostess asked if we'd prefer to attend the first show and eat later. Although it was only a few minutes to show time, we agreed. The hostess gave us a slip of paper which she said would get us into the Cabaret Room.

This was Kathleen and Joe's first time in the club, so Fred and I gave them the tour on the way down the hall. Each room we glanced into was full of people, it was a busy Saturday night.

The hostess in the Cabaret Room checked our pass and started toward the stage. A few steps down, she stopped, turned and gave us a strange look. I don't know what she was thinking. Wordlessly,she whirled and led us to the back of the room where we were seated at a tiny table on the left, near an aisle. This location offered a good vantage point, so I was glad that the hostess had changed her mind. I felt more comfortable there than I would have jammed in near the stage.

Although the room seemed full to me, more people were still being seated. Kathleen made some remark about the crowded conditions. While we waited for the show to begin, Fred spotted some friends of his being led toward the stage by the same hostess who'd seated us. Again, after a few steps, she turned and led them to a spacious booth behind where we were sitting. Fate, evidently, had turned her back both times.

Patrons were dancing to the orchestra's music on the large circular stage. One lady in particular, an especially skilled dancer, and her partner performed some fantastic steps, much to the delight of the audience. The performance was like a pre-show.

In a few moments, the music stopped, and the dancers cleared the floor as the lights dimmed. A short time after two comedians began their routine, a young man jumped to the stage, took the microphone and told us to get out of the building. I remember his instructions; "You people in the back, exit out the door you came in. Go straight or turn right, do not turn left. A small fire is occurring, and we need you to clear the building at once. Movequickly, but do not panic. When the fire has been extinguished, you will be re-seated."

Little did we realize that 18 year-old Walter Bailey was saving our lives. We got up to leave, observing that many people remained seated. Perhaps they thought his announcement was part of the act, or maybe they didn't want to chance losing their seats. Whatever the reason, the choice was a lethal one for some of them.

At that time, there was no smoke or fire in the room. People were slowly moving toward the exits. We had to go up three steps and turn left into the aisle that led to the door where we'd entered. Very quickly, overturnedchairs and assotteddebris littered the floor. Fred, using his military police training, locked his wrist with mine. I knew that his intent was, regardless of what happened, to keep us together. With his free hand, Fred tossed obstacles from our path.

A woman with lovely red hair and blue eyes stopped in front of us to light a cigarette. "Step aside or move on," Fred yelled, angrily. "There's a fire." Not moving, she calmly stood there. In a moment, she said, "Oh." Kathleen and Joe were initially behind us, but now pushed past, moving toward the exit. Fred and I finally got by her and moved on. Evacuation was not as simple as just **walking** out. Confusion and disorder set in quickly.

Eventually, we reached the exit. We turned right as the busboy had instructed. **Looking** to the left, I saw only a slight wisp of smoke hanging in the hallway. Fred later said that only a few seconds later, he looked behind us to see a solid wall of inky smoke roaring like a freight train down the hall toward us.

The narrow corridor ran about 60 feet between the showroom and the Garden Rooms. Once in the Garden Rooms, one could exit to outside. "Move faster," someone behind us yelled. "We're all going to die in here." Despite that, no one panicked, pushed or shoved. We all simply moved as quickly as possible. I whispered a little prayer of thanksgiving as Fred and I exited into the garden. I don't know how they got behind us, but I turned just in time to see Joe and Kathleen blown from the building by a blast of smoke. They appeared to come out the door riding on a coal-tar sea wave.

We were all uninjured, although badly shaken. Joe's white hair had turned black, and both he and Kathleen had their backs singed and blackened by soot. While Joe was unable to find his voice, Kathleen chattered continuously, telling about stumbling over some obstacle on the way out. She thought perhaps it was someone who'd been overcome by the smoke. Kathleen and Joe were the last people I saw come out that door. After them, oily, black smoke was the only thing coming out.

While we were standing in the garden, a young man dressed in a tuxedo rushed by us frantically calling a girl's name. After circling the garden, he dashed back into the building, still crying out for her. I did not see him again.

Dazed people were wandering all over the garden. I saw young Senator Bob Taft, who'd been speaking at a banquet, out there, and a sobbing John Davidson, sitting alone.

With concern for notifying our families, Fred and I obtained **permission** to walk down the hill. In the Oasis at the foot of the driveway, the television announced that 40 people had perished in the fire. By the time we got our calls made, the toll was up to 100. We looked at each other in unspoken horror. We'd survived a major disaster without realizing how serious it was. Outside, we were picked up and driven home by a kind stranger. Kathleen and Joe arrived a few minutes later in a taxi.

Safe at home, my thoughts turned to the people sitting around us. Did they get out? In particular, I wondered about the woman on the dance floor. She'd been laughing and twirling, having such a good time. Did she escape?

The next day, I learned that she did not. In the newspaper picture of the garden, I recognized her body lying on the grass. That was a very sad moment.

I **firmly** believe that my husband and I weren't taken because we still had work to do here on earth. Sometimes, I feel badly when people ask me if I know that parents of young children died in that fire. I reply, "Yes, I know and I'm sorry for them, but I can't help it. There's nothing I could have done." I consider such remarks very unfair.

Since the fire, I've felt a powerful urge to return to the site of the Beverly Hills. I do not understand why I feel this way, but I do. Above all my other feelings, I feel **thankful** for the calm, clear directions of Walter Bailey, the young man whose mature actions saved many lives, including the four in my party.

Eileen Druckman
Reservationist

On the day of the fire, I was taking reservations for dinner and the two shows that evening about as fast as I could answer the phone and write down the names. I was busily so involved when Ron Schilling stopped by and glanced at the reservation book. "My God, Eileen," he exclaimed. "Shut this thing down. Don't take any more reservations. We've got all we can handle now!"

As soon as he stopped speaking, the phone rang again. The caller was a man who insisted that he be booked for dinner and the first show. I told him that we were booked solid and that getting him in was not possible. In the ensuing argument, he got pretty rough with me and called me a few unpleasant names. In that job, being called unkind things was not unusual, but I angrily hung up on him for being so rude.

I'd no more than taken my hand off the receiver when the phone rang again. The same man again insisted on being booked and told me that he'd just keep calling until he got in. With a sigh, I reluctantly added his name to the list and closed the book for the night.

As soon as I was alerted to the fire, I got out safely, but several days later, I became sick from the toxic gases I'd inhaled. I eventually ended up in the UCLA Medical Center.

One day there, the phone rang in my room. The lady told me that she'd been calling hospitals all over the country trying to find me. Although puzzled, I asked, "What can I do for you?'

"Do you remember the man who gave you such a hard time about reservations on the day of the fire?' the caller inquired.

"How could I ever forget?"

Just before the line went dead, she said, "That was my husband. He was killed in the fire."

Garret Grover
Patron

The Institute of Financial Education's 1977 awards banquet for the Savings and Loan School of Cincinnati was scheduled for the Beverly Hills' Empire Room on May 28. We were expecting some 350 attendees. As past president, I would sit at the head table, right next to the podium.

I arrived about 5:45 PM and spent a few minutes chatting with the Schilling boys, whom I knew well from having scheduled many banquets with them over the years. In the course of our conversation, Rick invited my wife, Kay, and me to attend John **Davidson's** second show as his guests. We were excited about that and were anticipating a wonderful evening.

The dinner went off as planned. Shortly after the awards presentations began, a waitress dashed into the room through the door leading to the bar. In an excited voice, she announced, "There's a small fire in the building. We will have to vacate the premises, but we'll be able to return soon." When she finished speaking, she disappeared back out the door. The man making the awards presentations paused briefly, glancing at the door where she'd stood, then went right on with the next presentation.

In about a minute, the same woman reappeared and repeated her warning. As she was holding the doors open, I could observe smoke in the bar behind her. I grabbed the microphone and as calmly as possible said, "We're going to have to leave this room immediately. If possible, we'll come back later."

Everyone got up and started for the exits. Because I was at the head table, I had to wait briefly while everyone filed out the three exits from the room. When the crowd cleared a bit, I dropped from the stage, clasped Kay's hand and headed for the door on our right which I knew went into the kitchen. On the way, we picked up Helen and Ken Hanaver and led them along with us. Turning back to make sure everyone was getting out, I observed the band members, who had set up behind the stage, gathering their instruments. Sprinting back, I yelled, "Forget about the equipment. Get the hell out of here."

In the kitchen, we turned right, toward the rear of the building. The quickest way outside was by making another right out the door. That, however, led us into a smoke-filled service hall, so we veered left through a door that opened into a hallway which ran between the Garden Rooms and the Empire Room.

Amid the thick smoke in this corridor, waitress Pam Browning was directing traffic. Fortunately, some of us had thought to grab wet napkins before we left the Empire Room. Holding the damp cloth over our faces helped us to breathe. Just as we entered the hall, Pam shrieked, "Get out! Get out, here it comes!"

I looked up the hall to see what Pam had seen. The fire was roaring toward us, moving so swiftly that it reminded me of the effect you get when you squirt lighter fluid on a flame. We moved across the hall into the Garden Rooms in a hurry. The wall of flames came within ten feet of us. I am certain that another two second delay in our exit would have cost us our lives. I shall never forget how close I came to a horrible death that night.

Dashing through the Garden Room, I experienced an eerie feeling when I saw the tables still set with half-eaten dinners. Several people had collapsed on the floor. I gave only a fleeting thought to helping them; a roaring sheet of flames was right behind us! My major concern was getting myself, my wife and our friends to safety. As it was, the clothes on our backs were actually singed.

Outside, a gazebo blocked our path of escape. I kicked the lattice out, and we went through like a shot. As we joined a group standing at the base of the hill, I could still feel the heat on my back. Some men were entering the chapel in the garden and removing the pews to use as make-shift stretchers for the dead and injured. I saw Dave Downs and two other fellows go to the Cabaret Room exit and start pulling people out. They grabbed hands, arms, legs, or whatever they could get a hold on to save a victim. Although Dave is very modest about his efforts on that night, I consider him a true hero.

All over the garden, people were crying the names of lost loved ones. That sound haunts me yet. Dazed people, in shock, I suppose, ran frantically in every direction. A woman walked by me with her gown and bra molded to her body by the heat. "Help me," she sobbed.

"Stay calm," I replied. "Don't touch it. Help will be here soon." I don't know if that comforted her, but it was all I could do. I then started trying to calm some of the dazed people near me.

I lost all sense of time. I think it was around 11:00 PM when we were advised to leave the area. We were told that there was danger of a fuel storage tank exploding. We moved toward the parking lot behind the kitchen. I inspected the parked cars until I found one with a C. B. radio. On channel 21, I reached two base stations in Fort Thomas. Seeing what I was doing, people lined up at the door of the car to have me relay their names and relative's telephone numbers so the base stations could contact their relatives. After I'd been at this for about an hour, a man cut to the front of the line. "It's urgent that I use the radio," he said.

"Yours is no more urgent than anyone else," I told him. "Get in line."

"But it's my car," he protested.

"OK," I said. "You're next."

He made his call, then left the car to me. I continued working the radio for another two hours, when the authorities made us leave, explaining that they feared sparks flying over would ignite the cars.

On the way down the drive, I noticed a yellow Cadillac that had been squashed when a fire truck pushed it out of the way. I later learned that the car belonged to a member of the orchestra who was probably already dead by the time his car was damaged.

At the foot of the hill, we were offered a ride in the bed of a pickup truck by a passing stranger. He dropped us at the Southgate fire station. Ken called a relative who came to get us and delivered Kay and me to our home about 3:30 AM.

Early the next morning, I was on the phone attempting to contact our employees to see if anyone was missing. About 9:00 AM, I received the sad news that two of them, Marilyn Finch and Virginia Rambler, were dead. Evidently, they were in the ladies room across the hall from the Empire Room when the fire cut them off from safety. At church later that morning, we said prayers for all the victims, especially Marilyn and Virginia.

Kay remembers nothing about our escape or that evening. Some four years after the fire, however, when we drove by a large barn that was engulfed in flames, my wife dissolved into hysterics.

That fateful evening pointed out to me how useless I was in a catastrophe. In response, I joined the Southern Hills Life squad and took courses in C. P. R., E. M. T. and first aid. Eventually, I progressed to fire chief, a position I held until I injured my back and had to vacate the position.

Norm Catleman
Patron

S topping off at the kennel in Lockland, Ohio to feed my eight Afghans caused me to be late for the Afghan Hound Club banquet. My watch read about 8:30 PM when I drove my brand new car under the canopy at the entrance to the Beverly Hills. Because I gave the attendant an extra tip, he let me park it myself, about 100 feet right out from the front entrance. As I walked back to the door, I happened to glance up at the roof of the building. Nothing unusual was going on at that time.

Inside, the hostess directed me up the spiral staircase to where our party was being help upstairs. I sat the trophies that I'd carried in near where I was to sit and joined the line to pay my friends Peggy and Al Schard for the evening. There were approximately 100 dog owners in the room, mostly from Kentucky, Ohio, Indiana and Illinois, but some had come from as far away as Michigan, New York and California.

Being a non-drinker, I just milled around for a while, paying no attention to the time. Then I noticed some kind of commotion at the top of the stairwell. Moving in that direction, a faint aroma of smoke entered my nostrils, reminding me of childhood bonfires. In a very short time, the entire group was aroused. The fact that we'd all come up that way drove everyone instinctively toward the spiral stairs. Because the group on the other side of the hall was nearer the stairs than we, we found ourselves at the end of the line.

The banquet captain rushed by me pointing in the opposite direction. "Get out the back," he yelled. "Out the back." Everyone did an about-face, placing me at the front of the line. A waitress ushered us into a service hall where we found a set of stairs leading down to the brightly-lit kitchen. The kitchen personnel were going about their duties as usual, giving us a "What the hell are you doing?' look as we passed through. When someone pushed a loaded food cart out of the way, it hit a table and fell over, scattering food all over the floor. I remember thinking there'd be trouble about that.

Even though the kitchen was clear and I'd smelled, rather than seen, only a slight amount of smoke, I moved right on through the kitchen, out to the loading dock and on back to an area of raw dirt, about 100 yards from the building. Some other members of our group were there, talking about who was not present. Bob's Stein's two teen-agers were among the missing.

I really didn't know anything about the club's layout, but I walked back toward the building to look for the missing children. When I reached the garden, the ghastly sight of dead bodies lying on the ground dealt my mind such a severe blow that I was totally unable to recall what I saw until I finished counseling sessions at the University of Cincinnati Fire Aftermath Center, more than a month later.

Searching for the Stein children proved fruitless, so I returned to the raw dirt area. The kids were there, thank God, as well as some other members of the group that had been missing when I left. Our exchange of happy greetings was violently interrupted by a tremendous crashing noise as the back section of the roof collapsed into the flaming building. Debris and sparks flew into the sky around a great mushroom cloud of black smoke. We'd seen no flames before we escaped from the building only a few minutes earlier, but now the Club was an inferno. We watched in stunned silence as flames licked greedily at the doors of the structure until the entire back section was engulfed in consuming fire.

The firemen would not permit us to walk down the drive because of the emergency equipment, so we walked on the grass down a steep slope to U. S. 27. Just after we turned toward Newport, a man in an old station wagon stopped to offer us a ride. Inside the car were his wife and baby, and a load of wrought iron antiques. This kind man unloaded the antiques to make room for the four of us. He stayed with his booty while I held the baby so his wife could drive. She delivered us to a hotel in downtown Cincinnati, where one of the group was registered. I thought this was an amazing display of kindness by strangers. Whoever you folks were, I appreciate your aid.

From the hotel, I called some friends who came to take me home. Horrible nightmares of the tragic evening of May 28, 1977 haunted my sleep for a long, long time.

Joseph Braun, M.D.
Patron

Instead of the dessert course we were expecting, the young waiter brought a terse announcement. "There's a fire and it's out of control. Get out," he said. Thus ended the elegant dinner party hosted in the Viennese Room by Dr. and Mrs. Luis Davila.

My wife, Madonna, and I left quickly. Not knowing where we were going, we turned left which took us, unknowingly, light by the room where the fire was raging behind the closed doors. Smoke hanging from the ceiling of the bar forced us back the way we'd come. As we walked down the long hall, we went by the Cabaret Room where the show was still in progress.

In the garden, I encountered Dr. Richard Rust searching for his wife, Lorraine. Richard and I re-entered the building to find her. We searched the hallway and the Empire Room before finally locating her in the kitchen.

When we got back outside, I noticed a wisp of white smoke curling above the front part of the roof. A few people were coming out the back exit, rubbing their eyes. As I watched, the distress of those making their exit increased drastically. Richard and I began helping them out while Lorraine and Madonna escorted them away from the building. Many were having difficulty breathing. In fact, some of the last ones out were suffering considerable respiratory distress and had mild bums.

Dr. Davila established a triage system. We treated new arrivals on the lawn near the building, with the more seriously injured being carried further back to higher ground. We established an evacuation order for when help arrived.

Dr. Mark Schewgman worked with those exiting from the building at the north end, near the chapel. Dr. Rust worked at a side exit, while I remained on the south side near a fence. Where were the firemen and rescue squads?

My attention was distracted as gases exploded inside the Garden Room, turning it into an inferno. I climbed to the top of the fence where I could see a bumper-to-bumper line of emergency vehicles. 'We need help!" I screamed at the top of my lungs.

Dr. Schewgman was being overwhelmed by the number of victims being carried out of the rear of the Cabaret Room. Initially, clearing out airways and mouth-to-mouth resuscitation revived them. Most had vomited and some continued to do so. Expired air from their lungs was acrid and burning. Most were

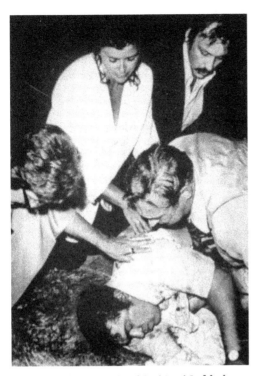

*Dr. Joseph Braun assisted by his **wife**. Madonna. (Dr. Fred Stine)*

not burned, but their upper bodies were dark with smoke and soot.

A woman, attired in a pink dress and impeccably jeweled and coiffured, was carried to me. Her appearance was perfectly fine and I expected her to sit up, but she remained motionless despite all efforts to revive her. For what seemed forever, I pumped her heart and lungs until, in a wave of depression, I was forced to admit that she was dead.

There was no time to mourn. Two more victims immediately arrived. An employee of the Beverly Hills volunteered to assist me, a grisly chore he performed admirably. We covered the faces of the dead as best we could. So many people were carried to me, limp and quiet. Soon the entire area was filled with rows of well-dressed corpses. Most looked well enough to speak to me, but they lay silently on the grass.

Saint Luke's administrator, John Hoyle, had summoned anesthetists and had a well-equipped resuscitation station set up in the chapel. Dr. Fred Stine, the Campbell County coroner, was in charge of the make-shift morgue. As I stared at the dead bodies of those I'd held in my arms, I decided it was time for me to leave; there was nothing more I could do.

With heavy hearts, Madonna and I walked hand-in-hand through the milling crowd to the front of the building. Television crews were busily photographing the front of the Beverly Hills, the solid wall of flames now a spectacular blaze visible for miles.

Ernie Pretot
Policeman

I was southbound on U. S. 27 in car #130 when I heard the alert that a fire was in progress at the Beverly Hills. The radio said that fire departments were **enroute** and that all emergency personnel were required. On the way, I was thinking, from previous experience, that a major fire up on that hill would be a difficult thing to deal with.

As it turned out, I was the first police officer on the scene. I saw no evidence of fire, but did witness several people staggering out the door, gasping and struggling for breath. As I approached the building, a **parking** attendant shouted, "Where are the fire trucks?"

"On the way," I assured him as I rushed toward the front door. Just inside, near the boutique, I saw an elderly lady in a gray dress wandering aimlessly. "Out that way," I directed, pointing her toward the front exit. "Get out!" Seeing a crowd of people coming up the hall, I started farther into the building, but a voice inside my head screamed, "Stop!" In a split second, I heard a loud noise and watched, helplessly, as a massive cloud of black smoke cut me off from the people coming toward me, although they were only a few steps away.

I raced back to the car and called my partner, Virgil Miller. "Get up here fast," I shouted into the microphone. "We've got a hell of a problem."

Fort Thomas officer Jack **McMullin** and I attempted to re-enter the building from another location, near the showroom. The instant we opened the door, a raging fire ball made a quick retreat our only option.

Defeated in that effort, I went to the rear of the building. There, I was dumbfounded by the bodies covering the ground. I counted more than 100 motionless figures scattered about on the grass.

I spent the remainder of the night doing whatever I could to control the situation and help with the removal of the corpses. What I witnessed that evening will never leave my mind.

Bruce Rath
Fort Thomas Volunteer Fireman

In the process of renovating the Beverly Hills, the new owners, Mr. Richard Schilling and his sons, not only remodeled the original facility, but also constructed new rooms around the existing structure. While this construction was in progress, I had occasion to lead a fire fighting crew in the battle against a fire that was deliberately set in the building. **Looking** up at the top of the old wall at the back of the building, I heard "popping" sounds which indicated to me that the roof was about to fall. I ordered my crew out just before it crashed, in flames, into where we'd just been working.

Mr. Schilling decided to rebuild the place again, even more elaborately than he'd originally planned. He did that, and through the next few years, he continually added to the structure. The Shilling's intent was to provide Las Vegas-style entertainment to the residents of the tri-state area. I knew all about it, because as a technician for the telephone company, I

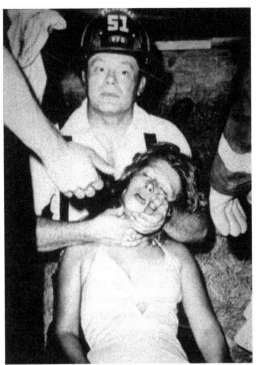

Fireman Bruce Rath's training, bravery and persistence helped him to rescue and save Karen Prugh from certain death. (Dr. Fred Stine).

had occasion to visit many times, both on business and pleasure.

On the evening of May 28, 1977, I was relaxing, watching television at home. My wife was slightly upset because, earlier in the evening, I'd refused to take her to see John Davidson's show. I'd told her that I had no desire to be a part of such a large crowd. Working in various areas of the club had led me to recently remark that if they ever experienced a fire, many people would probably die because the place was so large that getting out in a hurry would prove difficult.

Suddenly, the fire alarm tones went off in my living room. The message, repeated three times, announced, "Attention firemen, fire at Beverly Hills." I pulled on my bunker pants and dashed for the fire station.

The captain wasted no time. "Hurry up," he urged, "get on the truck. We gotta move." I jumped onto the truck and struggled into my bunker coat and helmet as we raced up North Fort Thomas Avenue. As we approached the site, I noticed a trace of smoke spiraling skyward. "It's probably another auto fire in the parking lot," I surmised to one of my mates. I lost sight of the smoke when the truck dipped into a valley in the road. In just an instant, when I saw it again, the trace of smoke had become a huge, thick column with flames lighting its sides.

Our plan was to hit the plug at the bottom of the hill with two 3-inch supply lines and take them to the base of the hill. The Newport fire department would supply two identical lines to connect up the driveway.

As soon as we stopped, the captain told me to get an air pack, which allows one to breathe in smoke, and jump onto the aerial truck as it turned into the drive. This I did, and rode up the hill with them. Pandemonium reigned at the top of the hill. People were frantically running around, screaming hysterically. I approached several to find out what they were trying to tell me, but they were beyond being calmed. I stood with a group of volunteers until a lieutenant called, "You take these guys to the U. S. 27 side and help people as they come out the exits." I dropped some men at the exit which would have been stage right in the showroom and went myself to the back exit, which would be stage left.

One of the men at the first exit later told me that the door was closed when they arrived, so their first chore was to get it open. That accomplished, they intended to block it to prevent the door from closing again. Before they could, however, a figure sheathed in white shot from the opening. A man had wrapped himself in a tablecloth and used ice from drink glasses to wet it down to protect himself from the heat and flames. The ploy worked. He knocked several firemen aside as he flew uninjured from the building.

Just as I rounded the corner of the building, a woman rushed up to me. "My God," she screamed, "there's a thousand people trapped in there!"

"Where?" I asked.

She was too hysterical to answer, mutely staring at me.

"Calm down and tell me where they're trapped," I tried again.

She took a deep breath, then said, "Go in that entrance right there," indicating the one she meant.

"OK," I replied. "Now you go to the front of the building and find a man wearing a white helmet. Tell him the same thing you just told me. Give him all the details, and tell him I need help. Do you understand?"

She nodded yes and acted just as I had instructed.

I placed the mask over my face and prepared to enter the door the woman had indicated. As I was getting ready, a couple of busboys approached me. "What can we do to help?" they asked.

"Just stay here," I said. "You can't go in there, there's too much smoke. When help arrives, tell them I'm inside finding out what we'll need."

I entered the hallway leading to the showroom. Smoke filled the area from the ceiling to about two feet from the floor. By crouching low, I could see that the showroom doors were open, some 30 feet away. When I'd penetrated about 10 feet, the smoke cleared enough to allow me to see electric lights and fires in the room. Then I saw a horrible sight. People had fallen or been knocked down in the door leading into the hall, and those behind had fallen like a row of dominoes. Bodies were stacked in the opening like cordwood, piled higher than I am tall!

Then I heard them. "Get me out! I'm burning!"

"I'm trapped, and I can't get out!" Other cries of pain and terror filled the hot, smoky air.

A movement attracted my attention. All I could see was a feminine hand, that apparently belonged to a woman desperately attempting to claw her way over the pile. I grabbed the hand and pulled the lady attached to it over the stack of bodies. She screamed hysterically as I draped her over my shoulder and wrapped an arm around her legs in the fireman's carry.

When I got her to the garden, I put her down on the grass and attempted to calm her. "You're out now," I said, soothingly. "Calm down. Breathe deeply. You're out and you're OK."

"My whole family's still in there," she shrieked.

No one had yet arrived to help me. I left that lady and re-entered the building. At the pile of bodies, I pulled two people off the stack and placed them on the floor. Grabbing each by the back of the collar, I walked backwards toward the exit, pulling them to safety. At the outside door, I turned them over to the waiting busboys.

I repeated this procedure several times, how many, I do not know. Some estimates say I rescued 30 to 35 people, but I have no idea. I just kept going back for more.

On one trip, a young woman, her clothes ablaze, streaked out of an opening that was a door before the fire consumed it. In a move born of hysteria, she dove over the stack of bodies into the showroom. I held on to the top of the door frame to get over the pile. I caught her, pushed her to the floor, and ignoring her screams, patted the fire out. Then I picked her up and carried her back to the stack of bodies, stumbling over tables, chairs, bodies and glasses on the way. I placed her on the top of the human mound, climbed back over into the hall and pulled her through.

By this time, I was nearly exhausted, but I knew I had to get this one out. I tied her wrists together with a short length of rope we carried for the purpose and placed her hands around my neck. In this way, I could "dogwalk" her out, me on my hands and knees while she rode on my back. As I started to crawl away, a woman near the bottom of the stack extended a free hand to me. "Please, mister," she gasped, "You've got to get me out of here. I've got babies at home."

"OK," I assured her. "I'll take you with us." As I turned to see if I could get her out of the tangle, she yanked the oxygen mask from my face just as I inhaled. Instantly, the smoke and hot gases caused me to lose consciousness.

When I awoke, I was lying atop the lady whose arms were still laced around my neck. The bell warning that the tank was low on oxygen was sounding. Groggily, I managed to drag the burned woman to the door, where I collapsed. Although I never saw the lady who was concerned about her babies at home again, her plaintive cries will never leave my mind.

My buddy, Covington fire fighter Jim **McDermitt,** found me lying in the door. Jerking my helmet off, he scolded, "Damn it, Rath, get the hell up! You've got to get out of here."

I felt like I was drunk. "Man, I can't get up," I slurred.

Jim grasped the straps holding the tank to my back and pulled me and the woman tied to me outside. Then he rolled me over so he could remove the tank and my bunker coat. Relieved of the extra weight, I was able to stand. I put my coat on the ground and placed the girl I'd drug out on it. Then, for the first time, I noticed that she was badly burned on her face, arms and breasts. I went to get a litter for her.

When I returned, a man was bending over her. "Pardon me, who are **you?**" I asked.

"I'm a doctor," he replied.

"Well, how's she doing?'

"I've just pronounced her dead," he said, emotionlessly.

"She can't be dead," I cried. "I talked to her when I brought her out not two minutes ago." I couldn't believe it.

"Well, she's dead now," he repeated as he left to help someone else.

Damn it, I thought, I'm not going to let her die. I heard the voice of my E. M. T. instructor from years before: "When you get involved with someone, do not stop **working** with them until you're absolutely certain that they're dead." I attempted to find a carotid pulse in her neck. No pulse.

I refused to give up, frantically searching for a pulse. Then I felt something throb. Maybe. Then I felt it again. For sure! Setting right to work, I performed serious C. P. R. on her for at least thirty minutes. During that time, a lady in a red dress approached. "Is there anything I can do to help? I'm a nurse."

"Get some oxygen," I said without pausing.

At last, the victim regained consciousness. Raising her to a sitting position, I talked to her, urging her to respond. "Who are you? Talk to me, damn it! What's your **name?**"

She fixed glazed eyes on me. "I'm Karen Prugh," she choked out. "My family's still in there," she managed to add.

Someone yelled. I looked to see the nurse in the red dress running up with an oxygen bottle. In the moment I looked away, Karen blacked out. We placed the oxygen mask on her and pumped the life-giving gas into her lungs. In a few moments, she was breathing normally.

While I was sitting on the ground, holding Karen's head in my hands, I heard someone yelling, "Hey, fireman. Hey, fireman number 51!" I looked up just as a photographer snapped a picture of me, bleary-eyed and exhausted, holding Karen Prugh.

Covington's Life Squad was on the scene, in charge of **taking** victims to the hospitals. I picked Karen up as gently as possible and carried her to an ambulance. She maintained a death grip on me, so I got into the ambulance with her and another badly burned victim. The only way we could fit in was with me sitting on a jump seat with her on my lap. She kept yelling, "My family. My family," all the way to Booth Hospital.

I stroked the back of her head and attempted to calm her. "Calm down, now. Calm down. It's going to be all right," I soothed.

She spotted the other victim on the floor. "Oh, my God," she cried. "That poor girl. Look how badly she's burned!" I was amazed that she could forget her own plight to feel concern for someone else.

By the time I got back to the fire, the roof had collapsed. We continued to battle the flames, trying to determine if we could safely enter the building to look for additional casualties. About **6:30** AM, the Captain walked up and looked into my face. "Get the hell out of here, Rath. You've had it."

I made no protest. I wandered around to the front of the building and sat down on a rock wall. Governor Julian Can-oil walked up and sat beside me. "Son, are you all right?' he asked, with true concern.

"I really don't know," I answered, truthfully. "This whole scene is so terrible."

He turned to the state policeman with him. "Trooper, go back to the car and get this man a drink of whiskey," he ordered.

While I sipped the restorative, Governor Carroll and I sat on the wall, discussing the night of horror.

After a while, I decided to return to duty. We were ordered to go into the building and examine anybody that we found to ascertain that they were dead. I was horrified to see a young woman's very pregnant body. In an effort to save herself and her baby, she had pulled the hem of her dress over her face. Both she and her unborn child had perished.

The Cabaret Room was filled with more horrors. At a table, six burned corpses still sat in place in their chairs. Adding to the ghastly vision, several bodies were piled on the table as if they'd tried to hurdle it in a frantic race for the exits. We placed the corpses in black body bags carefully **marking** the location where they were found and any other pertinent information.

At the bottom of the tangle lay a young woman, completely unburned. Bodies piled on her had protected all but the top of her head, which was totally burned away, leaving only a hollow skull.

About **9:30** AM the chief pulled me aside. "Rath," he said, "you've had enough. I want you to go home, take a shower and then report to the fire station. I need you there to take over the squad." As ordered, I walked out of the burned out structure. As soon as I got outside, the full impact of what I'd seen hit me like a blow from a baseball bat. Tears spurted from my eyes. I sobbed all the way home.

My face stared back at me from the front page of the Sunday morning paper. The picture of me holding Karen resulted in a bunch of phone calls.

Later, I visited Karen in the hospital. She burst into tears of happiness when she saw me. Somehow, she'd gotten the idea that I'd been **killed.** Her mother-in-law, father-in-law and brother-in-law had all perished in the fire, but, ironically, one of the badly burned victims I'd rescued was Karen's **sister-**

in-law, Shirley, who also survived. Karen was transferred to a hospital in Dayton, Ohio, her home town, where she eventually made a complete recovery. I still have the letters she and her parents wrote me expressing their gratitude.

Donald and Patricia Bezold. Taken at the fish pond under the spiral staircase in The Beverly Hills. They were two of the first known dead. The photo and poem are courtesy of the Bezold family.

AFTER GLOW

I'd like the memory of me
to be a happy one.
I'd like to leave an afterglow
of smiles when life is done.

I'd like to leave an echo whispering softly down the ways,
Of happy times and laughing times
and bright and sunny days.

I'd like the tears of those who grieve,
to dry before the sun
Of happy memories that I leave
When Life is done.

Carol Mirkel

Part Six

*E*PILOGUE

Chapter 21

When the law suits were settled, the Schillings went back into the restaurant business. Initially, they opened a disco/night club named *January's and Oodles* a couple of blocks from Riverfront Stadium in Cincinnati. They built that into a booming enterprise, then sold it.

Then they purchased two old barges, moored them in the Ohio River at Newport and converted them into *The Islands,* a huge, fabulous, restaurant complete with a disco room, a show room and a swimming pool. My youngest son, Ron, worked at both of these establishments.

The Islands eventually was moved down the river to Louisville and the Schillings replaced it in Newport with another, bigger and better. In a last minute deal, they sold that one the night it was to open. And I do mean last minute — patrons were sitting inside ready to order meals when they were told that the management had changed and that they'd have to come back later. Even though it was brand new, the new owners redecorated before they opened. That structure is now part of a gambling casino in Iowa.

From Louisville, *The Islands* moved to the Mississippi, just below Memphis, where it's now the gambling casino *Splash.* In December 1993, reports had the Schillings selling their interest in it to International Gaming Management of Minneapolis for $50,000,000, but that deal fell through. I understand that, at one time, Rick and Ron Schilling were involved in negotiations to open a riverboat casino on the Ohio in Indiana, but that hasn't happened, either.

Scott Schilling, the youngest brother, was always junior to his father and brothers in the restaurant business. His main interest is in the shop he owns in Covington where he makes and markets his own line of jewelry.

For those of us who survived, life went on with the fire as a major event. Some of my friends went on to productive careers, some in the restaurant business, some in other areas. One of the young men who was a busboy in 1977 evidently found his calling that night and is now a professional fire fighter. Others have died in the intervening years, Fran Oaks and my good friend, Fred Cianciolo (Mr. C.), among them.

Meanwhile, the property from which the Beverly Hills Supper Club once so grandly reined over the night club business remains vacant.

On May 28, 1982, I accompanied Fred Cianciolo, Judy Holiday and a few other former Beverly Hills' employees as we made the long climb up the winding drive to the weed-choked site of the fire to hold a small memorial service. In the middle of what little was left of the club, we stood in a circle, holding hands, and offered prayers in memory of those who had died there. In what was a very solemn occasion, we stood in silence, each lost in our own thoughts of what had taken place on that spot a mere five years before. I don't know what anyone else was thinking, but my thoughts were on the happiness and friendships I'd shared there as well as the trauma and tragedy. After about thirty minutes, we made the trek back down the hill. What little conversation we shared was subdued.

Another five years later, May 28, 1987, I felt compelled to do it again, so I organized a memorial service to be held at Saint Mary's Catholic Church in Alexandria. This time, as we'd gotten the word out, more than 600 people attended, including former employees, firemen and policemen who'd worked so hard the night of the fire, former Governor Julian Carroll, Ken Paul and several other local politicians, some people who were seriously burned and several members of victims' families, including Rose Dischar's parents.

This photo was taken at an employees' reunion several months after the fire. L to R; unknown waitress, Rick Schilling, bus boy Steve Wilson, and waitress Karen Watts Overby. (W. Dammert)

Fred Cianciola (Mr. C) violinist in clubs orchestra - one of the last persons to escape the fire alive. (W. Dammert)

The service received wide media coverage. The rear of the church was packed with television cameras and the parking lot was choked with satellite trucks. Additionally, radio and newspaper personnel from **Ashland**, Covington, Louisville, Maysville and Lexington provided Kentucky's contingent, while Ohio was represented by journalists from Cincinnati, Columbus and Dayton.

Once again, the occasion was solemn as we offered prayers in memory of those who'd perished ten years before. The personal highlights of the evening were hearing Mr. C. play the violin, and meeting survivor Janice Popp. Janice and a friend of her's had been badly burned, but managed to make a full recovery, while the other two members of their party died. She said that she was very happy to meet me, which made me feel good. The fact that she was in such fine spirits also helped me.

In 1992, I organized a reunion of former employees, a difficult chore. Locating them after fifteen years was one problem, and after I did, the conversation I had with many of them brought back a lot of sad memories. Some 90 of us attended, however, and we really enjoyed each other's company. Interestingly, the fire was not a major topic of conversation, — perhaps it was still too traumatic — but I know that each of us was remembering that fateful night and the victims.

It's now been nineteen years since the fire and over thirty-seven since Betty and I were married. Our four children, Richard, Wayne, Lisa and Ron are grown with families of their own. We are retired and enjoying our eight grandchildren, doing some traveling and volunteer work. We still live just ten miles from the site of the tragedy.

I actually began writing this story not long after the fire. It was not an easy task and many times I had to just put it aside, and if not for my friend, Mary **Macht's** encouragement, it might yet be undone. I cannot tell the number of times it brought tears to my eyes. I am now happy to be able to meet some of the victims' families. I feel very close to them.

The site of the Beverly Hills is still vacant, although it being the prime piece of real estate that it is, something eventually will, no doubt, go in there. Several developers have demonstrated great interest in the property over the years, but the zoning issues have yet to be resolved. We who survived and the families of the victims are actively involved in ensuring that some kind of memorial is incorporated into whatever goes on that spot. I think we should always endeavor to remember those who died there and the circumstances which allowed the tragedy to occur. I'd like to see the phrase "Lest we forget" inscribed on something up on that hill.

The Dammert children: Standing, L to R: Lisa and Wayne. Sitting, L to R: Rick and Ron. (W. Dammert)

Betty and Wayne Dammert in July 1995. (W. Dammert)

BIBLIOGRAPHY

Bright, Richard G., *Beverly Hills Supper Club Fire, Southgate, Kentucky, May 28, 1977 — An Analysis of the Development and Spread of Fire from the Room of Origin (Zebra Room) to the Cabaret Room,* US Department of Commerce, National Bureau of Standards, Washington, DC, September 1, 1977

Carroll, Julian, personal interview, May 8, 1996

The Cincinnati Enquirer, Cincinnati, May 10, 1961
The Cincinnati Enquirer, Cincinnati, October 23, 1961
The Cincinnati Enquirer, Cincinnati, October 28, 1961
The Cincinnati Enquirer, Cincinnati, November 9, 1961
The Cincinnati Enquirer, Cincinnati, September 19, 1977
The Cincinnati Enquirer, Cincinnati, September 20, 1977
The Cincinnati Enquirer, Cincinnati, April 8, 1979

The Courier-Journal, Louisville, August 4, 1978

Investigative Report to the Governor — Beverly Hills Supper Club Fire, May 28, 1977, Commonwealth of Kentucky, Frankfort, Kentucky, September 16, 1977

The Kentucky Post, Cincinnati, June 22, 1970
The Kentucky Post, Cincinnati, September 19, 1977
The Kentucky Post, Cincinnati, August 3, 1978

Lawson, Robert G., *Beverly Hills The Anatomy of a Nightclub Fire* Athens, Ohio University Press, 1984

The Saturday Evening Post. New York: March 26, 1960

Campbell County Coroners Report. July 8, 1977

Index

Above: Site of The Beverly Hills as it appears today. I-471 is seen in the background. Below: Entrance at the bottom of the hill to The Beverly Hills as it appears today. (John Snell)

CPSIA information can be obtained
at www.ICGtesting.com
Printed in the USA
BVHW08s1358150818
524588BV00004B/163/P